SALT of the EARTH

One Family's Journey Through the Violent American Landscape

SALT of the EARTH

JACK OLSEN

ST. MARTIN'S PRESS ❧ NEW YORK

SALT OF THE EARTH: ONE FAMILY'S JOURNEY THROUGH THE VIOLENT AMERICAN LANDSCAPE. Copyright © 1996 by Jack Olsen. All rights reserved. Printed in the United States of America. No part of this book may be used or reproduced in any manner whatsoever without written permission except in the case of brief quotations embodied in critical articles or reviews. For information, address St. Martin's Press, 175 Fifth Avenue, New York, N.Y. 10010.

Photographs courtesy of Elaine Gere.

Design by Nancy Resnick

Library of Congress Cataloging-in-Publication Data

Olsen, Jack.
    Salt of the earth : one family's journey through the violent American   landscape / by Jack Olsen.
      p. cm.
    ISBN 0-312-14406-7
    1. Abduction—United States—Case studies. 2. Missing children—United States—Case studies. 3. Problem families—United States—Case studies. 4. Mothers—United States—Biography. 5. Wives—United States—Biography.
6. Gere, Elaine. 7. Gere, Brenda, 1972–1985. I. Title.
  HV6574.U6057 1996
    364.1′523′0979771—dc20   96-474
                                        CIP

First Edition: May 1996

10 9 8 7 6 5 4 3 2 1

For Brenda, her memory

In our sleep, pain which cannot forget falls drop by drop upon the heart until, in our own despair, against our will, comes wisdom through the awful grace of God.
—Aeschylus

Dear God in heaven, where did she get the strength?
—Evelyn Mayzsak

I

BIG ED'S DAUGHTER

1

In later years, Elaine Mayzsak Gere described her old hometown as a "quicksand swamp." If you were from Fontana, she said, "it sucked you down and held you. People couldn't get away, still can't. It always pulled you back." In the darkest moments of her life, she never imagined that her husband and daughter would end up as permanent residents.

When she was a child in the late forties, Elaine was under the impression that the whole world looked and smelled like South Fontana: citrus blossoms in endless orchards, hog slop spilling from railroad cars, jasmine on melted adobe walls, diesel smoke from trucks and buses, congregations of chickens and turkeys, Concord grapes sweating in the sun, the sweet scent of wild plums, the steel mill's smelter tinting the undersides of clouds. Yodeling coyotes coursed jackrabbits in the nearby Jurupa Hills, and high winds off San Gorgonio Mountain blew dust and grit through cracks in the Mayzsaks' old house, into their sun-bleached clothes, their saggy furniture, into their sloppy joes and wieners.

On the hottest days of summer, rows of grapevines rippled as though freshly painted in oils. Residents popped salt tablets, fanned themselves with palm leaves, and wondered why they'd left Ohio. Heat ghosts formed and dissolved, and dust devils as tall as oil derricks sent the children inside howling. Their strong parents never seemed to mind the heat or the heavy smog, perhaps because the unhealthy air was the least of their problems.

"Big Ed" Mayzsak was a short, stumpy man, despite his nickname, with a lung diver's chest, a protuberant belly, and a bottomless capacity for women, beer and work. Tight brown tendrils grew everywhere but on his head. "One more hair," a doctor kidded him, "you'd be a bear." He was always the strongest man on his work crew. When he was knocked down by buckshot on a hunting trip, his partner fainted; Big Ed dragged him from the woods and drove them both to the hospital. For the rest of his life, his shoulder set off metal detectors.

His full name was James Ignatius Mayzsak, but no one called him anything but Ed or Big Ed. The family name, variously spelled Mayzsak, Misjak and Mizysak but always pronounced MAY-zak, meant "man of the cloth" in the original Slovene dialect. "Someone back there musta been a tailor," Ed liked to say.

He yearned for land and animals, even if it meant moving to the windswept hardpan that stretched from the eastern edge of Los Angeles to the base of a craggy massif sixty miles away. He retained an Eastern European lust for mud, manure, feathers and any foodstuff related to pork. His ancestors had converted hog raising (and cookery) into a fine art that seemed almost genetic. No one did pork like the Slovenians, or Big Ed Mayzsak.

Elaine's mother, Evelyn, was thirteen years younger and had milked Guernsey cows twice a day as a child. "I don't want no part of another farm," she complained when her husband announced that he was quitting his welding job in San Pedro so they could begin a life in the desert like homesteaders of old.

"Fontana ain't like your damned Wisconsin," Big Ed replied. He spread out a city map. "Here! Look at these street names: Orange Way, Lime Street, Tamarind, Mango. *Oleander*, for Chrisakes!"

It was true that fallen grapefruit and oranges lay untouched in the Fontana of the 1940s. At roadside stands, avocados sold for a quarter, pomegranates for thirty cents, oranges and lemons for a nickel. Not that Big Ed, a meat-and-potatoes man, intended to taste any of them.

After three days of tears, Evelyn gave in and signed the papers for the new house. But she never let her husband forget that the move to Fontana was *his* idea.

2

Daughter Elaine was born in 1945, and from the time she was old enough to recognize squalor, she was reluctant to bring friends into her home. The oversized shack at the foot of the Jurupa Hills consisted of two large rooms plus alcoves on twelve acres of land that were home to creosote and burro bush, mesquite, greasewood and more species of cactus than Elaine could count, all unfriendly. The roof sloped in one direction, making the house look as though it had been split lengthwise with an ax. The concrete-and-stucco walls were canted at every degree except ninety; ceilings sagged, and the lightest breeze set the house to groaning. Cracks in the linoleum revealed bare cement. The doors didn't quite close; Evelyn was always yelling "Git!" and shoving a chicken back outside. There were no built-in closets or shelves. The bathroom consisted of a sink and toilet bowl, separated from the kitchen by a drawstring curtain.

At three years of age, Elaine would curl up on the toilet seat and fall asleep. It was the only private place in the house. "Mom said I was a really good girl 'cause all I did was eat and sleep."

Big sister Beverly, three years older, was a livelier specimen, and Jimmy, the baby of the family, brought decapitated snakes into the house and conked Elaine with a hammer before he had graduated from soakers.

Neighbors were distant, few and odd. One family rustled cattle; the father would slit the animal's throat, and the wife and children would fall to their knees and butcher on the spot. Other neighbors lived behind eucalyptus windbreaks on the far side of several hundred acres of grapes and walnuts; they were usually too busy eking out a living to socialize.

A few miles to the north of the Mayzsaks, the world's largest citrus grove was fertilized by manure from a hog lot where fifty thousand pigs dined daily on five hundred tons of Los Angeles garbage, delivered fresh and pungent by the Santa Fe Railroad. So much silverware turned up in the garbage that the poorest Fontanans dined at place settings monogrammed by the Ambassador Hotel, the Hollywood Roosevelt, the Brown Derby, Chasen's and other tony establishments. To complete the cycle, trains returned fat Fontana hogs to L.A.

Despite the aesthetic limitations, the Mayzsak children spent joyous childhoods. In the searing summers and windy winters, they bonded so tightly that nearly four decades later, in Elaine's most desperate hours, brother Jimmy drove a thousand miles to her aid, stopping only to buy fuel, and found on arrival that older sister Beverly and mother Evelyn had already flown in to help out.

"We were three barefooted kids running through the rainbow sprinklers in the vineyards," said Elaine. "We swam in the irrigation weirs till a neighbor boy got caught in the pump and drowned. We played hide and seek and came home all purple from the grapes. We rode our bikes to a candy store a mile away. We had a heck of a time."

In their scraggly yard, wild wheat grew under a walnut tree left over from a back-to-nature scheme that had enriched its developers but no one else. Mother Evelyn planted a cactus garden—Spanish dagger, cat's-claw acacia, cholla, yucca—but spaded it under when the children kept impaling themselves. Bats hung from rafters in the garage. Everyone looked out for scorpions, although they were rare ("not goddamn rare enough!" Big Ed exclaimed as he shook one the size of a prawn from his Wellingtons). Tarantulas crawled into the house once or twice a year, and black widows were regular visitors. Ed squooshed them with his thumb till a bite cost him part of a finger. After that he executed all spiders with a ball-peen hammer.

The farm operation started small. While Evelyn wrangled the three children, Big Ed built a row of rabbit hutches and installed mating pairs. The children wanted a horse, but Ed told them, "You can't eat a horse. Maybe we can raise up a cow."

"How about a dog?" Elaine implored.

Ed observed that you couldn't eat a dog unless you were Chinese.

After two years he had his cow, and ex-dairymaid Evelyn taught Elaine and Beverly how to milk, churn and make cheese. At an auction Ed got a bargain price on a truckload of calves, then found out they had the scours.

"We rammed big pills down their throats," Elaine remembered. "We mixed powdered milk and bottle-fed twenty-nine calves, raised those babies up to three, four hundred pounds. Seemed like every pound they gained, the rest of us lost."

3

Big Ed was a dictator but also a loving father, warm, tactile and imaginative with his children. "Listen!" he would say, pulling Elaine onto his lap in the evening. "Hear that? Them trains come from every which place. Peoria, Chicago, St. Louis."

He would read aloud, invent silly stories, embroider on his boyhood in downstate Illinois and his parents' adventures in the old country.

"That there Dracula lived down the street from my great-uncle," he told Elaine and Jimmy one night as they listened with bulging eyes.

"Dracula came from Transylvania," Evelyn called from the kitchen. "That's Romania."

"In them days," Big Ed said without missing a beat, "it was in Slovenia."

"Oh, for God's sake," Evelyn replied.

There were no vacations or luxuries, and folding money was almost as scarce as coffee-table books or objets d'art. Evelyn traded with neighbors for perishables and stored them in a clammy wooden icebox that was never full. She made her daughters' dresses till they reached their teens. Elaine said, "We were the last kids in our school to wear flour sacks."

Sometimes the walls shook with Evelyn's scratchy 78-rpm polka records, played on a lo-fi phonograph from the forties. On Friday nights she shoved the kitchen furniture against the wall for dance parties, which were usually followed by intense sessions of Monopoly. When Elaine was five, she broke one of her mother's prized records, by Frankie Yankovic, "The Polka King," but three-year-old Jimmy took the blame. It was the way of their close relationship.

The Father, Son and Holy Ghost were considered family members, honorary Mayzsaks. A crucifix protected each bed. On Sundays Evelyn sent the children off to St. Joseph's Catholic Church, although she was usually too tired to go herself.

Little Elaine became religious but not churchy, with a firm attitude about the deity. "If I had any problem or frustrations, I'd do my best to solve them, and if that didn't work, I'd say, 'God, I'm gonna leave it in your hands. Please—you take care of it.'" Having issued her instructions, she felt she could dispense with the services of the bony old priest and his asparagus wand.

She turned into a docile, obedient, watchful child. Her Uncle Hank, who followed other Mayzsaks from Illinois to Fontana and became a homicide detective and later a real estate millionaire, described her as "a serious little kid, always helping her mom. Did cartwheels around the yard. Never said a bad word about anybody. Just a beautiful-type little person."

Her first ambition was to be a cosmetologist or nurse. Whenever her father shot a bird, she would administer first aid. "Sparrows, doves, quail, I never brought one back to life. After the funeral, Dad would go right out and shoot another one."

Big Ed became as fascinated with birds as he was with hogs. Over his wife's objections, he bought a mynah whose vocabulary was limited to "Go to hell." Evelyn came home one day to find a squadron of parakeets flying in formation in the house. "I hated to see 'em caged," her husband explained. She spent three days cleaning up.

4

By Elaine's eighth birthday in 1953, Big Ed had sold his rabbits and started raising chickens commercially. Soon hundreds of fowl were clucking and crowing and scratching up potato bugs and spiders. At market time, the three Mayzsak children had to wriggle into the pens headfirst and pull out the unhappy birds by their feet.

In true visionary manner, Big Ed sold off his chickens after someone advised that there was more profit in turkeys. Soon five hundred polts had multiplied into five thousand adults, and randy old toms with red wattles overran house and garden as they went about their task of deflowering virgins.

The children corralled, watered, fed and doctored birds that were as big as little brother Jimmy. Big Ed hired a helper, then another, and soon the family business counted nine employes, not including the Mayzsaks. He bought a small truck to haul the product to market, then a $30,000 semitrailer.

When the turkeys became overcrowded, Ed bought two adjacent ten-acre plots. Within a few years, the family was feeding 45,000 turkeys, and the operation was written up in a farm journal. Evelyn, still wearing homemade dresses, took receipts to the bank in brown grocery bags. Little Elaine tried to count one bundle and quit when she reached five figures.

Big Ed dug pits in the backyard and roasted hogs for barbecue parties that lasted all weekend. He was an easy touch for loans but tight with his children. When they complained that their friends got allowances, he said, "Yeah, and someday they'll be on welfare. But you kids—you'll be *independent*."

He had a standard reply to suggestions about moving to a nicer house: "What the hell's wrong with this dump?"

* * *

On a blowtorch-hot summer day, disaster arrived in the form of two truckloads of polts. "Put 'em in the pens with the others," Evelyn ordered. Big Ed was in L.A. on deliveries.

A few hours later, Evelyn looked out the window and saw a hen running in circles before falling flat on its back. The vet diagnosed turkey cholera. Within a few days the entire flock was down. Big Ed had never cared much about money, but he had a large Slovenian pride. He berated himself for not following his instincts and sticking to hogs. Nobody ever heard of a pig with turkey cholera.

After the bankruptcy proceedings, Evelyn went to work packing for Swift by day and sorting for Sunkist at night. Beverly, Elaine and Jimmy tended the farm as their father commiserated with himself in mill-town bars.

The loving home deteriorated. "My dad lost his drive," said Elaine, "and my mom was always ragging on him, cutting him down."

Soon after Elaine's tenth birthday in 1955, an angry Evelyn told her husband, "You're in bars so much. Why the hell don't you get one of your own?"

The next day Big Ed signed a promissory note to buy a Skid Road bar. With vodka optimism he explained that the monthly payments would be covered by profits, and if the family pitched in, it wouldn't be long before they had enough money to return to the livestock business.

"Raising what?" his wife cracked. "Mynah birds?"

The Town Pump was a beer joint, dance hall and meeting place for the Hell's Angels, the hoodlum bikers' club spawned in Fontana. Every weekend Elaine and her siblings were assigned to scrub out the bathroom, wash and wax the dance floor, and look for coins.

At first their mother refused to go near the place, correctly predicting that Big Ed would become his own best customer. He won a bet by drinking ninety-nine cans of beer in twenty-four hours, and his belly expanded accordingly. By his second year as a bar owner, he'd achieved alcoholic status, and the children's lives turned hard.

Every few weeks, Evelyn threatened divorce, and Big Ed would put his hand on the family Bible and promise to change. Then another skirmish would break out. After a 3:00 A.M. fight, Elaine watched as her father ripped the distributor cap from the family car and threw it in the bushes. "She ain't goin' nowhere till I finish with her," he declared.

The three children huddled in the darkness. "I'm scared," Elaine muttered. "He never did that before."

After a while there was a scream, and the children ran into the bedroom to see Big Ed choking their mother.

Elaine cocked a baseball bat over her shoulder. "No, Elaine," her mother squawked. *"No!"*

For the rest of his life, Ed had a bump on the back of his head. He never held it against the child.

"I was drunk," he apologized. "I'm proud of ya. You was protectin' your mom."

The day the divorce papers were served on Ed at the bar, he came home at five o'clock and demanded his supper as usual.

"Supper?" his wife said. "I wouldn't dirty a dish for you. Get the hell out of my house."

Two days later he returned and slumped into a chair. No one in the family had ever seen him cry. To Elaine, it was like watching the sun go black.

"Mom," he said, "I'll sell the joint."

Evelyn said she'd heard that before.

"No, no," he insisted. "I love you and I love the kids. I'll straighten up, I promise."

Evelyn scoffed.

"If I sell the bar," he said, still sniffling, "can I come back home?"

"Sell the damn place first!"

After the forced sale, the Mayzsak family turned into a matriarchy. Big Ed took a welding job in Kaiser's fabrication division and stopped at the Mexican grocery each evening to buy a few beers, which he would guzzle before dinner. Otherwise he was teetotal and quiet.

And at last he had his hogs, squealing, snorting, snuffling creatures that smashed out of their pens and occupied most of Elaine's free time. They were as bright and playful as children, and she named each one. Big Ed treated them as family till they reached two hundred pounds, and then stuck them in the throat.

"He'd put newborns in the oven to keep 'em warm," Elaine recalled. "We made blood sausage. Slovenians love it. When I found out what was inside, I never ate it again."

5

The three Mayzsak children attended nearby Slover Boyle Elementary School, where most of their schoolmates were Hispanic. Elaine didn't speak Spanish but learned some of the street language: *pinche puta, cabrón,* the various forms of *chingar.* The boys had a little rhyme:

> *No me chingas*
> *Juan Dominguez . . .*

The first time Elaine overheard an Anglo boy say the F-word, she was shocked to learn that it meant the same as *chingar.*

As a shy sixth-grader, she was a pretty child with a quick smile and a developing figure. With her friend Salvador Cruz, she reigned over the annual school fiesta, dancing to Latin music, munching on chimichangas, drinking red pop and taking first whack at the piñata. Boys stared at her, and she went home and told Evelyn that she didn't understand why.

Her mother said, "We better take you down to the mall." Both were surprised when the saleswoman suggested a B cup. "Imagine that," Evelyn told Big Ed on a note of pride. "From nothing to a B cup."

From that day on, Elaine had boyfriends. "I would go steady every two weeks. I wanted to be in love, but it never happened. In Sequoia Junior High three boys took turns walking me to class. I thought they were all cute. But . . . I was looking for somebody different."

Her IQ was above average, but there was no tradition of scholarship in her family, and she had to work for her As and Bs. She was class vice president and a champion dancer. Everyone wondered how the child had become so proficient at the polka, no small distinction in ethnic Fontana.

At thirteen, with the family finances bottomed out, she found a summer job typing case histories for an allergist in the city that she and her neighbors insisted on calling "San Berdeeno." She grew out of her last flour-sack dress and began wearing sister Beverly's hand-me-downs. She lunched daily at a hamburger joint called McDonald's, a business that was later sold to a man named Ray Kroc for $2 million. She couldn't afford a professional ear-piercing treatment, so she applied an ice cube and stuck a needle through the lobe and into a potato, a surgery so cheap and successful that she did the same for Beverly and some of her friends. Their mother declined the complimentary service with a shriek.

6

By the time Elaine entered Fontana High School, she'd developed into a leggy beauty with dark hazel eyes, a patrician nose and butterscotch hair to her waist. Years of farmyard twisting and stretching had created an hourglass physique without the bulges of a body-builder.

She made the cheerleading squad, but her small voice cracked when she yelled. Sometimes she broke into a twirpy giggle that sounded more like a hiccup or a gulp and seemed to come from a four-year-old girl inside.

She placed second in a contest for Miss Fontana, the local goddess of oranges, hogs and steel. Friends insisted she would have won except for class prejudice; three sets of tracks ran through town, and she was from the wrong side of all of them.

Her ideas about marriage took shape early. "I made up my mind I wouldn't promise to love, honor and obey unless I loved the boy enough to make it for life. My mom never really loved my dad—

that was their problem. I decided I would never divorce. I heard too much of that talk growing up."

She lacked tricks or wiles, and her personality kept suitors off balance. Years later a cousin recalled, "She was the original 'just do it' person, direct, always getting things done. Nothing was a big deal. I swear, if you said, 'Hey, we're invited to visit the president,' she'd say, 'What should I wear?' "

In 1963, when Elaine turned eighteen, she made a down payment on an anthracite-black 1958 Corvette with silver inserts. Her obsession with performance cars dated to a family visit from her third cousin, comedian Frank Gorshin, "the man of a million faces," who'd rolled into Fontana in a Jaguar XKE, performed his Jimmy Cagney and Burt Lancaster impressions in the Mayzsak kitchen, and left Elaine convinced that nothing less than a Jag would ever do for her, or maybe a Porsche or a Corvette.

Her fifteen-year-old brother showed her how to change fluids, filters, spark plugs and ignition wires. "You cut off the ends and put on new wires," he explained, "but you only do one at a time, or you get the timing off." Young men gawked as Elaine drove through town with her girlfriends, stomping the gas pedal with her black pumps and making the engine snarl and spit.

By day she attended typing and filing classes and daydreamed about an acting career. Her Aunt Shirley lived in the San Fernando Valley, dated George Raft and other stars, and had played a bit part in the film *Aaron Slick from Punkin Crick.*

Sometimes the vivacious woman brought visitors to the Mayzsak house: stars like Tony Curtis or Vince Edwards. "We're on our way to the Springs," she would call out from the front seat of a convertible.

Aunt Shirley got Elaine a job as an extra in a movie, but her big scene was cut.

7

College had never been in the picture for the three Mayzsak children. Who would pay the tuition, with Big Ed teetering toward his second bankruptcy? Most Fontana High graduates joined the eight thousand mill hands at Kaiser Steel, enlisted in the armed services or became artisans or laborers.

A week after graduation in 1963, Elaine was hired as a stenographer at the Mira Loma Air Force Station near Los Angeles. She couldn't believe her luck.

She'd been on the job for a year when she drove to San Bernardino to attend the Rolling Stones' first U.S. concert. With her friend Nancy Groff, she cruised Fontana on Friday night and, as usual, attracted male attention, as much for the black-and-silver Corvette as for her ensemble of black stretch pants, plum sweater and black boots. The two nineteen-year-olds headed east on Route 66 to the latest teenage hangout, the Cinnamon Cinder, a nonalcoholic nightclub. Inside the big concrete building they found two hundred teenagers dancing, swilling pop and filling the air with smoke, some of it from tobacco.

"This isn't for us," Nancy said.

They were on the way out when Elaine heard a male voice say, "Wanna dance?"

She turned and saw a tall young man in a fluffy brown mohair sweater that gave him a faint resemblance to a giant panda. She thought, What's this big guy doing with all these kids?

It was like dancing with Arthur Murray himself. He stood two or three inches over six feet, but he carried himself like a lightweight. Through her fingertips she felt the muscles twitching in his back.

He didn't seem inclined to talk. She asked, "Do you have a name?"

"Joe," he said in a deep baritone.

"How old are you?"

"Nineteen."

"How come I never saw you around here?"

"I'm at Berkeley. Premed. I'm here for the summer."

Up close, she took note of a baby face set off by dark and slightly slanty eyes. His tall shock of wavy brown hair was speckled with sun glints of blond and red. She looked for imperfections and found none.

At the end of the slow dance he thanked her politely and wandered off. She thought, Darn! That guy was *different.*

The giant panda lingered in her mind all summer. Living in an apartment in L.A. and working at an Air Force base, she dated often, but none of the men met her lofty standards for a wedding partner or even a steady.

After a few months she was transferred to Norton Air Force Station in San Bernardino and once again found herself cruising with Nancy Groff. They dropped in at a teenage gathering and saw five or six couples mooning and dipping around the big open living room.

The University of California student sat on a couch. "Hey," Elaine blurted out. "I know you!"

He smiled but didn't invite her to dance or sit. After a while the partygoers migrated to another house, and Elaine found herself talking to two men on her left and another on her right while trying to keep track of the big head of brown wavy hair among the dancers. It annoyed her that he didn't seem interested.

She was dancing with a boy a head shorter when the familiar deep voice broke in. "C'mon, Elaine."

He still seemed shy. She figured he was preoccupied with school. The fall semester started in a few days. No one became a doctor without years of hard work and study.

After another dance she began to worry that he would wander off again. She decided to take him outside and show him her 'Vette. Every young Fontanan was obsessed with cars.

Joe looked appropriately impressed. "Yours?" he asked.

"Well, of course."

She offered him a demonstration ride.

"Uh . . . let's just sit," he said. He reached across the leather seats and took her hand. She allowed him a brief kiss and he turned into the usual teenage octopus. Well, Elaine told herself, he's not *that* different. Her figure was always a provocation, no matter how demurely she dressed, and her small voice made her sound like the pushover that she wasn't.

She said, *"No!"* and pulled away. She hoped he wasn't offended. She thought, I bet he'd make a good husband! Her mother had always said that it was okay if a man didn't try to kiss on the first date, but if he didn't try on the second, he was undersexed and the marriage would fail.

Joe murmured something about Aphrodite.

Elaine asked, "Who?"

"Venus," he said.

"The star?"

"The goddess."

Hercules and Zeus were the only mythical gods she'd ever heard of. "Goddess of what?" she asked.

He giggled and didn't answer.

They exchanged last names and phone numbers. She didn't quite catch the name. *"Gary?"* she asked.

"Gere," he said. "G-E-R-E. It's Hungarian." When he pronounced the name, it still sounded like "Gary."

At home Elaine looked up *Aphrodite* and gulped. She'd always been nervous around college men. Big words, big ideas, BMOCs full of beer, hot air and quotes. They reminded her that she'd been raised with hogs. Besides, it seemed a little early to be invoking the goddess of love.

The next morning she was dressing for church when an ugly green station wagon with a Fontana H. S. Steelers sticker bumped down the driveway ahead of a cloud of bluish exhaust. "That's *yours?*" she asked.

"Hell, no," Joe Gere said as though it was a silly question. "It's my parents'. Mine's in the shop for a tuck."

She canceled church in favor of a stroll, and they'd hardly reached the grapes before he told her he had a confession to make. Oh God, she said to herself, he's a dope dealer; he's wanted by the police; he's engaged; he's married; he's got three kids—

"I don't go to Berkeley," he said. "I'm, uh—I'm in school."

"School?" she asked. "Where?"

He said he'd just finished his junior year at Fontana High.

Elaine let go of his hand and asked, "How old *are* you?"

He said he'd just turned seventeen.

She realized that if she'd known his age, she wouldn't have looked twice at him. Now she was halfway hooked, and by a high school kid.

"What's the difference? he said. "You're not that old yourself. How old are you? Thirty?" He had a smart-ass grin on his face.

"I was nineteen in May."

"Jeez. Elderly."

She asked how he knew about the Greek gods if he wasn't in college. "You don't have to be in college to read books," he said.

I thought I'd heard all the lines, she said to herself, but this guy is unusual.

When he asked for a date, she gulped and put him off. "Joe, I gotta think about this."

He said he would drop by in the morning.

Jimmy Mayzsak was working on his 1956 Chevy convertible when the tall kid drove up and walked into the garage as though he were a member of the family.

Elaine's little brother removed his nose from the gear box and stood up, a greasy wrench in hand. Even at seventeen, he was an intimidating figure, a sandy-haired road warrior who was already tearing up bars and challenging town bullies, including Hell's Angels. At five-ten, he had a thin waist, no backside, twenty-two-inch biceps, and his father's barrel chest and shoulders. He won bets by bending beer can openers one-handed. His mother described him as "his dad without the gut."

"Who the hell are *you?*" Jimmy asked.

"I'm here to see Elaine."

"What the hell for?"

The kid ignored the question. Jimmy took a step forward. "Aren't you kinda young for my sister?"

"Old enough," the kid said evenly.

Jimmy was impressed. Like most Fontana boys, he divided his fellow males into two classes: you took on the tough guys and won or lost. The others were dogshit.

He smacked the wrench against his palm two or three times, and the kid didn't blink. Jimmy thought, If he's really Elaine's friend, I better back off. "Wait here," he said. "I think she's inside."

"Thanks," the kid said. It was the beginning of a friendship that would last until violent death.

II

MAN AMONG MEN

1

When Joe Gere was a small child in Appalachia, his family lifestyle was as Hungarian as if he'd lived in Budapest. In bituminous coal towns like Pursglove, West Virginia (population two hundred), the citizens were classified as "wops," "Johnny Bulls," "micks," "Polocks" and other racist names. Hungarians were "hunkies." Second-generation Americans like little Joey were taught to stand straight when they were called such names, and if the insult was repeated, they were instructed to knock the offender on his *bal sege*, a family phrase which was pronounced "ball sheggee" and meant "left ass."

Little Joey's mother, Reva Dawson Gere, was six years younger than her husband Joe Sr. and had luxuriant finespun hair that she passed to her four children. She cooked Hungarian-style, laboring over lamb and pork dishes called *porkolt*, thick cherry soup, and *csirke* (chicken) paprikas, served with thimbles of Tokay. At her husband's request, Reva omitted the soupy stew called *gulyas* from their cuisine. "I'm all goulashed out," Joe Sr. informed her after their marriage in 1946.

Their first son, Joey, was born in 1947 while the family lived in a company shack in Pursglove No. 2 Hollow, pronounced "Holler." Everyone in the village had one of two addresses: "Number One" or "Number Two." The miners called their home state "West by

God Virginia'' and Pennsylvania "Northern West by God Virginia.''
(Later, when some of them migrated west, they dubbed their new
home "Fontucky'' and "Morgantown with sunshine.'')

In No. 2 Holler, the rare good times were fueled with a drink
known as corn. Family friend Mike Pompura remembered exactly
how the birth of baby Joey Gere was celebrated, " 'cause it's the way
we celebrated everything. Our motto was 'I'll drink to that.' We
drank to Truman's birthday, floods, card tricks. We drank corn when
the Pirates and the Steelers won and lost. We drank corn like other
folks breathe.''

Reva and her infant son Joey seemed unusually close. An Eastern
European principle held that male children should be toughened
rather than cuddled or squeezed. Reva adhered to the teaching with
her later children, but her firstborn was seldom far from her arms.

When the boy was eighteen months old, she bent over his crib
and the hem of her nightgown curled into a gas heater. She rolled
herself in a blanket and passed out.

Joe Sr. drove her to the hospital. Doctors found her bra and
nightgown fused to her skin. Her long dark hair, rolled into rats,
had shielded her head and face, but her back and underarms were
as black as Pursglove coal.

Medics told the sturdy mountain woman that she could bear no
more children; toxins from the burns had damaged major organs
and weakened her heart. Her fingernails and three fingertips were
gone. Reddish patches marked grafts removed from her thighs.

She begged Joe Sr. to divorce her and start a new life with little
Joey. "Nah," said the tough little miner.

Reva tried to resume her usual busy schedule, but visitors would
often see her in her black rocking chair, exhausted. Little Joey would
toddle toward her and she would push him away. She tried to explain
that she couldn't raise her arms without pain, but the child was too
young to comprehend.

Three hurtful years passed before she was able to hold her firstborn
again. When she picked him up, they were both so happy they cried.

2

In 1952, the coal vein ran out. Joey was five and his younger brother Bob (a major surprise to the family doctor) had just turned one. Reva, pregnant with her third son, Rick, took a job in a Morgantown shirt factory.

Two years later, Joe Gere Sr. was still unemployed, his loved ones living on gravy and pole beans and wearing clothes that were mostly patches. Little Joey, a second-grader, wore the same short pants all winter. Joe told his wife, "I don't want these three boys workin' in mines. We're gittin' where it's warm."

Reva and her sons stayed behind in Pursglove No. 2 Holler while the family head nursed a rattly 1953 Ford nearly three thousand miles to Fontana, where an older brother already worked at the Kaiser mill. A few days after arrival, Joe Sr. found himself on his knees again, this time bundling steel plates at $1.62 an hour. "After the mines," he wrote home, "this here's like a vacation."

In August 1954, he made a down payment on a small ranch house and retrieved his family. The Geres impressed their new neighbors. Joey played in abandoned fields and ammunition bunkers and called the women "may-em." Father and son became known as Big Joe and Little Joe. Reva served West Virginia breakfasts and became a Brownie leader and PTA president. Her half-pint husband managed Little League teams and took on other extracurricular duties. Pursglove No. 2 was a memory.

Along with just about every other Fontanan, Joe Sr. drank his share of Coors and Bud. Every Saturday night the steelworkers replaced their chaws with Sen-sen and Pine Bros. glycerine tablets and sallied off, spending so much time in bars that even nonsmokers eventually died of lung cancer, their bronchi black and gray with a hint of red from the mineral dust that floated off the Kaiser slag like windblown talc.

Little Joey observed the drinking that went on around him and considered it normal behavior. He'd been offered his first sip of Tokay at five. Later he told Elaine that his mother seemed to think it was cute to make him tipsy. In constant pain, Reva had escalated from wine to vodka. The Geres' youngest child, Linda, recalled, "We were an alcoholic family. Plenty of denial, plenty of arguments. First it cursed us, then it killed."

3

Like Elaine Mayzsak, Joey acted more mature than his years. He raised pigeons and sold them at a nickel profit. He dug machine-gun rounds from an old firing range and hawked them as mementos of World War II. From ten on, he had pocket money to share with his brothers. He told a friend he could never work eight to five like his father. "There's gotta be a better way." His favorite book was *Tom Sawyer* and his favorite scene the painting of the fence.

An uncle said, "Joey always had a blue suit. Everybody said it made him look like a lawyer. That's what he should've been. Joey could talk the devil into going to church."

In retrospect, family members felt that in some odd way Reva's accident fused the souls of mother and son. They often talked about his plan to become a doctor, even though both knew that higher education was beyond the family's means. Joey did housework and cajoled his siblings into keeping quiet. He told his sickly little sister Linda that his mother's flaming silhouette staggered toward him every night in his dreams. Sometimes he saved her; sometimes she burned off like steam.

* * *

In a town where machismo was learned in nursery school and a teenage boy who didn't know how to ride a "motorsickle" was considered backward, Joey also served as his little brother's protector.

"He didn't know fear," said his father. "He'd take on anybody. I asked him one time, 'Son, do you know this guy so-and-so?' He was a dope dealer, six or seven years older. Joey said, 'Yeah, I already knocked him on his *bal sege.*'"

Five young males beat up brother Bob in the sixth grade, and Joey exacted revenge one by one.

Early in his junior year at Fontana High School, while Elaine Mayzsak was working as a civil service stenographer, the lean young man was discovered by girls. "You couldn't keep 'em away," said Bob. "Two or three came over at a time."

In a working-class town where boys dressed down, his physique brought gulps. At sixteen he carried his six feet "tall and straight," a friend recalled, "very proud of his height, with a long hunter's stride." The narrowness of his dark eyes produced an exotic effect; some thought he looked a little Oriental. He experimented with various styles of mustaches and sideburns. One local admirer said he had "looks like Ricky Nelson, style like John Wayne, and a body like Attila's Hun." Some saw a resemblance to the young Elvis.

He had a commanding voice, soft but authoritative, and looked his listeners straight on. He smelled faintly of Old Spice, like his father, smoked Marlboros and snapped a Zippo lighter in the manner of Humphrey Bogart. In some ways he seemed naive. A supermarket checker snapped a bare-chested picture of him smiling in her line and presented a copy of the print with a wink. He thanked her for the kindness and gave the picture to his mother.

Late in his junior year he went on a date with the daughter of conservative Baptists, and soon was accompanying the family to church in Riverside. At their urging, he was baptized. When the romance faded he dropped religion and began snaking up Sierra Street in his hot car, hanging out at Pepe's, attending dances and parties and working on his line of chatter.

Then he went dancing at the Cinnamon Cinder and met Elaine Mayzsak.

III

COMBUSTION

1

Elaine and her panda-bear friend strolled between the heavy-hanging rows of the Tudor Winery's grapes. A rheumy disk of sun flickered through clouds and smog; her father had joked that "some of the steelworkers are goin' back to Pittsburgh for a breath of air." Calves huddled under a plywood lean-to that Big Ed had built for shade.

Elaine asked Joe why she'd never seen him on the football field. He said he'd been a sub defensive lineman for the Fontana High School Steelers, but the team was so poor he'd lost interest and quit. He preferred hunting and fishing in the mountains.

She asked if he had a steady girlfriend and he said no. His dad worked at Kaiser's and his mom ran a nursery school. He had two younger brothers and a little sister, and Elaine could tell by the way he talked that they were as tight as the Mayzsak kids.

On their first date, he took her to a monster movie. A few nights later they drove to Pepe's in his newly renovated Pontiac for cherry Cokes and pastrami grinders. Unlike previous boyfriends, he didn't try to show off his driving skills. Even when she let him take the wheel of her black Corvette, he obeyed the laws. Fontana boys weren't usually so mature.

Most of her boyfriends had traveled in packs and introduced her around as though she were an ornament, but Joe kept trying to get her alone. He made a big impression on her mother and sister. "He's so tall!" Beverly commented. "So big. So handsome—"

"—so taken," said Elaine.

Joe seemed embarrassed when Elaine's gorgeous cousin gave him a squeeze and a peck on the cheek. Later he asked, "You didn't get mad about that?"

Elaine explained, "We're a huggy-kissy family. Haven't you noticed by now? We hug everybody."

Joe said his people were more reserved. "I tried to kiss my mom the other day and she pulled away. She's just that way."

He told Elaine that Hungarians didn't show much physical affection and considered public displays to be vulgar. My goodness, Elaine said to herself, I've got a lot of work to do.

Despite his youth, Joe spewed out more big words than any male she'd ever known. If he wasn't yammering away about Edgar Rice Burroughs or Zane Grey, he was pointing out the constellations and spinning tales about Cassiopeia and Sagittarius and other unpronounceable names. He tried to teach her chess, and she was flattered that he treated her like an intellectual equal, but when he tried to teach her his favorite gambit, she pleaded a headache. After that, she turned their conversations to school and cars.

Some nights he barely stopped talking long enough to kiss. They would park for an hour or two, and he wouldn't make his move till it was almost time to go home.

Now that he'd accepted her ground rules, she found him exciting. For a seventeen-year-old, he was an accomplished kisser. She wondered where he'd learned. They didn't talk about love. She was still nervous about robbing the cradle.

She was surprised to see how small his father was and how tall and stolid the mother. The Geres were polite but made her wonder if they bore her some unspoken resentment. It was plain that Joe was the family hero. She'd seen the same pattern before; her holy-terror brother Jimmy was treated like a tin god. She guessed it was the Eastern European way.

A puzzling quote came back from a friend: "Joe said, 'I like Elaine but I don't know what to make of her. I go over there one night and she's sewing some kind of doily thing, and the next night she's butchering a pig.'"

She performed a quick makeover in the direction of ultrafemininity. A friend warned her that if she became any more ladylike, she and her parasol would be carried off on the next dust devil. She'd never had to alter her style for her previous boyfriends, but this elongated kid was worth the trouble.

After four or five dates, he drove her along a dirt road to an old stone chapel with a terra-cotta roof. The one-room building, a mile from her house in the Jurupa Hills, had been built for migrant workers in 1908 and was a minor tourist attraction, but the parking lot was deserted after dark. Elaine asked how many girls he'd taken there, and he insisted that she was the first. Moonlight glinted off the outside mirror like a diamond on an engagement ring.

In the middle of a kiss, he broke off and said, "You're not going out with anybody else, are ya?"

"No," she said. "What about you?"

"No." His nose nuzzled her ear. "So," he said, "it's kinda like, uh—we're going together. Right?"

"Well, sure!"

She realized that she should have said, Hey, let me think about it. But there was nothing to think about, and she'd never been much of an actress. Except for his age, Joe Gere was exactly what she wanted. And he was more mature than some twenty-year-olds she'd dated. He sometimes nipped at a bottle he kept under the seat, but that just made him a typical Fontanan like her father and Joe's father and every other male she knew.

"Well, okay then," Joe said nonchalantly. He could have been discussing a new camshaft. "I guess we're going together."

Another month passed before he brought up the delicate subject of love. It was January 1965, and sticky-hot in Fontana. A popcorn smell mingled with gasoline fumes as a lone coyote critiqued the drive-in film from a nearby knoll.

"I love you, Elaine," Joe whispered.

"Oh, I love you too," she said.

He seemed a little embarrassed. He was plainly more interested in kissing.

2

By February, four months after they'd met, Elaine was still working as an Air Force steno and Joe was in his senior year at Fontana High. To their friends, they seemed joined at the lips, camping, hunting, fishing, dating, parking. Sometimes he borrowed her black Corvette to drive to school. One night he took her bowling with his parents. The families drew closer when Joe began to hang out with her brother Jimmy. Since the staredown in the Mayzsak driveway, the two young men had developed a mutual respect based on the outdoors, guns, pool, beer and the internal combustion engine.

On a winter afternoon during one of the frequent smog alerts, Elaine was wondering if her allergy shots had been a waste of money when Joe phoned to ask if she would mind if he went out that night with his friend Vince "and the boys."

Big Ed's daughter was indoctrinated into the cultural attitudes of steelworkers and hog farmers and members of the armed services, and it still seemed natural to her that males did as they pleased and females adapted. At nineteen, she'd barely set foot outside San Bernardino County, and then only to work for the military, and an acceptance of male arrogance was as much a part of her makeup as a knowledge of how to boil the bristles off a boar.

"Have fun," she said.

Around ten at night she was practicing her shorthand in the kitchen of the old house in the Jurupa Hills when an adolescent neighbor burst into the Mayzsak home. "Hey, Elaine," the girl said, "can I tell you something and you won't get mad?"

"Sure," she said.

"Joe's out on a date tonight. They went to a movie."

Elaine was doubly perplexed. She knew her rival slightly; she was brunette, short, and shaped like a T-paper roll.

Elaine thought, Have I been taking Joe for granted? Getting careless? She didn't think so. Every morning she got up before anyone else, showered, spent almost an hour on her hair and makeup. She'd always enjoyed feeling neat and clean, and besides, she never knew when Joe might come to call.

Her mood went from bafflement to pique to rage. What did going steady mean, for gosh sakes? Joe had plenty of admirers, but so did she. If he's cheating on me already, she thought, what'll he do in a year or two? *What kind of husband would he make?*

Just after eleven, she headed for the other woman's house. Joe's car was parked in front, and she saw two heads in silhouette. Apparently the lovebirds had just returned from the movie.

She yanked the girl out by her hair and called Joe every name she'd ever heard in her father's bar or read on its bathroom walls. "You want her?" she yelled. *"You can have her!"*

She laid a smear of rubber as she left.

Back home, she perched on the front edge of a kitchen chair and watched for his headlights. He pulled in at midnight and jumped from his car babbling. He said he was thrilled that she loved him enough to fight for him; he hadn't realized how much he loved her; he would never cheat on her again; the date was the girl's idea, she'd insisted that Vince fix them up; it was a combination of errors and poor judgment; blah blah and *blah* . . .

She told him she would have to think things over.

In the morning she decided to take direct action and phoned her rival. "We need to talk," she said.

"Why not?" the girl answered. "I'll drive right over." She sounded defiant.

An hour later an old Ford rattled up the Mayzsak driveway. The girl stepped out while another female stayed behind the wheel.

Elaine thought, Whatever happens, I'm not backing down. She'd had only one brief fight in her whole life, with some biker mamas who'd stolen her wallet, but she'd spent years roughhousing with one of the toughest guys in town, her brother Jimmy.

The rival was shorter but about the same weight. Elaine said, "You leave my boyfriend alone!" When the girl cocked a fist, Elaine punched her in the face.

The girl dived to safety and the old Ford accelerated behind an explosion of gravel.

Jimmy appeared on the porch. "Hey," he said, "I thought you guys were gonna have a talk."

"That was our talk," Elaine said.

3
___

Joe Gere graduated with his class in June 1965 and went into instant debt for a black 1960 Corvette with foot-wide slicks, mag wheels, headers and a supercharged engine. His racing convertible blew the doors off Elaine's car every time they dragged. She'd always been amused by machismo. When a gas station attendant cracked that she was hanging around Joe for his car, she said, "*My* 'Vette's parked at home."

Joe was eighteen now, two years and two months younger than Elaine, and they were lovers, committed for life. Together, they hammered out a plan. Joe would begin the long climb toward a medical degree by attending junior college in nearby Upland. Elaine would quit her civil service job and take a prenursing course at the same school. Someday they would have a family practice or work as a surgical team, flying off to the Third World to save lives and hunt bushbuck.

Every morning they made the tedious commute, alternating in their Corvettes. Joe breezed through his classes but didn't seem motivated. Elaine had been out of school for two years, hated math, and had no background in chemistry, a required subject. On her first day in the lab, the instructor said, "Now take your Bunsen burner . . ."

"Joe," Elaine whispered, "what's a Bunsen burner?"

On the drive back to Fontana she announced that she was dropping chemistry.

Joe reminded her that she couldn't be a nurse without it. "Then I'll be something else," she replied.

"Like what?"

"A—a lab tech."

"That takes chemistry, too."

She complained that she couldn't relate to scientific subjects; the college brochures always talked about dissecting frogs and mixing weird bubbly concoctions, but in the classroom everything came down to numbers. She was beginning to wonder if she belonged in college.

"Hey," Joe said, turning his tanned face toward hers, "I feel the same way."

"Don't you want to be a doctor?"

"That was Mom's idea."

Two weeks after the school year had begun, Joe took a job at Rohr Aircraft in nearby Riverside as an apprentice metal bonder on Boeing 707s, and Elaine enrolled in Ferguson's Beauty School. For nine weeks she wrapped permanents on dummies, learned the bone structure of the head and how to cut, rat, tease, bleach, mix colors, add toners, and create high-fashion hairdos. She became a virtuoso of the bouffant, so skilled at arranging hair in gravity-defying stacks that Ferguson's manager invited her to stay on as an instructor.

She applied her new skills to her mother's graying hair until Big Ed complained, "People come up to your mom and ask her what she's doing with an old guy like me. It's that goddamn new hairdo."

Elaine had always noticed that Joe seemed attracted to blondes. She'd been a blonde as a child, before her hair had darkened to a deep honey brown. On a whim she decided to use her training on herself.

"My God!" Joe said when he saw the results. "It's, it's—Marilyn Monroe!"

Overnight the runner-up for Miss Fontana seemed to have transformed herself into a public spectacle, drawing all eyes. She decided to dye her gleaming blond coiffure back to plain old brown. "I don't like attention," she explained to Joe.

He grumbled but accepted her decision. For years afterward, he pressured her to return to blonde, until she finally gave in.

After that, she noticed that he seemed to enjoy showing her off. Her mother explained, "Men love to be seen with blondies."

"*Blondies?*" Elaine said. The word sounded so cheap. "Well, I guess it's okay, as long as I'm the blondie."

4

Early in 1966, Joe was drafted. On his first home leave, he proposed, but Big Ed warned his daughter, "Don't even think about no weddin'. I got a million things to do first."

"What kind of things?" Elaine asked.

"Just . . . weddin' things," the old welder answered.

Elaine tried to be understanding. Her parents had been upset when her older sister Beverly married in Mexico. They wanted their children to marry in the old Slovenian tradition. Big Ed was always looking for an excuse to dig a pit, roast a pig and have a party. What better excuse than the middle child's wedding?

A few days later, Elaine watched as her father unloaded calves, piglets and turkey polts from his truck. The ceremony was set for July 1967, when Joe was scheduled to complete Army Officer Candidate School, but he fell down an embankment and dislocated his hip, causing a postponement. Then, after the Mayzsaks had mailed five hundred new invitations to the rescheduled August nuptials of "Miss Elaine Mayzsak" and "Second Lieutenant Joseph Paul Gere," Joe beat up a superior and was cashiered from the program. He wrote home, "They only want West Pointers to have commissions."

Three days before the grand final revised wedding date of September 16, Private Joe Gere, now a slim 180 pounds and either six-three or six-five, depending on whether his big hair was included in the measurement, arrived in Fontana to find everyone gabbling about the wedding. It was said that Ed Mayzsak planned the social event of the decade. Joe wanted a simple civil ceremony, but Elaine reminded him that she'd been confirmed in the Catholic Church and didn't intend to marry under any other auspices. He signed a paper agreeing to bring up their children in the faith, clearing the way for a ceremony at St. Joseph's.

Elaine took the words of the service to heart. "When I got married," she explained later, "it was for life. That's the way I was raised. Look how my mom and dad put up with each other.

"The priest told me and Joe, 'Remember, God is head of the church just like the man is head of the household.' That was fine with me. I waited to find somebody I would *always* love. Divorce would never happen."

The bride's family had hired Fontana's Italian-American Club to celebrate this symbolic reconstitution of the ancient kingdom of Austria-Hungary, and the drafty old building was barely big enough to hold the food and drinks, let alone dozens of guests and crashers. Big Ed had spent the previous day and night butchering livestock and preparing turkeys that were so overstuffed they could barely gobble. Evelyn Mayzsak's garlic potato salad was heaped in a mound on a reinforced table. Three silver tureens held the traditional Hungarian cherry soup, topped with crème fraîche and laced with Tokay. There were foot-high stacks of wursts, including knack- and brat-, cheeses ranging from Parmesan as hard as San Gorgonio Mountain to a Port du Salut runny enough to be sipped. The lemon-vanilla wedding cake measured four feet across, each layer six inches thick, surrounded by beds of marzipan, fudge, divinity, candy truffles and the Italian hard candy called *cicci*.

"Twenty thousand people lived in Fontana," Elaine recalled years later, "and I think my dad invited every one. Either he'd served 'em at his bar or drunk with 'em at somebody else's bar or knew 'em at Kaiser. My sister Beverly was married to a Sclafani—thirteen kids in their family—so a bunch of I-talians showed up. Joe's 'Uncle' Mikey Pompura brought the Slavs. Somebody else tipped off the Serbs, and the Slovenian hall gave up and shut down for the day. Mom's people flew in from Wisconsin and Dad's from Illinois. The band must've played 'The Beer Barrel Polka' ten times, czardas, polkas, tarantellas, mazurkas."

Joe's younger brother Bobby gawked at a trio of Croats playing tamburitza music during the hired orchestra's break. "Half these guys are speaking American and half are speaking Hungarian," he shouted into the ear of his brother Rick.

"Yeah," the youngest brother said, "and the other half are Polocks."

Joe's Aunt Marjorie Cirillo, his father's younger sister, blinked back tears. "My goodness, look at those two," sighed the gracious woman, who'd been known to her nieces and nephews as "Aunt Mogie" since their babyhood difficulties with pronunciation. "They're so *matched*. Perfect specimens. A picture-book couple."

As far as Elaine knew, there were no Greeks in attendance, but every few minutes a glass shattered against the floor, and after a while it sounded as though they were dancing on grit. Mike Pompura sold bridal dances for outrageous prices.

"It's okay to step on my toes, honey," a Kaiser worker whispered in her ear. "We all wear steel caps."

At midnight the newlyweds climbed into their new convertible Corvette and made a beeline for Joe's station at Fort Eustis, Virginia, honeymooning cross-country at ninety miles an hour. They found out later that Big Ed's wedding party reconvened at the Mayzsak farm and lasted three days.

IV

EARLY SORROW

1

After a few months, Private Joe Gere was ordered to Korea with the Him Jim Scouts of the 2nd Infantry Division, and Elaine went back to work for her thirteen colonels at Norton Air Force Base in San Bernardino. She thought of herself as a war bride. Joe told her not to worry; the fighting in Korea had been over for fifteen years.

He wrote colorful letters in a schoolboyish handwriting as easy to read as letterpress. After a few months she became surprised at his romantic intensity. She threw away the mushiest notes so her mother wouldn't see them.

Some of his buddies, he wrote, were receiving "Dear John" letters. "What about you?" he wrote. "Are you sure you still love me?"

When she replied that she loved him more every minute, he fired back, "Are you being faithful?"

For a moment she was annoyed. He was like a child. What did she have to do to prove her love, pitch herself off the top of Mount Baldy? But then she pictured him standing guard duty in a Korean ice storm, and she thought of his cold parents, and she remembered how Reva hadn't been able to pick him up when he was an infant. She said to herself, Of *course* he's jealous and insecure, way over there with a bunch of foreigners. Who wouldn't be?

She took an evening sales job at Marian's Dress Shop in the Inland Center Mall in San Bernardino. Every night at ten she dragged herself home from work and wrote him a long letter—*every* night.

Then she would read herself to sleep with *Journey to the Center of the Earth* or another book in the Mars Series, his favorites, so she could quote passages and make him realize that she went to bed with no one except him and Edgar Rice Burroughs.

"Looks like you're keeping busy," he wrote, "but how are you spending your weekends?"

She replied that she'd attended one party since he'd left, with her brother. "Jimmy wouldn't let me out of his sight the whole time," she wrote. "He had his arm around me and told everybody I was his date so nobody would scheme on me. Somebody lit a joint and he got me out of there. So you see—you don't have to worry about your wife."

When Joe still seemed insecure, she began to spend weekends at the Geres' house. She taught his thirteen-year-old sister Linda how to use makeup, how to knit, how to style her hair so she looked older. The child was a diabetic, in and out of hospitals, and her exhausted mother was grateful for assistance. The women baked cookies and cakes, and Elaine mailed them off, buffered by popcorn in monstrous boxes. Joe's platoon sent her a letter of thanks.

"Now," she wrote after a few months of the frenzied routine, "do you believe you have a faithful wife?"

Joe replied that he sure hoped so.

For the first six months or so, he didn't write much about his activities, and she took him at his word that summer camp had been far more dangerous. But gradually the truth crept into his letters. The Him Jim Scouts, predecessors of the Green Berets, pulled two-week reconnaissance patrols that brought them into the fire zones of North Korean soldiers in the heart of the DMZ, the most unsettled piece of real estate in the country. Two of Joe's fellow scouts were killed by infiltrators. Then his last-minute replacement on a night patrol was picked off by a sniper. "It should've been me," he apologized in a letter. "I guess it wasn't my time to go." Whenever he discussed the incident, he seemed ashamed. Later Elaine wondered if it had contributed to the load of guilt that eventually dragged him down.

She was excited to see him in the February 2, 1968, edition of *Life*, walking point in the snow-covered DMZ, but the picture also reminded her that he was engaged in hazardous duty. His letters always ended on an up note:

Well, honey, I'm going to go & mail this letter now, so I'll be closing. I love you & miss you very much, honey. Don't worry about me, honey, because as you can see, I can take care of myself. Be good, honey, & I'll be home before you know it. Only 94 days left. I love you.

Your loving husband
x Joe x

In November 1969, Sergeant Joe Gere returned to Fontana. His little sister Linda described the scene when the family hero appeared on the Gere front walk with armloads of presents:

"I heard Dad holler, 'My God!' I thought he was having a heart attack or something. He's looking out the kitchen window and yelling, 'It's Joey! *It's Joey!'* He started choking. I ran over to help and saw that he was crying. I didn't know what to do. The tears just streamed down. When Mom saw Joey, she broke down too."

Later Elaine said to herself, How stupid it is to pass judgment. Never again would she think of the Geres as cold or unemotional. Hungarians just had a different style.

2

The young Geres took a claustrophobic little apartment in nearby Rialto, and Joe, fresh from three years of military discipline, began carousing with his hard-drinking brothers, Rick and Bob, and his rowdy brother-in-law, Jim. At first, Elaine didn't object. She'd grown up with a wandering father—"I thought that running around and drinking all night was what men did," she explained later.

Joe didn't get drunk, so what was the harm? He could mix rivers of Jack Daniel's with estuaries of Coors and Bud and still drive in a straight line. If he planned to get up at three in the morning to hunt ducks at Tule Lake, he would be awake and alert no matter how big a load he'd taken on the night before.

And it wasn't as though he were trying to avoid his wife, like so many of their studly male friends. He'd tried hard to turn Elaine into his drinking partner, but she couldn't keep up with him even when she ordered "ladies' drinks" and sipped them as though they were distilled from foxglove leaves. Joe would be on his third or fourth drink while she rushed toward the rest room for another look at her Brandy Alexander. Liquor irritated her system and gave her migraines. She didn't think she was missing out on much.

She was soon reminded that Joe still despised drunks. "If you can't hold your liquor," she heard him snap at his brother Bob, "drink milk!"

Whenever his mother poured herself a drink in his presence, Joe would find an excuse to leave. Privately he told Elaine that Reva was committing suicide one ounce at a time, and nobody in the family seemed to give a damn.

"What can they do?" Elaine asked.

Joe said he wished he knew. She could see that he felt guilty about that, too.

3

Big Ed Mayzsak, freshly retired after thirteen years at Kaiser, moved a seven-hundred-square-foot "free house" from Fullerton to Fontana and placed it next to his own home in the Jurupa Hills. "This is for you kids," the old welder said proudly. He beckoned toward the small pasture in back. "A fella could feed up some pigs."

Joe had always said that he wanted to live on a farm, but there wasn't much farm left. As a result of two bankruptcies, Big Ed had sold off all but four acres and now raised his animals and birds at close range. He supplemented his retirement check by parting out junk cars with an acetylene torch and selling the scrap. His yard was littered with metal carcasses, and Elaine remembered with a twinge how he'd once earned his living skillfully joining metals together.

The young couple paid Big Ed $2,000 for transporting the little Spanish-style house across the desert. After they moved in, Joe seemed content to remain on indefinite R&R. Elaine enjoyed the sight of him on the couch, long legs stretched out, size-13 feet splayed on the coffee table. He went on long hunting and drinking trips with relatives, cronies and a few old friends from the Hell's Angels. As near as Elaine could determine, the main idea was to slaughter as many birds and fish as possible before falling into the water or driving into a ditch.

Joe's industrious father urged him to apply at Kaiser, where he would receive priority as a veteran and an employee's son. Joe put him off and told Elaine, "Look at Dad. Bundles those big steel plates, never takes a sick day, never clocks in late. He drags himself home, drinks a six-pack, and watches TV till he falls asleep in his chair. He's a goddamn machine. No dreams, hasn't read a book in ten years. That's not for me."

He helped Elaine dig a vegetable garden and build some pens, and the young couple turned a small profit feeding up calves, chickens, turkeys, goats and yellow Labrador retrievers.

"I can tell ya how to do cows," Big Ed yelled from his backyard, "but I never butchered no retrievers."

As the months of civilian life passed, Joe stayed out later and later. Elaine still wasn't concerned. After three years in the Army, the guy deserved a break. He gave her no complaints in or out of bed. Relatives whispered that he'd inherited his sex drive from Joe Sr., whose bedroom schedule had remained the same since he was twenty-five (or so said his sickly wife, looking at the ceiling).

A bigger threat to the young marriage seemed to be Joe's insatiable need for demonstrations of love. "Six times a day I had to tell him I loved him," Elaine recalled. "I was always hugging and kissing him, and then he'd complain that I didn't show him enough affection."

For someone who demanded total attention, he volunteered little in return. In public, he couldn't seem to bring himself to hold Elaine's hand or put his arm around her. At home the only pet name he used was "honey." She just figured he was a Gere.

She was surprised that his jealousy didn't ease now that they were married and living under the same roof. He bridled when other men gawked at her but insisted that she continue lightening her hair, which only brought more unwanted attention. One Saturday a lieutenant colonel from the air base paid a social call, and when he left, Joe grabbed her by the shoulders and said, "Don't you ever let that guy come around here again!"

"Why?" she asked. "He's so nice."

"That son of a bitch sat around drinking my liquor and telling me how much he loves you."

Elaine didn't know what to make of the incident until she thought it over. Then she realized that the colonel had probably made an innocent comment—"I think the world of Elaine," or "Your wife's a fine lady," a typical compliment that friends make about one another's spouse after a few drinks. Joe's jealous nature had taken over from there.

She never knew exactly when the cheating started. She discounted the first rumors she heard, taking solace from a remark her mother had made after Big Ed started womanizing in his bar: "Why would a husband go out for hamburger when he's got steak at home?"

As Joe's sister Linda saw the problem, "Elaine and Joe looked like they walked off the cover of *Modern Screen*. They had chances to cheat every time they left the house. Joe strayed, Elaine didn't. Joe loved her, but he just had a roving eye. And he was young, so he didn't always use good judgment. He borrowed our brother Bob's Olds Cutlass to go drinking with one of our neighbors. Things like that. It was hard to keep it quiet."

If Elaine knew what was going on, she neither sought consolation nor confided in her friends or relatives. Linda paid a visit to the little Spanish house and said, "Elaine, why do you give Joe such a long rope?"

There was an uncomfortable silence. Linda said, "I guess you must really love him, huh?"

Elaine replied softly, "Now you're getting it, Linda." To herself, she said, You love a man or you don't. It's not as though I have a choice.

4

After Joe had been out of uniform for four months, he sent a job application to the San Bernardino County Sheriff's Office. Elaine's Uncle Hank Mizysak, a detective on the burglary-arson squad at the time, provided a "juice card" to smooth the way. There was a minor glitch when a background check showed that a mafioso had attended Joe's wedding, but it was explained that the man was a friend of a relative.

Before Joe left for the police academy in the nearby mountains, one of his future supervisors took Elaine aside and said, "You understand, don't you, that police officers have the highest divorce rate . . . ?"

She nodded.

"The highest suicide rate . . ."

She nodded again.

"The highest rate of alcoholism?"

"Yes."

"And one of the highest mortality rates?"

To Elaine, they were only words. How could a law enforcement career be more dangerous than firefights in the DMZ and claymore mines and screaming assassins with bugles and bayonets? Besides, her good shepherd uncle would keep watch. Hank and his wife Dorothy had endured the deaths of two small children, and the Mayzsaks and Mizysaks and other spellings had drawn closer than ever. Uncle Hank had always been one of Elaine's heroes. It was exciting that her husband had chosen the same career.

With his military experience, Joe finished the police academy near the top of his class. "A cakewalk," he announced to Elaine.

The new deputy sheriff was issued a six-inch Trooper Mark III .357 magnum with a swivel holster. When he complained that he couldn't draw such a cannon fast enough, even after hours of practice in front of the mirror, his proud dad handed over his personal .38 revolver.

The graduation party developed into a wild free-for-all. "Everybody showed—clerks, forensics people, street cops, bailiffs, jailers," a deputy recalled. "At four in the morning three motorcycle cops were dragging up and down the block. One of the neighbors hollered, 'Stop that or I'm calling the police!'

"Somebody yelled, 'We *are* the police!'

"One of our party cold-cocked a civilian, and by the time we got the guy to the hospital, his head looked like a beachball. Everybody was afraid the sheriff would find out, but we managed to shine it on. It's a good thing. Sheriff Bland would've lifted about twenty badges."

Every member of the department walked in the shadow of Frank Bland, variously known as "the cowboy sheriff," "last of the whitehats," and "the colossus of roads." The former Marine gunnery sergeant held his five hundred troopers to rigid standards. Solid-white police cruisers were polished till they twinkled. If a deputy used profanity in front of women, he could be fired. Married officers were expected to be faithful. "A wife would complain that her husband was sleeping around," a former deputy said. "Sheriff Bland would drag the guy in and say, 'Make your choice right now. Be true or be gone.'"

The cowboy sheriff discouraged personal debt, and several deputies were decommissioned after bill collectors made repeat visits to headquarters. Bland constantly warned deputies about his three Bs: "booze, bills and broads." His officers patroled from the eastern edge of Los Angeles to the borders of Nevada and Arizona, an area large enough to contain Rhode Island, Delaware, Connecticut and New Jersey with space left over for half of Massachusetts. The trip between the most distant substations took an hour in the department's Cessna 210.

In temperatures ranging from below zero to 120, deputies covered plane crashes and climbing accidents on fifty peaks over five thousand feet, including the 11,485-foot San Gorgonio Mountain, where

Frank Sinatra's mother and Dean Martin's jet-pilot son, among others, died in separate crashes.

The exhilarated Joe told Elaine that there were no "normal" days on patrol. He counted the pressure as a plus; boredom had always been his enemy. He grew a dark mustache that made him resemble Kubla Khan. Elaine was shocked. "What happened to that baby face?" she asked.

"Honey," he said, offering her a rare kiss, "them days are over." She hoped so. She'd never seen him so contented. If he'd been a woman, she would have called him radiant.

One of his earliest assignments was jail transport, a typical rookie chore, picking up prisoners in desolate spots like Barstow and Needles and making the long drive back to the county jail in San Bernardino. Then he was transferred to patrol and complained to Elaine that the dispatcher was sending him on dog complaints, treed cats, roadkills, and scorpions in bedrooms. After a few months he caught a few 415s, domestic disputes, then some petty thieveries and car thefts, and finally ascended the crime numerology to 165, assault with a deadly weapon, and 187, murder.

Along the way he made beginner's mistakes, some nearly final. When he unhitched his pants in a restaurant rest room, his father's .38 clattered to the floor and fired. The slug lodged in the mirror.

"J.D.!" he yelled to his partner. "Let's get outa here."

"We just ordered dinner," said J. D. Brown, a big bear who performed Kenny Rogers imitations at police parties.

As they were pulling away, Joe said, "That damn bullet passed my head four times."

At home he seemed reluctant to discuss the darker side of his work. "He didn't want to worry me," said Elaine.

He was first in at the scene of a high-speed accident and found an unconscious man lying alongside the road, his heart apparently stopped. Joe pressed so hard that he broke several of the victim's ribs. He grieved for weeks while Elaine tried to convince him that it wouldn't have made any difference.

On another night his voice shook as he described five young teenagers burning to death in a Volkswagen. His own hands were blistered and his arms denuded of hair. It was his third Volkswagen fire, all fatal.

"Jesus, honey," he said, "it could've been you, or Rick, or Dad." He wiped his uniform sleeve across his eyes and murmured, "It could've been Bobbie—or Mom."

Elaine had been commuting to Norton AFB in a Beetle. Joe put the car up for sale.

5

Toward the end of Joe's first year as a deputy, Elaine suffered a miscarriage. Something about losing his child seemed to revive Joe's restlessness. He complained about being hemmed in, chained, "stuck in this dump for the rest of my life."

It was true that the quality of Fontana life hadn't improved. The bulging slag heap at the west edge was becoming a town signature, noted by drivers on Interstate 10 and mentioned in every disparaging article. By official measurement, the local air was now the unhealthiest in California. Under the stained skies, citrus trees produced insipid fruit that no one would eat, much less purchase. An outbreak of Newcastle disease killed more chickens than there were citizens of the county, and Big Ed lost his latest flock of Rhode Island Whites and seemed demoralized.

After a rare heated argument in early 1972, Joe didn't come home at all. Elaine tracked him to his old room at his parents' house. He explained that he hadn't dated seriously as a young man and felt that he'd missed out. Maybe after a few months they could get back together.

"Joe!" she yelped. "We're *married*!" He was beginning to remind her of her father. Big Ed felt he'd been missing out, too, but when Evelyn slapped the divorce papers on him, he reverted to monogamy fast.

Background information began arriving over the police wives' private network. Joe had been making bar checks a few weeks back when he'd heard a chanteuse with a V-cut dress and a slinky voice sing, "It's your thing. Do what you wanna do." He'd driven her home, and her husband had put a rock through the window of his car. The dalliance continued.

Elaine tried to figure out what to do. Should she go to the bar and confront the woman? That would get Joe's attention, but also Sheriff Bland's. Unemployment wouldn't be much of a basis for reconciliation.

She wondered if she should send an anonymous letter, but the gossips had said that the lounge singer's husband was already aware of the problem. Should she appeal to Joe's common sense? At the moment, she didn't think he had any, mooning around like a sixteen-year-old with a runaway libido and a bad haircut.

But Joe Gere was coming home to his wife, and fast. Of that she was certain.

After another lonely evening, she bleached her hair, painted her nails tangerine red, applied toner, foundation, blusher, mascara, eyeliner, and a few exotic chemicals that she'd encountered at Ferguson's Beauty School, and selected a dress that Joe hated because it accentuated the voluptuousness that she usually played down. Her final touch was a pair of dangly rhinestone earrings and a diamanté brooch that she'd bought when she was single and hardly ever wore because it attracted too much attention.

With her old friend Nancy Groff, she headed for the most conspicuous nightspot in Fontana: the Italian-American Club on Sierra Avenue, site of her wedding party. It was another hot night. A muffled roar and a glow in the sky showed that the Kaiser smelter was firing.

As the two beauties walked into the bar, the entertainer was singing, "Where the air is fresh and free. Oh, oh, oh, Cantina . . ." He looked and sounded like Eddie Fisher.

The last notes had barely died before he popped up like a ventriloquist's dummy between Elaine and Nancy. Would the ladies like a drink? He resembled a weasel under his stage makeup, but his looks weren't the point to Elaine.

"I would dearly love a Coke," she said coyly.

The crooner sang his next set directly to Elaine, and when the lights blinked for last call he invited her to Denny's for breakfast. Good, she said to herself. That's conspicuous enough.

At one in the morning she drove herself home to the Jurupa Hills and went to bed.

The next morning, Joe burst into the house as she was dressing for work. "Goddamn it," he yelled, "you went *out!*"

She arched her eyebrows and asked, "Didn't you?"

He demanded every detail of her evening, the name of each drink, the full text of her conversations with "that goddamn wop" at the bar, at Denny's, and points between. Every set of questions, every tirade, ended with "Did you sleep with him? *Did you sleep with him?*"

Elaine thought of responding, *Did you sleep with her?* But she didn't want to know.

Somehow Joe managed to transform himself into the aggrieved party, one of his favorite postures. It didn't seem to matter that he'd been AWOL for almost a week. Apparently that was acceptable behavior, but having a few Cokes and some scrambled eggs with a harmless putz was a wanton act.

"How do you think that looked, Elaine?" Joe whined. "Everybody in town thinks you slept with the guy."

"What makes them think that?"

"You left in his car!"

"I just wanted you to come home, Joe," she said, and couldn't help giggling. "And here you are!"

Elaine couldn't resist repeating the whole story to her mother, to Linda, and to Nancy Groff and several females at work. The women agreed that the entire experience could be explained in a single word:

Men!

6

When word circulated in the sheriff's department about Joe's multiple talents, he began to draw elite assignments, including infiltrating "hot-seat" poker games, ferreting out street scammers, and busting bunco artists who preyed on the elderly. Top scores at the shooting range brought a stint with the sniper squad. At a cop killer's trial, he and other riflemen were posted in the eaves of the courtroom. He worked in intelligence and vice, "the pussy posse," and conducted interviews with pimps and madams while Elaine took notes in shorthand on the other phone. He was frequently teamed with detectives, and everyone predicted he'd be in plainclothes by his twenty-sixth birthday, if he could just keep his private life under control.

"Gere didn't go out of his way to chase," a former colleague explained, "but if the opportunity presented itself, he might take advantage, especially after a few drinks. Of course, this didn't make him that much different from the rest of us."

After a neighbor spotted Joe drinking with a redhead, he explained to Elaine that he'd been working undercover. When a distraught woman called the house, he claimed it was part of a sting operation. Police work gave him a steady supply of excuses, and Joe and his buddies covered for each other. One of them had a wife and four kids and a sexy English girlfriend. Elaine thought he was an interesting guy—so, apparently, did most women—but she wished he'd find a new hang-out partner.

7

Early in 1972, Elaine's pregnancy test killed another rabbit, and the doctor predicted that she would carry to term. Joe carpeted the baby's room and told everyone that his son would be the third straight Joe Gere in the family, although none was called Junior or weighted down with Roman numerals. Elaine perused a paperback book called *Name Your Baby*. Reva and Aunt Mogie and sister Beverly and the other relatives kept running over with ancient jumpers, bibs and footie pajamas smelling of mothballs and stained with applesauce and Similac. Joe brought home a tiny pair of Oshkosh B'Gosh overalls and said they were for the baby's first birthday— "Won't he look cute in 'em?"

"Yes," Elaine said, "she will."

Joe and some friends were playing poker in the front room when she went into labor. She left quietly and checked into the obstetrics ward at Fontana Kaiser Foundation Hospital. An hour later Joe and his brother Rick burst in, their faces chalky white. Rick stared anxiously at his brother. Hey, Elaine thought, who's the patient here?

The baby arrived at 8:46 A.M., eight pounds eleven ounces of enraged protoplasm with a red face as wrinkled as a walnut and a voice like a burglar alarm.

Joe ran out and bought a dozen roses. "Don't ever do that again!" said his frugal wife. "They cost too much and they die in three days."

He bought a box of cigars marked IT'S A GIRL and confided, "We'll get you pregnant again, hon. I need a hunting partner."

He sat by the bed and held her hand for hours. He acted as though the newborn were made of spun glass and referred to her as "it." Elaine could see that he was chagrined at fathering a penis-deprived human being, and even more so after a nurse informed him that a child's sex was determined by the father's genes. But he softened when the baby looked up at him and smiled. Elaine didn't tell him that it was her first burp.

"Would you like to hold her?" she asked.

"Let's not push things, Elaine. Okay?"

It turned out that he didn't like the names she'd selected. "We're not French, hon," he pointed out. "Fontana people don't name their kids Michelle and Denise."

They decided to look for a name common to their ethnic backgrounds, but couldn't agree on whether the child was Austrian, Slovene, German, Hungarian, Choctaw, Umatilla, Scotch, Irish, English or plain American. They wanted to honor Joe's mother, but Elaine thought that "Reva" sounded too nineteenth-century. So did "Evelyn," her own mother's name. Baby Girl Gere was two days old when Joe showed up with another book of names. Elaine ran a manicured fingernail down eleven pages before she came to "Brenda."

" 'Brenda'?" Joe said. "Where's that come from?"

"It says 'Irish Gaelic. Firebrand. A dark beauty who kindled a flame of love in every heart.' "

"That's her!" Joe said.

Elaine was too weak to argue. Just before she went to sleep that night, she opened her baby diary, a gift from her sister. On the first page she read:

> *Whenever a little child is born*
> *All night a soft wind*
> *Rocks the corn;*
> *One more buttercup wakes to the morn,*
> *Somewhere, somewhere.*

At the bottom, she added in her neat schoolgirl penmanship, "This book belongs to Brenda Sue Gere." She wondered why she felt like crying. It was the first time she'd written her daughter's name.

In a tradition familiar to many mothers, the father who'd desperately wanted a boy fell in love with his baby girl, making a fool of himself at cribside and elsewhere. He turned the little Spanish house into a combined nursery and shrine and bought enough dolls and teddy bears to supply a foundling home.

Elaine shopped around till she found a self-stick wallpaper patterned in pink and blue balloons at the Standard Brand paint store. She studied a brochure and papered the baby's room herself, dipping the paper in water, slapping it on, trimming top and bottom. She installed red shag polyester carpet in their bedroom and redid the bedroom wall in bright red velveteen. When she began to measure the living room, Joe rebelled. "That's it! One goddamn red wall's enough." But after a while he relented.

Joe's friend J. D. Brown kidded him: "I see you've divided the work. Elaine does the working and you do the drinking." It was true that Joe was still self-indulgent and dominating. Elaine realized that he'd never known any other lifestyle, whether at home, in the Army or on the job. And anyway, he wasn't nearly as interested in being the boss as in *acting* like one, especially in front of others. It was a little game they played.

Some of the relatives remained convinced that Elaine was in thrall to a tyrant. Marjorie Cirillo, Joe's beloved Aunt Mogie, had helped slosh his diapers back in West Virginia and still called him Joey, even on ceremonial occasions when he wore his deputy's dress uniform with brasswork and ribbons. Years later she described a morning when she dropped in on Elaine and little Brenda just as Joe was returning from the night shift. "That brat Joey hugs me and then starts giving orders to Elaine. He says, 'I want the lawn mowed today. Wash the truck, too. And you better make sure the pee-pees are fed.' That's the baby chicks. Then he pours himself a drink and goes to bed.

"I said to Elaine, 'Who crowned him king?'

"She just smiled. She seemed happy with the situation. I see her in the mud, long blond hair flying. She always reminded me of Eva Gabor in her beautiful robes, chasing after Arnold the pig in the TV show *Green Acres*. If she was put upon, she didn't know it. So I just shut up."

Elaine knew how the situation was perceived but didn't care. "I never wanted equality," she explained. "I only wanted Joe."

* * *

With another hungry mouth on the scene, Joe took on extra security jobs until his financial adviser, the two-time bankrupt Ed Mayzsak, convinced him that there was big money in animals.

"They had their heads together all the time," Elaine remembered. "At heart Joe and my dad were farmers, pet-store operators, zookeepers—I don't know which. They looked their most natural in John Deere caps and rubber boots. I wasn't surprised when Joe ordered rabbits and half of them died. We took in a sick horse from the sheriff's posse and kept shooting him with penicillin in the garage. Then a semi pulls up and the driver says, 'Hey, lady, where d'ya want these calves?'

"So now we had ten newborn calves in the breezeway, all with the runs. I stuffed big pills down their throats every four hours. I'd feed Brenda, then run outside and bottle-feed the calves. I kept thinking about the twenty-nine calves I took care of when I was a kid. I thought, I always wanted to get away from the farm, and now I'm running one.

"One calf survived, and Joe didn't know how to castrate him, so an old neighbor did the job with a sharp knife and a tablespoon. He poured a container of Morton salt in the wound and the calf dropped to his knees like it'd been hit with an ax. The guy said, 'The old way didn't hurt 'em as much.' Joe said, 'What was the old way?' and the guy said, 'With your teeth.' After that, Joe always managed to be at work when we butchered. Didn't bother me. But I had to keep scrubbing up for Brenda."

8

Elaine heard worrisome news about her father. At sixty-five, Big Ed had developed chills, hot flashes and shakes. The doctors thought he might have Rocky Mountain spotted fever, but tests were negative. After $40,000 worth of treatment and study, the ailment remained undiagnosed.

Big Ed's wife had her own theory. "It's all those damn animals," said Evelyn. "We oughta take him to the vet."

One night the old welder accused Evelyn of being a priest and attempted to choke her. He took to wandering through the vineyards at 3:00 A.M., doing polka steps. Once he turned up a mile from home in his robe and slippers, balancing in the bed of a truck, and explained that he was surfing at Waikiki.

His strong son Jimmy was summoned from Wyoming to put him in a home.

9

In the perpetual hubbub of their lives, Joe and Elaine had wasted no time worrying about Joe's personal safety on the job. "We never lived in dread," she observed later.

During his three years as a deputy, two of his colleagues had been killed and several injured, but Joe seemed impervious to danger. As one of his colleagues noted, Joe was an imposing figure, seldom challenged on the street. "He had that hard-eyed police look. He wasn't a guy you wanted to fuck with." Evildoers skated when he appeared.

Then one night he answered a family dispute call, solo as usual, and walked straight into the barrel of a .38 Chief's Special.

"Honey," Joe told Elaine later, "I can still hear that sound. *Click. Click. Click.* It misfired three times. We found the indentations on the rims."

The incident was recorded as a 245B, assault on an officer. Elaine was concerned, but she still thought of her husband as immortal at twenty-six.

Joe was working security at a Hispanic dance when a drunk charged his blind side with a knife. A sixth sense made him turn and slam the attacker to the floor.

"He came home shook," Elaine said later. "I was relieved when he took the detective's test. Criminal Intelligence wanted him; he'd worked with several of their investigators. It was the elite, the best."

On Thursday, May 17, 1973, two days after he was notified that he'd passed with a high score, Joe left home at 3:30 P.M. to float in the Central District till midnight. It was Elaine's twenty-eighth birthday, and as he left the house he yelled, "Happy birthday, hon! We'll celebrate later."

Just before dark, she was smoothing his favorite frosting on a double-stack angel food cake when her Uncle Hank and Aunt Dorothy entered without knocking. Three-month-old Brenda cooed in her crib.

"Elaine, honey," Hank said, "there's been an accident. You'd better come with me. Aunt Dorothy'll stay with the baby."

"Is Joe all right?"

"Well, uh—"

Aunt Dorothy exclaimed, "Tell her he's all right!"

"We hope so," Uncle Hank said. "He's at Community Hospital right now. He's, uh—" His voice dropped. "He's pretty bad."

Joe was strapped to a gurney in the hall. A bandage covered an eye and half his head. His left arm was strapped to his side, and blood seeped through the dressing. A doctor reported that his temporal artery had been lacerated and he had a concussion. Elaine tried to follow as an attendant wheeled him away, but a nurse shooed her into a waiting room.

Rick Gere showed up with the family's close friend and next-door neighbor, Battalion Chief Gene Shutten. They'd been making preparations for Joe Sr.'s fifty-fifth birthday luau the next day when the fire chief's scanner picked up a 999 call and an urgent request for an ambulance.

Elaine and Rick gripped hands as Joe's brother officers poured in. It took a while to piece the story together.

Joe had spotted a burning 1955 Buick in a section of North San Bernardino once known as "the Iron Triangle" but nicknamed "the Black Triangle" by police. The streets were littered with broken bottles, stripped cars, hypodermic syringes and trash, and the area was considered off-limits after dark, especially to whites.

As Joe pulled up, he noticed a noisy crowd watching from the east side of California Street. He yanked open the trunk of his police cruiser and grabbed an extinguisher.

"Let it burn!" someone shouted, and another added, "Burn, baby, burn!"—the rallying cry of the Watts fires in Los Angeles.

A burly man with a goatee and a neat Afro was darting in and out of the flames, waving an ax handle. "Fuck the car!" he yelled in a slurred voice. "I'd rather ride a tricycle, man." When he saw Joe, he said, "Here come the motherfuckin' pigs!" and drew back the weapon.

Joe aimed the nozzle at the base of the flames. "Hey, whatchew doin'?" the man said. "Hey, that's my motherfuckin' car, man. I'll burn it if I want to, man! I have my motherfuckin' rights, man."

The firebug, a twenty-five-year-old man named George Edward "Oatmeal" Gray, swung the ax handle and missed by three feet. Joe ran to his car to radio for the arson unit. While he was talking, one of Chief Shutten's pumpers pulled up, but the firefighters were driven off by Gray and others.

Joe became concerned about crowd control. On muggy May afternoons, any fuse could set off a riot. He called for backup, pulled on the weighted sap gloves that were worn by most San Bernardino deputies, and grabbed his nightstick. Oatmeal Gray was standing on the sidewalk, his weapon cocked over his shoulder.

"Drop it!" Joe ordered, and informed him he was under arrest for interfering with firefighters.

Someone yelled, "That's my brother! *Leave him alone!*" The crowd pressed in as Gray rammed the ax handle into Joe's chest and shoved him against a fence.

Joe turned in the direction of the voice and was hit with a baseball bat. He jerked to the left to avoid the next blow and saw the firefighters watching from their rig. "Help me!" he called.

Someone in the crowd yelled, "Kill the pig!" A bottle crashed at Joe's feet, and a blow knocked him flat. As he lay faceup, George Gray swung the ax handle again. Joe warded off the blow, tried to strike back, but discovered that he couldn't move his arm. Shattered bone pierced the skin. Blood smarted in his eyes like saltwater. The action pinwheeled in a crimson haze: trees, flames, fire truck, firemen, angry faces, the Gray brothers' cold black eyes.

He tried to draw his father's revolver but was too weak. The gun clattered to the street, and an older black man kicked the weapon under Joe's body. Someone landed another hard blow with Joe's own nightstick. He crawled to his car, radioed a 999, and blacked out.

At last he was wheeled from the operating room, dark eyes open, arm in a cast. Elaine bent over to kiss him, and he awarded her a crooked smile. She mumbled a prayer of thanks as she followed the gurney down the hall. Uniforms filled Joe's private room, and a loud argument was in progress. One of the sergeants told Gene Shutten that his firefighters were pussies. The two men were squaring off when a nurse yelled, "Stop it!" Everyone fell silent, and she added, "There's too damn many people in here."

A voice came from the bed. "Tell her to shut up. I got a headache."

George Gray and some of his fellow troublemakers were beaten in jail. Later a story circulated that George was kicked to death in San Quentin by a gang of Hell's Angels loyal to Joe Gere, but it wasn't true. In the traditions of modern American justice, both brothers soon returned to the street.

10

After Joe's release from the hospital, he seemed grim and disheartened. He exchanged gallows humor with comrades when they visited, but Elaine could see that it was forced.

He told her how frustrated he'd felt during the assault. "It's sickening to fight somebody you're trying to help. I thought I was gonna die. I said to myself, 'How'd this happen? I'm not even *mad* at these guys.'"

His resemblance to Rock Hudson had become indistinct. Nineteen stitches crossed his eye socket. Doctors told him that scar tissue impinged on the optic nerve and might eventually render him blind. His face looked as though it had been squeezed in one of Big Ed's vises. His left arm and hand were immobilized. The hearing was gone in his left ear and diminished in his right. He might continue to hunt and fish, a police doctor said, but he would never return to the sniper squad or float in a one-man car.

Joe couldn't forgive the firemen who'd sat on their axes fifty yards away while he was being mauled. He found out later that his life had been saved by a quick-thinking African-American named Rufus Minnifield who saw what was happening and drew the drug-crazed George Gray into his car with a ruse.

Joe's desk sergeant kept dropping by the little house to check on his progress. Paul Bruce was one of the department's token blacks and most highly respected supervisors. A few days earlier, he'd cracked at roll call, "Gere, you do a lot of duck hunting. How come you don't bring your sergeant nothin'?"

At the end of the shift, Joe had dumped a flattened roadkill on Bruce's neat desk. "You wanted a duck, Sarge? Here's a duck."

Bruce told Elaine he was sick over the beating. "I love Joe Gere," he said with tears in his eyes. "I *love* Joe Gere! Why did it have to be him?"

After the assault, the two lawmen remained close, even though Joe's racial attitudes seemed to harden. He retained a few other black friends but made no new ones.

"We used to hang out with everybody, every color," his brother Bob recalled. "Went to school with 'em, worked with 'em, partied, hunted, fished, even socialized. Our dad brought a little leftover prejudice from West Virginia, but it didn't come through to the rest of us—not till Joe got hurt."

Elaine didn't notice the change till her husband had been home for a few weeks. He'd always enjoyed *The Jeffersons* and *The Cosby Show* on TV, but now he switched them off, explaining that black skin made him nervous.

"Bill Cosby?" she asked. "George Jefferson?"

"They're black, aren't they?" Joe said.

Later he told her, "I don't want you driving on Mount Vernon Avenue."

She asked why.

"You know why."

"Joe, I've been driving on Mount Vernon for years. I can take care of myself."

He began a rambling lecture about black crime. She said, "Joe, are you talking about black people or *poor* people?"

"I'm talking about spades," he said. She'd never heard him use the word. "No control, no pride . . ."

He was still yakking when she tuned him out. She knew that his attitude would soften when he returned to work.

V

ON THE ROAD AGAIN

1

Elaine had seen her husband in many roles, but never as a total mope and layabout. For a while, it was almost as pleasant as his days on R&R. During his early convalescence, he was home most of the time, and she enjoyed waiting on him. His damaged arm began to heal, but there was a lump where the bone had thrust through the skin, and the muscle bulged oddly. He had sharp pains where the ax handle had punished his skull.

It didn't take him long to turn to his mother's favorite analgesic. Elaine would tell him, "Honey, why don't you get some real painkiller from the doctor?"

He would explain that he'd seen too many burnt-out junkies in his work. "I don't want to get hooked."

He didn't seem to see any danger in heavy drinking, and life in the Gere house turned into a reprise of Elaine's years as a Mayzsak, when Big Ed used to stagger home from his saloon only to eat. Joe hung around the 10-7, a cop hangout with red lights, a Visibar and other police artifacts, trading war stories, drinks and condolences. Elaine was patient; "I never wanted to be his ball and chain."

She overheard him boast to a friend, "She lets me go out whenever I want." She didn't think it was up to her to "let" him. Despite his occasional misstep, she trusted him. She knew how much he missed the excitement that came with his uniform. At the 10-7, he could hear a siren once in a while.

* * *

He seldom got drunk, but sometimes he became morose and sullen, especially after a sheriff's physician confirmed that he couldn't return to full duty. A desk job might work out, they said, but with his weakened eyesight that could also be problematical.

Joe stormed around the house. "Goddamn it," he yelled at Elaine, "I can still do the job."

He filed a lawsuit against the firemen who'd failed to come to his aid, but he didn't follow through. He went before police and medical boards, begging to be returned to full duty. He was downcast when he came home and told Elaine that he'd been forced to accept a disability retirement of $650 a month. He said, "I feel like a failure."

"Joe," she said, "most people have to wait all their lives for this, and you're retiring at twenty-six."

"I'd rather suck a pistol," he said. How she hated those hard police expressions.

As the months of healing passed, he complained of backaches and headaches but refused to take the Percodan and codeine prescribed by the police doctor. Instead he continued to drink.

It wasn't long before his lawman's strut became a slouch. He seemed careless, rushed into things, unconcerned about results. "I don't have time for this shit," he would tell Elaine as they worked on a household project. "Let's speed it up."

She wondered if he'd suffered brain damage. Once he'd been a perfectionist; now he performed slapdash repair jobs, left tools on the garage floor, and expected her to tidy up. After a minor disagreement, he slammed a book to the floor. A few nights later he threw a plate of spaghetti against her red velveteen wallpaper.

"He's not the same Joe," Bob Gere told Elaine. She agreed with the younger brother. She was living with a stranger. But she'd stayed at his side when he was a handsome young cop, and she would stay with him now.

She came across a magazine article with advice on how to pump up unemployed husbands. "It's just a bad period, hon," she told him. "Your self-worth is down, but it's temporary."

They'd always led cheers for each other. "Thank God for you, honey," he told her, and hung his head.

* * *

Then late one afternoon he hit her. She'd been feeding Brenda in her high chair, and Joe was insisting that they should make room for Bob and his wife and baby. "My God, Joe," Elaine said, "we've got seven hundred square feet in this house."

"If they were your family," he said, "you'd take 'em in."

"My family wouldn't ask."

He slapped her hard. She picked up Brenda and ran outside. When she returned, he apologized over and over, made a show of diapering Brenda and preparing dinner, picked a bouquet of flowers and presented it with a flourish. "I just want to say one thing, honey," he told her in bed. "This'll never happen again. Never, never, *never*."

"You're right about that," she said, and turned away.

A month later he was trying to hang a picture when his weakened left hand lost its grip and the glass shattered on the floor. "God *damn* it!" he said, and slammed his other fist through the wall.

When Elaine remonstrated, he said, "Would you rather I put my fist through the wall or hit *you?*"

She couldn't help remembering a Hungarian saying she'd heard from the Geres: "Money is for counting, women are for hitting." No matter how blindly she loved him, she would have to draw the line right there.

2

Two months after the start of Joe's forced retirement, Elaine's latest pregnancy test came out positive. The next morning she awoke to the sound of sledgehammer blows against a wall. "What on earth are you *doing?*" she asked.

"Home improvement," Joe announced, hugging her and dusting her nightgown with plaster. "A nursery for Joey."

With his one good arm and hand he ripped and hammered and

planed and sawed till three or four every morning. Elaine tried to figure out this latest edition of the man she'd married. Were male children *that* important to Hungarians? She'd always known he would turn out to be a good husband and father. He was a family man— you could see it in the way he hovered over his parents and brothers, as concerned about them as if he still lived at home. He was openly loving with baby Brenda but bored with details like burping and diaper changing. She decided that Hungarians loved kids but wanted them full-grown.

As one wall after another crumbled, the little Spanish house expanded to a thousand square feet, then fifteen hundred. Most of the original construction had been flimsy, but the outer walls were made of old-fashioned hard plaster and chicken wire. Joe rented a jackhammer and operated it with one arm. He forbade Elaine to touch the powerful machine. "Wait till Joey's born," he said. "Then you can try."

He hired framers, electricians, carpenters and drywallers, studied them as they worked, then copied their techniques in a rare concern for expenses. He ended up doing much of the work himself. Rick and Bob also helped, and sometimes the master artisan Joe Sr. showed up with spools of wire, kegs of nails, paint, turpentine and tools that he'd liberated from Kaiser Steel. The company had a relaxed policy about minor requisitions.

Elaine and her home ballooned together. When she was eight months pregnant, she was climbing stepladders, taping and texturing the Sheetrock that the Gere brothers had hung. She also wallpapered and stuccoed. When Joe showed up with rolls of shag carpet, she elbowed him aside and said she'd learned wall-to-wall from her father. She laid the pad and shag carpet strips, sewed the backsides with industrial-size needles, and was the only one who wasn't surprised when the finished product covered the available space exactly.

And when the renovations were finished and a healthy baby son was born, with a squall like Brenda's and Magyar eyes like his dad's, what did Joe want to do?

He wanted to move. He said he needed to be a cop again, but not in Fontana. He was unnerved by the bickering that went on in his father's house, and by his mother's and brothers' drinking (he still seemed unconcerned about his own), and by the heat and smog and lethargic atmosphere in his hometown. Newborn Joey and thirteen-month-old Brenda, he said, deserved something better than the Jurupa Hills.

It took him a few more days to admit that there was another reason. He said that someone had put out a contract. "I can protect myself, honey," he told Elaine, "but they're threatening to kill you and the kids."

They decided to scramble north and made down payments on a twenty-three-foot travel trailer and a 1973 Dodge pickup off the showroom floor. Elaine scribbled in her baby diary, "Brenda loves to go bye-bye in a car and also loves to go outside. She also started twirling and gets dizzy and falls down."

In the fall of 1974, the family pulled out of Fontana. Along the way, Joe applied for police jobs, but no one was hiring. For three months they lived in the trailer while he worked at a forge in Portland, Oregon, hammering iron in 130-degree temperatures, sweating down to the hard physique of his teens.

When the job played out, they continued north to Seattle, where Joe called on city and county police departments and security companies. An aunt and uncle baby-sat Brenda and Joey while Elaine took a secretarial job at the Washington Bureau of Recreation and Joe temporarily sold used cars in suburban Bellevue.

With his line of talk, he was soon averaging $500 a week and talking about moving out of the trailer and into a house. But Elaine could see how much he missed his job as a deputy. He applied at the Bellevue Police Department and signed his name on the tag end of a long waiting list. No matter how much money he earned selling cars, he never considered himself anything but a cop, or stopped grieving for his job.

On a dreary, wet weekend the Geres crossed the Cascades on Interstate 90, heading for the Idaho panhandle to visit old friends. At the Columbia River they saw blue sky for the first time in days. Just west of Spokane the spikes of a low mountain range were mantled in fresh snow. Elaine watched as a familiar look crept across her husband's face.

"Jesus, hon," he said as they approached the old mining town of

Coeur d'Alene, "what the hell are we doing living in a trailer in West Seattle? Look at this country."

As they drove into Sandpoint, a town of five thousand at the foot of the Selkirk Mountains, Joe said, "Every single thing we need is here."

"Except jobs," Elaine put in.

"We can live off the land," Joe said excitedly. "I'll always be able to take care of you guys out here. There's trout in the streams, deer, quail."

The want ad in the Sandpoint paper was fortuitously timed. "Experienced officer needed," it said. "Apply Bonners Ferry, Idaho, Police Department."

Joe insisted that they drive straight up. He'd always been impatient. Elaine liked action herself. If either of them wanted something, they wanted it now.

The bare-boned little town lay due north of Sandpoint toward the Canadian border. An assistant police chief invited them to dinner, and after the sharing of a half-bottle of Canadian and some war stories, Joe was hired at $600 a month.

He moved his family into a slump-walled farmhouse on the outskirts of town and sowed an acre of potatoes, corn, cabbage and broccoli. "He planted so thick," Elaine said, "that we couldn't keep it weeded." On the side, he hayed, harvested hops, shoveled snow and bounced at clubs. He ice-fished and brought home two hundred perch; Elaine filleted and breaded till four in the morning, filling the freezer. They started feeding up a fractious Black Angus calf that sometimes broke through their fence and trotted downtown to gawk at window displays like a shopper.

When their bank account ran low, Elaine hired a baby-sitter and went to work for the U.S. Forest Service, typing letters, cleaning windows, chopping wood, whatever was required in the undermanned district. Joe's little brother Rick and two of his uncles came to visit, and he took them partridge hunting. Elaine didn't mind missing out on the trip; Joe always made her carry the decoys. Once he'd shouted, "Duck!" and fired a blast a few inches from her ear. Then he deafened her other ear with another volley. She enjoyed tromping through the woods with her husband but felt she could use a few days of quiet.

The hunters got home as she was arriving from work in nylons and heels. Rick told Elaine's mother later, "She just dove into those birds and started guttin' and pickin' 'em. I couldn't believe it."

"I could," Evelyn Mayzsak said.

After a few months on duty, Joe began to have adjustment problems. "I'm bored shitless, honey," he complained. "This place makes Fontana look like Vegas."

It was a big night in rustic Bonners Ferry when Joe drove home a sodden Kootenai Indian, or when he exchanged a few words with old Fred, a superannuated delinquent with his own set of game laws. If a bear wandered onto old Fred's property, he would shoot it and then buy a bear tag. One night Joe stopped Fred's pickup truck and found a legless deer hidden under a blanket. "Takin' it to the vet, officer," Fred explained. "Poor thing took sick."

Joe complained to Elaine, "Jeez, honey, I'm worried about myself. I'm looking forward to seeing old Fred."

Night after night she watched as he sat in his favorite chair, sipping bourbon and staring into space. She knew where his mind was and she had no idea how to bring him back to reality. He was on a windy desert highway, headed toward Barstow, turning 110 on lights and siren.

She kept hoping he would snap back to the real world.

3

By the summer of 1975, Brenda was two and a half and already acting motherly, an echo of Elaine's behavior on the turkey farm in Fontana. One morning she found the child sitting on the front porch spooning Shredded Wheat into the birdlike mouth of year-old Joey. Soon the morning feeding became a habit.

Like most intelligent children, the blond scamp went from mischief to mischief. She put a kitten in the freezer and a cat in the clothes dryer; both were rescued short of death. She loved dogs, horses, chickens, white mice and rabbits. She had a succession of guinea pigs, each named Teddy because they put her in mind of bear cubs. One day she picked up her pet male and five babies slid out.

After a while, Brenda decided that she would rather care for siblings than pets. She and Joey were thirteen months apart, and wherever the toddler toddled, she followed. Friends said they acted like twins. Before she was three, she saved her mother and brother from fire. Elaine recalled:

"We had turkey polts under a heat lamp in the dining room. I was reading to the kids at nap time and we fell asleep upstairs, me and Joey and Brenda.

"Next thing I know, Brenda's pulling me. 'Mommy, Mommy! Turkeys, *turkeys!*' I looked down the stairs and saw flames. We got out okay, just a few blisters, and our good neighbor Jim Nash heard the windows breaking out and called the fire department. We might have died except for Brenda.

"Joe was as shook as I've ever seen him, much worse than when he was hurt on the job. The fire brought back his mom's burning hair. It was eerie, how both those fires started from heaters."

Reva flew up to visit, and Joe gave her the grand tour. It was touching to see the love between mother and son. But the Gere family curse shadowed both. One night she became almost incoherent, and Joe told Elaine, "She needs help, hon. She's drinking herself to death."

Elaine wondered how long it would be before Fontana sucked them back.

4

Joe asked for two weeks off in elk season and resigned when he was refused. It was as though he'd been waiting for an excuse.

"Now what?" Elaine asked, as though she didn't know.

"Home," he answered. "Where else?"

She felt heartsick. "Joe," she said, *"why?"*

"Mom's goin' fast. My sister's bad, too. Dad says real estate's jumpin'. We won't have to live in Fontana, hon. I'll get us a place at the beach."

Elaine hated to leave the north woods. She tried to convince herself that Joe needed to be in a place where he had friends and admirers, where he'd been something other than a small-town cop rousting tramps and drunks. She figured she owed him that much consideration after what he'd been through.

They rented a house at Dana Point, on the ocean just south of Laguna Beach and a seventy-minute drive to Fontana, and Joe leaped into real estate as he'd once leaped into law enforcement. He passed the agents' test on his first try and hooked up with a Fontana broker who specialized in big-ticket properties, buying promising units of land and selling them at high markups to commercial developers who were flooding into the badlands east of L.A. Joe knew the back country and showed an early genius for sniffing out hot properties. Within a few months, he'd added a $10,000 bonus to his regular commissions.

Elaine took a nine-week course and began selling real estate on her own. For the first time in their married lives, money came in faster than they could spend it. The only drawback was that Joe was involved in projects as far away as Palm Springs and Needles, and the commute to and from the coast kept him away from his family. One night he announced that he'd rented a house with a pool on a quiet street lined with pepper and lemon trees.

"Where?" Elaine asked.

His reply was so soft she could hardly hear. "Fontana," he said.

It was a long drive in their new his-'n'-her Corvettes, dragging their U-Hauls behind.

Soon Elaine was earning $2,000 a month and Joe was making more. With each financial triumph, he seemed more like his old self. His company was written up in a business magazine, just as her father's turkey operation had once found its way into print. He bought her a red Corvette and began to make payments on a forty-two-foot Concord yacht with fly bridge, salon and galley, moored next to John Wayne's slip at Newport Beach.

The young tycoon frequently donned a $400 white suit that made him resemble an elongated Don Ho and entertained clients on *Moana*'s polished teak afterdeck. To Elaine it seemed that every transaction floated on Scotch, bourbon, gin and French champagne. On weekends the realtors, brokers and agents played golf, sailed, hunted and fished, their energies buoyed by 86-proof liquids and shaved ice.

One afternoon Joe dropped in on his Aunt Marjorie and Uncle Junior and threw down a shot of bourbon before splashing another few fingers into a water glass. "Wow!" she said. "Isn't that a lot, Joey?"

"Don't worry, Aunt Mogie," he said. "I'll just sip." When he left an hour later, the bottle was empty.

Elaine remembered how her father had turned grouchy and snappy when he started imbibing the profits at the Town Pump. Sometimes she heard her father speaking through Joe's mouth.

"Goddamn it, where're my cuff links?" he yelled as he dressed for a real estate closing.

"In your drawer," Elaine said softly.

"That's bullshit!" He lifted them from the drawer and said, "Who put 'em here?"

"You did."

"Don't ever tell me I did something I didn't. I hate that! Just leave my stuff alone!"

His flashpoint seemed to lower with every drink. He began to consider the phone a personal enemy. "If that thing rings one more time," he raged one night, "I'm gonna shoot it."

"Joe," Elaine said gently, "it's not alive. You can't get mad at a phone."

The phone rang and he blasted it to pieces.

A few evenings later, his good mood was dispelled by a salad that didn't measure up to his rigid standards. "It always had to be perfect," Elaine said. "A piece of lettuce for a base, a scoop of cottage cheese, three or four slices of Del Monte peaches, a dab of mayonnaise. If I didn't make it exactly the same, he wouldn't eat."

For a few minutes he sat at their $300 coffee table and glared. Then he picked up the kidney-shaped slab of glass and shattered it against the stone fireplace. "Please, Elaine," he said, "a little more mayo the next time, okay?"

Some of the family members continued to speculate that he had brain damage. Elaine decided that he was just being Joe. He didn't often apologize, but there were occasional signs of contrition, usually in the form of a gift or a night out or a compliment on her hair or her figure. Like his daughter Brenda, he wasn't much of a hugger; they showed their love in other ways. Elaine decided that living with a Gere was like reading a book in a foreign language. You had to learn the vocabulary.

5

By the time Reva Gere's oldest son had been back in Fontana for a year, she was into the final stages of alcoholism. Joe tried to commit his mother to a program at Patton State Hospital, a mental institution, but his father balked at signing the papers.

"Joey," the old man said, "I just can't put your mom in a place like that."

*   *   *

Two weeks later, Reva blacked out and was rushed to the hospital. Joe burst from the emergency room in a rage.

"Goddamn it, Mom's dying!" he yelled at family members. "Couldn't you see that? Did you have to wait till she's almost dead?"

Doctors explained that she'd never fully recovered from the effects of her burns. Her organs had been put under such a strain that she was especially vulnerable to toxins like alcohol. Now she had terminal cirrhosis. Joe went from rage to shame to inconsolable grief.

On Sunday, August 14, 1977, Reva spent her fifty-third birthday on life support. The next night at eight, with the family at her bedside, she shuddered and stopped breathing.

Joe pushed back her hair, kissed her, and slipped off her wedding band and engagement ring. He passed them to his sobbing sister Linda. "Mom wanted you to have these."

Linda said she would accept the rings for someone else. "Brenda was Mom's first granddaughter," she said, "and I'll save the rings for her wedding day."

For months Joe berated himself. Part of his reason for returning to Fontana had been to watch over his mother, but instead he'd concentrated on making money.

"If I'd only known how bad she was," he told Elaine.

"You're not a doctor," Elaine said.

"I'm the oldest son, the one she depended on." Joe always took too much blame.

6

Like other TV viewers at the time, Brenda and Joey became fascinated by a cute little boy named Mikey who devoured Life cereal.

"Mommy, Mommy," Brenda kept saying, "can we have a Mikey?"

"We want a Mikey!" little Joey would chime in.

Elaine went off her birth-control pills, and on Thanksgiving Day, 1978, three months after her mother-in-law's death, she checked into San Bernardino Community Hospital to give birth to the child who would be known jokingly as "Joe and Elaine's Thanksgiving turkey."

Michael Gere was a dark-haired butterball and a medical mystery from the beginning. At two and a half weeks he underwent corrective surgery for an overdeveloped muscle wall in the upper intestine. Elaine sat by his crib three days and nights without sleep.

After the intestinal problem was corrected, he was found to be severely lactose-intolerant. Then a rattling developed in his lungs and he proved to be suffering from reactive airways passage disease, "allergic to the twentieth century," as a specialist put it after tests. Elaine had similar problems, although her medical needs were usually ignored in the pressure of caring for others.

Before he was six months old, the new baby developed tonsillitis and bronchitis and endured the first of four operations for strabismus, a condition which causes crossed eyes. At eleven months, doctors inserted tubes into his infected ears and started him on what was to become a lifetime regimen of antibiotics.

The situation was scary, Elaine commented later, because Mikey could wind up in the hospital if someone brought a rose into the house or fed him a gumdrop. Luckily, he was a stoical little boy, possessed of a sweet disposition and his family's tolerance for aggravation.

* * *

Brenda Sue Gere, approaching seven, considered the new baby her personal doll, arranging him in front of the TV to watch her favorite shows: *The Brady Bunch, Adam 12, Dragnet,* monster movies.

"See, Mikey?" Brenda would say. "That's a broncosaurus!" The baby would blink and spit up.

He grew fast and soon overflowed the sides of Brenda's toy buggy. She tried to wheel him to the Burger King on Sierra Street, but her parents intervened.

One day Elaine arrived home to find her frowning daughter standing over the baby's crib like a sentinel. "Mom," she said, "do you know what the baby-sitter did? She fed Mikey, but she did *not* heat up his food. She fed it *cold*! And I had to change him 'cause she doesn't change him enough."

Elaine noted later, "Brenda was so grown-up, so responsible. From the age of two she used big words. 'Dipsipline.' 'Refringerator.' 'Liberry.' She never liked a lot of hugging—I guess that was her Hungarian side. She had Joe's personality, his intelligence, independence. From first grade on, she got good grades, never had to study hard.

"She'd have a slumber party and invite girls two or three years older. She worked on her scrapbooks—page after page of purple and red and pink and yellow ribbons, merit awards, citations. This was her favorite: 'In recognition of earned achievement in self-propelled transport through an aqueous medium.' That means she learned to swim."

If there was a puzzling aspect to the oldest child's personality, it was her fearfulness. She was afraid of the dark, the boogeyman, spiders, snakes, the monsters she watched on TV. Sometimes it seemed she went out of her way to scare herself. She had a peculiar fear of her mother's Uncle Hank, a warm gentle man who'd lost two children of his own to cystic fibrosis.

"Maybe it had something to do with what happened to her dad when she was little," the retired homicide detective theorized later. "She always shrieked when I walked into the house, especially when

I was in uniform. Even when she got older, she'd run to her mom. I used to laugh about it. 'Why's that little girl afraid of me?' "

No one had any idea.

7

Toward the end of 1978, Elaine began to see signs of another big change in her life with Joe. The real estate business was in trouble, and he was ranging farther and wider, taking bigger chances, overextending himself by assuming ownership of high-priced properties on the slimmest of margins.

Soon they began liquidating, staring with *Moana*. Elaine hired a nanny and returned once again to her colonels at Norton Air Force Base. She thought how quickly success came and went. The last three years had been dreamlike, as insubstantial as her father's success with his turkeys. She just hoped her and Joe's story would have a different ending.

On an evening when a cap of bilious smog settled on Fontana like a punctured blimp, Joe returned from an unproductive sales meeting to find his wife chairbound by allergies and his baby son wheezing in his crib.

"Goddamn it, hon," he said, "I can't take this town anymore."

"I never could," Elaine admitted.

"Nothing's moving," he said. "No sales. No profits. No air. What the hell we doin' here, anyway?"

Before the night was over, he'd made one of his famous unilateral decisions, based on insight, experience and a pint of Jack Daniel's. If they had to ride out the real estate recession, he explained on a rising note of cheer, they might as well live in a place where you began each day shooing pheasants and deer from the garden: Idaho,

the Gem State, land of deferred dreams, the state where every car
license read FAMOUS POTATOES.

Elaine's heart lightened. She'd begun to wonder if she would ever
butcher another bear.

8

I n September 1979, Joe headed north to Idaho to enroll Joey in
kindergarten. Elaine and her half-pint helper Brenda stayed behind
with baby Mikey to sell their house. It took two months to unload
the property at a loss.

By Christmas the family was reunited in a mobile home on a bench
above the Moyie River, just east of Bonners Ferry on the road to
Troy, Montana. Joe cleared acreage for a new house, harvested a
crop of Christmas trees, and trucked them to Nevada for a $1,000
windfall. But there were few other ways to turn a profit in the north
woods and hardly any regular jobs, and the Geres faced persistent
demands for cash for their Southern California condos and other
speculations.

A friend from Seattle tipped them that Boeing was hiring, and
Joe told Elaine they had no choice but to head for Seattle. "This
time we won't be gone for three years, hon," he promised. "We
can both get jobs. Real estate'll pick up and we'll bounce back here."

By the time they removed Brenda and Joey from school and disen-
gaged from the Idaho panhandle in their pickup truck, Boeing had
put on a hiring freeze. "Goddamn it," Joe complained, "Dad was
right. If I didn't have bad luck, I'd have no luck at all."

He visited every Northwest police department, car lot and real
estate agency, and couldn't catch on. The family squeezed into a
tiny apartment in a Seattle suburb in time to receive notice that
a nine-thousand-dollar payment was due or they would lose their

investment in their last California condo. The payment was out of the question.

Elaine got a job as a stenographer in the Veterans Administration Medical Center while Joe continued to peruse want ads. One day he announced that he was applying for a job as a foreman in a factory. "Joe," she said gently, "you're a cop. You're a salesman. You're—"

"I'm a paint foreman," he said.

Even with two regular paychecks, the Geres fell behind. They were earning hundreds but owed thousands. Joe pawned his .400 Weatherby and his bicentennial shotgun. He took out a bank loan at 22 percent and a personal loan at 25, and Elaine borrowed to the limit from the federal credit union. "Just a few more months," he kept saying. "Things'll turn."

They did, but not soon enough. Joe's voice was almost inaudible as he stared at his feet and recited the news. They were bankrupt.

Elaine wondered why she wasn't more upset. She figured she didn't possess anything too precious to lose except what no court could take away. Besides, she knew about bankruptcy. "My dad went through it twice," she reminded Joe. "It didn't kill us."

Joe looked glum. "Honey," she persisted, "we had nothing when we started, and we still have nothing. What the heck have we lost?"

He didn't respond.

"And, and . . . look at the experience!" she went on. "We learned you can only eat so many steaks, drink so many drinks and drive so many cars. We've got all we need, hon. We've still got your retirement check, our jobs, our kids. We're *lucky*, Joe."

He took a few days off, then dragged himself back to the paint plant. Word came that Big Ed Mayzsak, suffering from advanced Alzheimer's disease, had died in his Wyoming rest home. With the despondent Joe on her hands, Elaine barely had time to mourn. She comforted herself that God was good and her father was feeding up every fat hog in heaven.

By the time the bankruptcy referee had made his last ruling, the Geres were left with a spavined old car, their wardrobes, and a few pieces of furniture stored in Fontana. Elaine was almost relieved. A year earlier, they'd owned the world. A few months ago, they'd *owed* the world. Now, at least, they were solvent. She was thirty-eight, Joe thirty-six, and it was time to return to the lifestyle she'd learned at Big Ed's knee in Fontana:

Hard work, and plenty of it.

9

In a few months their cash flow began to steady, and within a year they were able to move into a rambling house sixty miles south of Seattle. It wasn't Idaho and it wasn't Dana Point or the Newport marina, but there was enough land to plant a garden and raise a few animals.

Joe worked overtime and drove his crew to production records. He bought the children an Appaloosa colt and an old Shetland pony and taught Brenda to ride. For the first time since her birth seven years before, he was acting like an involved parent and not just buying pets and presents.

But he was still the stereotypical gloomy Hungarian. He even worried about worry. When Elaine came home and told him she'd had a flat tire, he said, "Damn, hon, did you have to walk right in the door and tell me that? Couldn't it have waited till later? I was finally in a good mood and now you've ruined it."

Elaine was convinced that he had a deep-seated need to feel anxious, even if he had to invent a cause. She was glad they'd never won the lottery; he'd have been crushed. Big Ed's daughter considered worry a self-indulgence. Mikey became so ill in kindercollege that she had to quit her job to watch over him full-time, but she didn't waste time brooding. As she told Joe in one of her cheerleading sessions, "Life never goes smooth. Once you're dead, you won't feel *anything*. At least you're alive, Joe. You're feeling life, you're breathing. *So quit your darn worrying!*"

Every time she looked at little Mikey, she was relieved that she wasn't a worrier. When his health took one of its periodic nosedives, the

Geres gave up their country house to move closer to Seattle, and Elaine returned to work at the VA hospital. Every weekday morning she drove Brenda and Joey to a sitter, dropped Mikey off at a day-care near her office in case he had to be rushed to the emergency room, and then drove Joe to his job in an industrial flatland where he wouldn't draw a breath of fresh air for nine hours. He was the wrong man in the wrong job, and yet he was persisting into his third year at the paint plant.

After work every afternoon, she picked him up at a cops' bar near Seattle's South Precinct headquarters, where he would drink beer, shoot darts and listen to war stories. He took little part in the conversations and explained to Elaine that he didn't want to be considered a wannabe—"Cops hate that." It was more likely that he didn't feel worthy. Gosh, she thought, these Seattle cops should've seen him in his uniform. He'd looked like a magazine ad.

"If I'd've accepted that desk job in San Bernardino," Joe complained one night on the drive home from the plant, "I'd be back on a beat by now."

"That isn't what the doctor said," Elaine reminded him.

"Screw the doctor," Joe said, and didn't speak for the rest of the drive.

His drunken mood shifts worsened. He became so angry after an ordeal in the dentist's chair that he ground the gears on their car and burned out the transmission. When a driver hit Brenda's Appaloosa mare, Joe had to be restrained.

A fellow worker invited him to an Alcoholics Anonymous session. He attended but refused to return. "That's for wimps that can't handle booze," he explained to Elaine. "You know me. I can out-drink anybody."

Not anymore, she thought. The pattern was plain, and it didn't take a psychologist to make it out. He'd always loathed drunks, and now he was becoming one. Soon he would be turning his aversion against himself, which would make him drink more. Somehow they had to break the cycle.

10

Early in his fourth year as a paint plant supervisor, Joe told Elaine that he'd begun to suffer steady headaches and thought they might be caused by the fumes. "Five minutes after I clock in, my head starts pounding."

She reminded him that a company chemist had warned that he would be exposed to carcinogens and run substantial risk of cancer. She urged him to quit the job and clear out his lungs. "You're an outdoors guy, hon," she said. "We'll get by."

Joe returned to the used-car business. He was a natural-born salesman with an unusual technique. "I tell the truth," he explained to Elaine. "If a car's a piece of junk, I say so. That makes people believe in me. Then they look around the lot and buy another one." On nights when he worked late, Elaine would prepare a hot meal and deliver it with Brenda and the boys in the backseat.

Their seesaw finances improved again, and Joe bought the children a pedigreed yellow Labrador retriever named Tracker and a bright red Honda three-wheeler with balloon tires and a gasoline engine. He brought home the fanciest Nintendo, a children's TV and VCR, a pinball machine with sirens and flashing lights, and a Christmas tree so wide that he had to unhinge the front door to get it into the house.

He started taking Joey on hunting and fishing trips to the Cascade and Olympic mountains. He had high expectations for his older son and showed it in his demands, fixing attention with his loud ex-soldier's voice.

"Look, kid," Elaine heard him tell his namesake before a bird-shooting trip, "I brought you into this world and I can take you out." It seemed a harsh way to put such matters, especially when they were both carrying shotguns.

* * *

Joe could be unreasonably tough on his older son, but he'd always been patient with the sickly Mikey, and he still kept Brenda on a pedestal in the old family tradition. Gere females might end up as household drudges, but they were also expected to be fragile, feminine and dependent, protected by their men.

Joe never seemed to catch on that Brenda was miscast in the Hungarian princess role. She could be dainty and feminine, but her main quality was the inner strength that seemed to run in a straight line through the maternal side of the family.

For her tenth birthday, Joe gave her a dozen red roses and a $100 bill; a family photograph showed father and daughter in a rare hug. She had trouble with spelling and bombed out in a spelling bee on her first word, *barrel,* which she spelled *barrol.* Her father joked, "You must be a Mayzsak."

Brenda complained to her mother, "Dad didn't want me 'cause I wasn't a boy."

Elaine smoothed it over. "He *did* want a boy, honey," she said, "but when he found out how special you were, he would rather have you." The child frowned.

Like both her parents, Brenda seemed obsessed by speed. Before she'd learned how to skip rope double-Dutch, she was driving her three-wheeler so fast that passengers tipped out on turns. After a couple of bad bruises, her father installed a governor, which she defeated with a screwdriver. She was a daredevil gymnast and horse-woman, short on finesse but unafraid of injury.

There were times when the child's intuitive intelligence made Elaine feel stupid. Homework never took more than ten or fifteen minutes. She was a pretty girl, with dark hazel eyes, brown hair, and a slender, almost gawky body. She wore $2,500 worth of braces to correct a gap in her front teeth. Like her father, she was relaxed about money but always seemed to have cash. She was even-tempered and sometimes slightly impudent. "She was very good about putting up with me," Elaine summed up later, laughing.

From the child's earliest years, she had her own stubborn ways. She combed back her bangs till Elaine gave up. As soon as the issue was settled, Brenda went back to bangs.

She refused to wear dresses after the first grade. "My figure's right for jeans, Mom," said the child, who was built like a pencil. Elaine nodded and thought, Why argue? I'll only lose.

From eight on, Brenda insisted on selecting her own clothes. "She was independent, but she wanted my opinion on everything," Elaine recalled. "She'd say, 'What should I wear today?' and if I picked something out, she'd say, 'Oh, *gross!*' Then she'd wear it. She wouldn't go near the mall without me. She'd say, 'Mom, you're taking me shopping today,' and off we'd go. She treated me like a lackey and Joe like an equal."

When Brenda was ten, Mikey was a chubby four-year-old, and she still considered him her doll. Joey, going on nine, was her fall guy and protégé. She shaved him with her father's razor and slapped on shaving lotion. When he screamed, she splashed water on his face and ordered him not to tell.

If Joey tried to squeeze her, she shoved him away. "I only hug Mikey," she explained. "He's my baby. You're my brother."

Joey thrived under her protectorate. "She was my brain," he said later. "I saw everything through her eyes." She taught him that spruces had hard prickly needles and Douglas firs soft, and if you became lost in the woods you followed a creekbed downstream to a road. She was a logician and debunker and had little patience with childish mythology and nonsense.

Joey became dubious after she explained that frogs didn't cause warts.

"I'll check that out with Mom," he said.

"Don't bother," Brenda answered.

She was sturdy for her age and not shy about protecting her brothers from tormentors. Joey recalled:

"We were in another new school, and this bully kicked Brenda's shin. They went to the parking lot and duked it out. She beat the crap out of that girl, left her face all bloody. Brenda knew how to fight 'cause she'd fought with Dad and us boys. The principal said he was gonna tell our parents. Brenda said, 'Go ahead. My dad told me to take nothin' from nobody, and he won't care.' Dad didn't."

At Christmastime, Brenda converted Joey into Santa Claus by pasting shreds of toilet paper to his face. Mikey played Rudolph the Red-

Nosed Reindeer with the aid of Elaine's lipstick. Brenda had always used the boys as foils and props in household plays and pageants. A friend remembered her chasing Joey through a fern gully, the boy giggling as she squirted him with liquid soap. They drenched the house in water fights. She showed Joey how to ditch school for a supermarket opening—"They're giving away candy!" Brother and sister returned home a pale shade of green.

"It was the perfect crime," Elaine recalled. "I didn't find out till Joey was sixteen. Brenda did all the planning. The instigator, as usual."

Brenda was as good at placating the two boys as she was at stirring them up. When Mikey was three he was afraid of a monster that had taken up residence in his bedroom closet. At nap time, Brenda filled an atomizer with water and said, "This is monster spray."

She sprayed the closet and said, "There! Now they're gone." Mikey smiled and fell asleep.

She loved animals and wrote in her journal, "When I grow up I want to be a veteranarian. I'd do anything for animals and I'm going to get a cocker spaniel. A great Dane, a german shepeard, a yellow lab a yellow retriever, St. Bernard a Springer spaniel, a white persian kitten, a black persian kitten, a gray Hymalyan, a Siamese, and a russian Blue."

She stuffed five wild ducklings under Joey's shirt and said, "Run!" The child took off, pursued by a quacking mother. Elaine made her return the birds to the pond.

The family's nomadic ways sometimes upset the boys, but Brenda seemed at home anywhere. A week or two after each move, she would have a new best friend, a favorite teacher, a new hangout. When other students enrolled, she took them under her wing. "There's a new girl in school," she wrote in her journal. "I'll have to make sure to try to be her friend."

Undemonstrative at home, she wrote poems of praise to friends:

> *Karen was a friend that had faith,*
> *She worried for everybody,*
> *And had such a kind heart*
> *She bought everything from K-mart.*

She stayed in touch with old classmates and never quit on a friendship. She wrote in her journal, "I think having friends is more important than having money because if you have money it always makes you crazy and then you act so big and hot and then nobody likes you. If you have friends its better."

Elaine drove her daughter thirty or forty miles to parties or class functions in neighborhoods they'd left a year or two earlier. The weary mother told her husband that there was only one Christmas gift that she really needed: a black peaked cap with the word CHAUFFEUR in gold.

At home Brenda continued to function as the baby-sitters' overseer, making sure the boys were properly attended. In a family with a history of strong females, she flowed into the role of adviser and guide. She'd never been intimidated by her father and often stood between him and her brothers. "Well, Dad," she would say, one hand on her skinny hip, nose aloft, "weren't you ever a little boy? No, I guess *not*."

On a trip to Fontana, she took over the care of her father's diabetic sister, Linda, who was going blind in her right eye and suffering spiderweb bleeding in her left.

"She grabbed my arm," Linda said, "and led me all around Knotts Berry Farm. She'd say, 'C'mon, Aunt Linda, you can't see good. I'll help you.' She gave up her own fun for me. She was always caring."

And always fearful. No one understood why. Such a resolute child shouldn't have been afraid of birdcalls and shadows. After she saw the devil appear in a farmer's field in a Satanic movie called *The Children of the Corn*, she took long detours to avoid pastures. She was traumatized by Freddy Kruger of *Nightmare on Elm Street*, and for months after seeing the movie she couldn't sleep without the family dog.

For a while the Geres lived south of Seattle in the Kent Valley, hunting grounds of the "Green River Killer." Hardly a day went by without media mention of the nation's most notorious uncaptured murderer, and Brenda and her fellow students were preoccupied with the crimes.

"Maybe it was because she'd been raised around cops and guns," Elaine recalled. "She'd heard talk about Joe's injury since she was a baby. I think she picked up on his attitude—he was fearless about himself but scared to death for everybody else: me, the kids, his dad and his sister, his brothers, *everybody*. He called home three times a day to check on us. He taught us self-defense. Some of our friends never discussed abduction and murder with their kids—they said the odds were so slim, it wasn't worth putting the fear in their heads. But Joe said he didn't want to play Russian roulette with his family. He briefed Brenda and the boys on every possibility. The bad guys were always on his mind."

Brenda acted panicky when police were summoned to check out an intruder on the school grounds. For a classroom exercise, she wrote, "I would like to invent a different kind of car. It would be totally invisible. It would be made out of plexiglass or somthing. . . . If your a police officer it would be an advantage because you could see if any body was a murderer and had a dead body in the trunk of the car."

Teachers thought it was a macabre concept from a child who'd just received a Barbie Town House for Christmas and talked constantly about her motorized three-wheeler and her pony.

Neither her parents nor her teachers considered the possibility that she was prescient.

11

One afternoon at the height of the Green River Killer hysteria, Brenda was home alone when a late-model sedan pulled up in front of the house and a tall white male in a business suit stepped out. She locked the doors and windows and spoke to him through a slit. He said he was looking for someone in the neighborhood. "May I just step in and use your phone?"

"It's out of order."

After the car pulled away, she opened the back door and brought her dog Tracker inside. Ten minutes later an African-American man knocked and identified himself as the plumber.

"We didn't call a plumber," she said through the same crack.

"Your mom called," the man said in a pleasant voice. "I'm supposed to fix your pipes."

"I don't think so," said the well-briefed child. "My mom would've told me."

The door rattled and Tracker let out a hoarse Labrador howl. After the man hurried off, Brenda ran to a neighbor's house to await her parents.

When Joe phoned the local police station, he sounded like a watch commander barking orders. "You're goddamn right I want a detective. . . . Don't give me that *yeah yeah yeah!* The guy tried to get into my *house*, for God's sakes!"

Two detectives showed up at bedtime and took a report in the dining room. Brenda described the white car down to its CB antenna and a dent in the passenger's side. When the plainclothesmen heard the description, they bore down for more details. Brenda apologized for missing the license number, but her angle of vision had been bad.

After the child went to bed, the detectives confided to Joe and Elaine that a team of pedophiles had been working the suburbs south of Seattle. Usually such perverts worked alone; in tandem, they were far more dangerous. Two days earlier the pair had grabbed a five-year-old boy and violated him. An all-points bulletin was out.

"What color are the perps?" Joe asked.

"Salt 'n' pepper." It was standard police nomenclature.

After they left, Joe said, "See, hon? For all we know, those guys coulda been the Green River Killer. Maybe that's why he hasn't been caught. Maybe he's *two* guys."

Elaine had seldom seen him so perturbed. "Goddamn it," he said as she prepared for bed, "I can't protect you and the kids in this neighborhood. Nobody could."

After a few minutes, he said, "Listen, honey, I don't want the kids outa your sight unless they're in school, understand?"

She didn't have to be told.

The next morning Debbie Simmons asked her favorite student to recount the ordeal to the class—"It'll be good to learn how well you handled this." The teacher admired the child's stage presence; a few weeks earlier Brenda and a classmate had done a comedy turn and made everyone laugh.

Two and a half months later, another Green River body was found a mile down the road from the Geres' house, bringing the total into the mid-forties. Then a young girl vanished from the next block.

"That's it," Joe said.

They rented a three-room bungalow in Bothell, a pleasant town twenty miles north of Seattle at the upper end of Lake Washington, and Elaine wangled a transfer to the local office of FEMA, the Federal Emergency Management Agency, a ten-minute drive from her new home.

"Honey," Joe told her a few months later, "we made a mistake. This is no place for Brenda. She can't even have a horse." The unsaddled child had quickly joined 4-H so she could help out at the club's livestock shows.

Elaine said, "You mean we have to . . . move?"

She didn't mind. Friends and fellow workers kidded her about rootlessness, but she liked to renovate, add on, reline, shore up and refurbish as much as some wives enjoyed luncheons and golf. "Seems to me," she would tell Joe, "all this room needs is a little paint here, a little plaster there." Pretty soon she would be pulling on her overalls.

As the 1984–85 school year approached an end, the real estate market was reviving, and Joe talked about returning to the Idaho panhandle. "I can sell houses or cars in Idaho same as I sell 'em here," he told Elaine. "I can sell any damn thing. And you can always find a job."

This time Brenda wasn't pleased at the prospect of another move. Lately she'd been unusually upbeat about herself, her latest school and new friends. She'd written a fantasy newspaper article for an English class: "On Saturday the fourth of March, Brenda Gere won the biggest award that America ever saw. It stands sixty three feet high and fourty two feet wide. It's made out of pure gold. It stands in her back yard. She has guards standing all around."

In her exuberance, she drew up an "I like" list, which included "I like barbecued ribs and Pietro's pizza only." "I like Karen Oberhelman (she's my best friend)." "I like the name Sharon." "I like the octupus at the fair." "I like all the Star Wars series."

But she didn't like the idea of another disruption in her life. On June 5, 1985, four months after her twelfth birthday, she wrote in her journal, "I'll go crazy if we move to Idaho."

She told her mother, "If I had it my way I would never leave Washington."

"It's drier there," said the woman who'd been raised in the desert. "I like it dry."

"I like it rainy," said her daughter.

Brenda finished the discussion in her journal, "I like states like California, Reno, Las Vegas, Florida and you know how some people love Hawii and they'd give up anything to go there. Well I hate Hawii, I think I'd throw up if I had to go there. . . ."

She moped around the house till her father promised to reconsider the out-of-state move. On June 18, she wrote, "I'm sad because today's the last day of school, I've been telling everybody that I'm going to move to Idaho this summer and I finaly found out we might not. I hope we don't. I'm going to miss Heather, Crista, Annie and Cristen, Sheila, Alicia, Terese, Sue, Jenifer, and I already miss Nicole but she moved. I'm also going to miss alot of other people who are in these 3 classes, the people who made me laugh, cry, be happy, and also be sad. It's just to sad to leave this school. . . .

"This is how I feel: 1. Happy cause schools out. 2. Sad to leave all my friends. 3. And not sure."

12

On a Saturday drive with the kids, Elaine spotted the log house. She couldn't wait to tell Joe about the big place a few miles from downtown Bothell on a two-lane country road that was named, with typical rustic panache, Thirty-fifth Avenue Southeast. The house sat at the edge of a rural community called Clearview, a scattered region of tall fences, weathered barns, pastures, hedgerows, deep woods, algae-covered ponds, and cedar-water lakes. The property included a paddle tennis court, a corral, a run for Brenda's new Hungarian vizsla Kanga, and so many berry bushes, roses, rhododendrons, vine maples, red cedars and Douglas firs that the place could hardly be seen from the road. It was for sale, and if the Geres would be willing to show it to potential buyers, they could rent for $550 a month, almost exactly what they were paying for their cinder-block cracker-box in Bothell.

Elaine was disappointed at Joe's reaction when they looked the bargain over.

"Honey," he said, "I don't like the vibes. Look at the woods in back. I couldn't protect you guys here."

Elaine thought, He wouldn't consider his family safe if we lived in a castle with a moat and crocodiles.

"Joe," she said. "The kids need space. Who's gonna come way out here to hurt somebody? We'll find something better later."

Brenda's reaction was as complex as Brenda. She was pleased to have a bedroom upstairs in an A-shaped area formed by rough-hewn wooden logs, while her brothers would share a room on the first floor. She leaned far out the second-story window and said, "Look, Mom! If we had a fire I could drop right out." Fire was a special terror. She remembered the turkey fire in Bonners Ferry and the stories about her grandmother Gere's burns.

Brenda seemed wary as they checked out the yard. She kept staring at two windows that resembled eyesockets. "Mom," the child said, "this looks like Amityville to me."

Elaine told her to lighten up on the imagination and give the place a chance. Amityville was three thousand miles away.

The Geres took over the log house in the summer of 1985, a few months after Elaine's fortieth birthday. The moving truck turned a corner too sharply and their living-room mirror shattered. My God, she thought, that's all we need: the Amityville Horror plus seven years of bad luck. The omen stuck in her mind.

The first time Brenda washed her hair in the new house, she called from behind the shower curtain, "Hey, Mom, I haven't heard if they found any more Green River victims lately."

Without thinking, Elaine looked up from her newspaper and said, "They found one yesterday."

Brenda said, "Oh, I spoke too soon." She sounded disappointed. Elaine wondered when the fearfulness would end. You could expect it in a four- or five-year-old, but Brenda was twelve and very grown-up. Elaine wished the police would catch that darn Green River guy. Seventh-grade girls should be thinking about horses and cars, boys, dances, not killers named after rivers.

A few midnights later Brenda called out, "Mom, could you come in and sleep with me?"

Elaine thought carefully before she answered. To pad down the hall and climb into bed with her tremulous daughter, she decided, would be a confirmation that there was something to fear.

"Not tonight, honey," she said in her softest voice. "We're right here if you need us. You and Kanga go to sleep now. Everything's fine."

It took several weeks for the Geres to learn that the rustic neighborhood was less peaceable than it appeared. Most of the homes were set back from the road and separated by heavy landscaping or high fences. BEWARE OF DOG signs abounded. Pit bulls and Rottweilers were called "Snohomish County retrievers." Every now and then one retrieved someone's skin.

"We're too far out in the tules," the world-class worrier Joe complained to his wife. "No street cops, no beat cars, no pedestrians. It'd take a half hour or an hour to get a deputy. That's too damn long."

13

Brenda soon had her usual complement of playmates and admirers. Her best friend was Annie DeSantis, a vivacious child and a good match, who lived a quarter mile down the country road. They arranged to get off at the same bus stop every afternoon so Brenda could walk Annie home. The girls attended Annie's church and carpooled to their soccer team, "the Daisies," in the Northshore Soccer League. Sometimes they overnighted and shared ghost stories.

Annie and Brenda agreed that males were likable—at a distance. If boys drove by and shouted remarks, Brenda would duck or turn away. "I think he's so *cute*," she would whisper later to Annie. She informed her mother that boys were okay, but too many of them thought it was clever to belch and gas.

With another classmate, Crista Crownover, she made a few tentative approaches to the opposite sex. "She'd get me to call some boy she liked," Crista recalled, "and I'd say, 'Hi! Are you going to the dance? My friend Brenda really likes you. Say, I'm kinda curious. How do you feel about her?' Brenda would listen on the other line. Then we'd hang up and giggle."

Brenda wrote Annie DeSantis, "How much do you like Petie?" and blocked off four squares marked 25%, 50%, 75%, 100%. She began applying touches of her mother's eye makeup and importuning the orthodontist to remove her braces. In a school paper, she wrote that she admired model Christie Brinkley, "but I would have better taste than her because I wouldn't marry Billy Joel at all. He's so gross. She's so pretty you'd think that she could get someone better looking. . . . I think that if I had any idol that I wanted I'd pick Christy Brinkly. I used to like Stephanie Powers. Yuck."

In midsummer, Brenda was packed off to Carson City, Nevada, to spend a few weeks with her grandmother, Evelyn Mayzsak. Every night the child called home. "I guess she's not so independent after all," Elaine told her mother over the phone.

"It's an act they put on," Evelyn whispered. "You were the same."

Brenda felt better when her grandmother took her to the mall to buy school clothes. She wrote a friend, "We ate out at the Nugget and Ormsbee and the Spike every night. Then I also visited my Aunt Beverly who also lives in Carson."

She failed to mention that once again she'd suffered twinges of anxiety, even though she was six hundred miles from the Green River Killer.

On one of their nightly calls, Evelyn told Elaine, "Last night when I put her to bed, she said, 'Grandma, did you lock the door?' I told her, 'Don't worry, there's a deadbolt.' Elaine, what's the child so afraid of?"

A few nights later, Evelyn asked Brenda why she was sleeping with her light on, and the child answered, "Monsters, I guess. You know, Grandma. The boogeyman."

"There's no boogeyman, honey," her grandmother said.

"Yeah, there is. I see him in my dreams."

They slept together in the grandmother's bed.

14

On Sunday, September 15, 1985, Brenda was confirmed in the Roman Catholic Church. Joe donned a new suit for the rare church appearance, and Brenda wore ruffles and white lace.

After Elaine put the boys to bed that night, she tiptoed into her daughter's bedroom. Brenda reclined on her comforter with the rainbow design, playing with her toy horses. Mother and child discussed Brenda's first singing lesson and the Halloween dance that was coming up. They'd already shopped for her Cleopatra outfit.

Brenda was still put out that her dad had missed the school's father-daughter banquet, but she understood that he had to sell cars or they wouldn't eat.

In a sleepy voice, she said, "Ya know, Mom, I just wanna do everything I can. Ya know, Mom? In the time I've got left?" She paused and said, "I mean . . . before it's too late."

Elaine was exhausted from the long day, and she'd never been one to analyze nuances, even those of her children. "That's a good idea, honey," she said, and hugged her daughter good night.

At work on Monday, Elaine found the phrase sticking in her mind. She stared out the window at the unusually dry September day. "I was thinking how short life is," she said later. "Brenda was right. Make every minute count, 'cause you never know when something's gonna happen."

The children had been pestering her to drive them to a school skating party on Wednesday night, and she'd put them off with the old reliable phrase "We'll see."

She still didn't think she could do it, what with working a full-time job and running the house and supplying Joe with home-cooked meals at the car lot and keeping up on Mikey's medical problems and getting Joey off to school. She leaned toward a veto, but Brenda's comment made her reconsider. Didn't every minute count?

The next afternoon she stopped at a mall to select a school outfit for Brenda; the child had grown out of most of last year's wardrobe. Elaine knew better than to trust her own taste, and she asked for help from an Asian-American clerk who didn't look much older than Brenda. The girl recommended bright red stretch pants with stirrups, an oversized gold-and-black checked shirt, and a wide red patent-leather belt.

"Are you sure this is okay for a twelve-year-old?" Elaine asked. She couldn't remember seeing anyone at Slover Boyle Elementary or Fontana High in bright red stretch pants.

The saleswoman said, "Trust me. She'll *love* it."

"Mom," Brenda said after birdlike tiltings of her head and balletic wavings of her matchstick arms, "did *you* pick this out?"

"Uh, yeah," Elaine said.

"Oh, Mom, it's cool!"

"Well," Elaine admitted, "I had help."

15

At 2:30 P.M. the next day, Wanda Munson, a dark-haired nurse in her mid-thirties, left her secluded home a few hundred yards from the Geres' log house and headed for Evergreen Hospital. She'd barely driven a block when she realized that she'd forgotten her brown-bag lunch, which consisted in its entirety of a banana.

A small off-white Toyota blocked the entrance to her long circular driveway. She stopped in her lane and flicked a turn signal. The intruder didn't budge. Wanda squinted against the glare on the car's windshield and made out the form of a man who seemed to fill every inch of the driver's side. "He wasn't just big," she told her husband later, "he was *huge*. He looked like the Hulk."

She thought, Who *is* this joker and why is he blocking me from my own driveway? Her three children were in the house, and she certainly didn't intend to give way. The man's broad face was deeply tanned and topped by brown waves or curls. He looked annoyed.

Wanda was already late for work. The longer the impasse continued, the meaner the man looked. She told herself, I don't care what kind of frown that idiot puts on. This is *my* driveway.

After a few more minutes, the Toyota eased away. Wanda drove up and rushed inside. "Some guy was blocking the driveway," she told her fourteen-year-old daughter Michelle. "Did you see somebody come up and turn around here?"

The child said, "No."

"Is Jeffrey okay?" Her son was five. "And Rachel?" The other daughter was ten.

"Yeah, Mom. Why shouldn't they be?"

Wanda looked at her watch again and wondered if she was over-reacting. No, she decided. The big man was definitely out of place.

It was too late to call for a replacement at the hospital. "Listen, Michelle," she said, "it's probably nothing, but after I leave, lock up. And don't let *anybody* in."

She drove back down the long driveway and stopped before turning into the street. The Toyota was parked forty or fifty yards away on the shoulder. The man seemed to be staring at her house.

Wanda asked herself, What is this guy's *problem?* Why is he scoping out our neighborhood?

She waited. Another five minutes passed. Then the man headed north. His brake lights flickered as he crawled along the two-lane asphalt road. Wanda had the impression that he was watching her in his mirror.

When she arrived at the hospital fifteen minutes later, she called home. "Michelle," she said, "I really feel uneasy. Did you lock the doors and windows?"

"I'm doing it, Mom."

"Well, I want you to go around the house and check every one."
Michelle told her not to worry.

The teenager put down the phone and was locking the back door when she heard a scratching sound at the front. She thought it was her friend, the Geres' fourteen-year-old next-door neighbor, Melanie Bonadore.

Before Michelle could open up, she glimpsed a face. A man with dark hair and close-set piggy eyes was trying to get a grip on the bottom of the front window. She stepped back as he tried other doors and windows.

The noises stopped, and she peered through the curtains at an unusually large man standing in the front pasture. He looked confused and irritated. He left in an odd spraddled duck walk, his thighs so big that they rubbed together. She was relieved when he passed from sight.

Gordon Munson, graying, middle-aged and native to the area, arrived home from his vending business and immediately got a breathless briefing from ten-year-old Rachel.

"Good grief!" he said. "Did Mom call the police?"

Rachel said she didn't think so. Mom had been late for work when she left.

Munson dialed the Snohomish County Sheriff's Department and told a policewoman, "I had an interesting experience here at my house today. Somebody came up and tried to get in the front door, went all the way around the house checking the slider and the garage door and stood in front and was quite disgusted and left. Very strange behavior."

The officer commented, "That *is* strange. Let us know if anything happens again."

Munson was a little surprised by the woman's nonchalance and blurted out, "Sure will."

Within a few hours, most of the neighbors along the rural road had learned about the incident via back fence and telephone. Most put it down to eccentric behavior. A burglar wouldn't be operating in broad daylight, and child molesters prowled school and shopping areas, not wide-open areas where they stood out distinctly.

The Geres, newcomers to Clearview, heard nothing. For most of the day the log house had stood empty, and in the evening Joe worked overtime at the car lot while Elaine took the children skating.

Everyone was home by nine-thirty. It was an Indian-summer night, and the only sounds came from an occasional passing car and the croaking of a few lusty frogs that mistook the warm air for another mating season.

Despite Brenda's apprehensiveness and Joe's eternal concern about his family, the big Dutch doors of the log house were usually kept unlocked. The head of the household didn't like to fumble for his keys when he came home late at night. It didn't seem significant at the time.

VI

WHERE'S BRENDA?

1

The next morning, Elaine awoke at six, showered, dressed, improved her pretty face with practiced expertise, and was juicing oranges by the time her children shuffled into the big open kitchen at six-thirty. It was Thursday, September 19, 1985, and she was due at FEMA at seven-thirty. After eight hours of sleep, miniature skaters still pirouetted in her brain. She would be working the phones at the office, and she hoped the images would fade.

The days were already shortening. Pacific Daylight Time had six weeks to run, which meant that the Gere children and their school-mates would continue to grope toward the bus stop in darkness, a common complaint at 48 degrees north latitude. It was Joe's day off, but he planned to go to work. Christmas was a big event in the extravagant father's life, and he needed some extra commissions.

Elaine pulled a curtain aside and looked into a wall of trees that shaded from green to black. A few scattered glints of watery light shone through the topmost branches of the red cedars and Douglas firs, up where hawks and bald eagles sometimes posed. Two or three hours would pass before the direct rays of the sun warmed the log walls and the sunflowers began to rotate degree by degree.

She felt a little thrill of accomplishment when Brenda pranced into the kitchen like a runway model. She was wearing the bright new outfit with the loud belt and red stirrup pants along with a yellow checked shirt and black go-go boots. She'd just bought her first bra, even though she didn't need one. Elaine remembered how embarrassing the subject had been when she was a child.

As always, Brenda's day was planned to the minute. Her first class would start at eight and she would get home at two-thirty and receive a checkup call from Elaine. This was the children's first year without a baby-sitter, after years of listening to Brenda complain that they were all incompetent, and the parents still made several daily calls and felt nervous if the phone wasn't answered on the first or second ring.

After school, Brenda would let Kanga out for a romp in the fenced yard, then call in the hound and do her homework. The boys would come galumphing through the front door around three-thirty, right in the middle of *General Hospital*, and she would usually have to threaten them or promise rewards to get them to shush.

At ten after four, Elaine would arrive to drive Brenda and her friend Annie DeSantis to soccer practice with the Daisies. Annie's father Julio would drive them home. That was the plan for the day.

En route to work in the morning, Elaine dropped Brenda at Annie's house so the girls could walk together to the bus stop. "Now, Mom," her daughter said in her schoolmarmish tone, "what time do you get off work?"

"The same as always. Four o'clock."

Elaine maintained a serious look even though she felt like giggling. Brenda always acted as though she were dealing with a backward child, just as Elaine had acted with her own mother back in Fontana.

"Now, Mom," Brenda said, "be sure to come *straight* home. We have to be at the field at four-twenty."

"Yes, hon, I know," Elaine said gently. The Daisies had won three straight games and planned to go the whole season without losing.

"Well, okay then," Brenda said. She skipped up Annie's front steps, turned, and waved. The porch light reflected off her patent-leather belt, and for an instant Elaine wondered if the outfit might be a mistake. She'd read somewhere that bright colors were not recommended for young girls; they attracted weirdos. She decided that the idea was a silly overreach, like so many ideas about crime these days. It was so easy to become as paranoid as Joe. The DeSantises' front door opened and her only daughter was gone.

* * *

At the beginning of her lunch hour, Elaine rushed home to do the breakfast dishes, tidy up the house and get a head start on dinner. It was her daily routine. Otherwise she would never catch up.

She was a little surprised to find Kanga inside. She didn't know whether the boys had forgotten to put the rufous-furred hound outside or if Joe had let her back in again before leaving for work.

"Out!" she said, and shooed Brenda's pet into her run in the backyard. Then Elaine returned to her office to gulp a half sandwich at the reception desk.

Around 1:45 P.M., a Gere neighbor named Katherine Murray answered her doorbell to find a tall, wide body standing between her and the sun. She was relieved when the man smiled and asked politely, "Do you happen to know where one-nine-eight-one-five is? It's the Simpsons'." He paused. "They're selling a car."

"I don't know any Simpsons," she said, "but that address is north of here."

The man apologized for bothering her and returned to a white car that looked like a Toyota or Datsun. He had an odd way of walking.

About thirty minutes later, Barbara Adams, who lived a quarter mile north of the Geres, was looking out her front window when a small white car appeared in her long driveway, a man at the wheel.

The elderly woman had become accustomed to the varied sizes and shapes of rolling stock that used her driveway for a turnaround; it was a little like birdwatching. The car turned and drove off.

Just after 2:00 P.M., Gordon Munson left his office for home. As he drove, he wondered what the hell was going on in his neighborhood. An avid newspaper reader, he'd long been aware that the woodsy suburb wasn't as peaceful or as safe as it appeared. Bodies from Seattle killings popped up like toadstools in the surrounding woods or floated to the top of the reddish-tinted ponds that were left over from abandoned cedar-shake mills and logging operations. Only a few miles over the ridge from the Gere and Munson homes, an enraged ex-con on work release had broken into a house and slashed the throats of the rape victim who'd testified against him, the woman's young daughter, and a female visitor. After a twelve-year legal delay, Charles Campbell was hanged.

Munson usually worked a longer day, but he and Wanda were concerned about the events of Wednesday and didn't want to leave the children alone a minute longer than necessary. He reached home at two-thirty, greeted the kids, and went out to reconnoiter in his pickup.

At the corner of Thirty-fifth and Grannis, a block from his home, Munson spotted a compact white car parked in a grassy V at the side of the road. A large man, apparently the driver, was walking on the shoulder toward the Geres' house, a few hundred yards north. He looked to be two or three inches over six feet tall and at least two-sixty in weight.

As Munson drove past, he noticed that the man's thigh muscles bulged against tight-fitting pants and his upper body strained a white sport shirt. His first thought was innocent wonderment. Isn't this strange? he said to himself. What an interesting thing! Here's this great big guy and this little car, and they both match Wanda's description of the guy who came up to the door yesterday. He asked himself, Is this another Sunlock Gas Appliance salesman? A Century 21 agent?

Munson eased past the Geres' log house, then U-turned to swing back for a front view of the stranger. After the walking man shot what looked like a bold smirk, Munson continued south to the off-white car and noted its green-and-white Washington license number: LJS090. It looked like a 1981 four-door Toyota Corona. Then he spotted his stepdaughter Michelle and her friend Melanie Bonadore talking at the school bus stop.

"Don't go home yet," he warned the Bonadore girl. Her house was in the direction the giant was headed. "I just saw that man down the street in his car. I'm gonna have the cops check him out. Melanie, go to our house with Michelle."

As Munson continued on, he passed the Gere girl, skipping toward her house in her black go-go boots, wearing a yellow checked shirt and a bright red belt. She smiled as he drove by, and he thought, What a sweet child. The family was new in the neighborhood, but he knew her name was Brenda. The stranger was walking in the same northward direction on Thirty-fifth, but he was a hundred yards ahead of the girl.

Later an anguished Munson described his state of mind as he

dialed police from his home: "I knew I had to check this guy out. I mean, it was a strange and unusual situation. But damn—I didn't see any evil connection. That thought never came to my mind. It didn't relate to me that he'd tried to get into the house to get Michelle. It only related that he tried to get into the house. I just couldn't think that evil. Unless you live in that kind of framework, you don't conjure up such thoughts. I never thought something horrendous would happen. I thought, He's just an aggressive individual doing surveys, or—some kind of salesperson going door to door."

The sheriff's log showed that it was two forty-five when Munson called 911. After hearing his story, the dispatcher asked, "Would you like for us to come down and check?"

Once again Munson was taken aback by the professional coolness of the response. He said in a surprised voice, "Don't you think you *should?*"

The dispatcher told him to stay put; a car would check the area and give him a full report. The conversation took three minutes.

Munson thought, Maybe I should go outside and check things out. But it might cause him to miss the deputy. He told himself that this was just a neighborhood incident, not the Lindbergh kidnapping, and decided to sit tight.

Ed Bonadore, Melanie's father, was taking advantage of the radiant afternoon to mow his front lawn before leaving for the swing shift at his garage and service station. At about ten minutes to three, his wife brought him an ice cream bar and he took a short break on his front porch. They'd lived in Clearview since 1972 and didn't worry much about security. The neighbors were bright and alert, and he'd heard that the new guy next door was a retired deputy sheriff from California.

From his vantage point Bonadore couldn't quite see over the hedges and wild shrubbery to the top edge of the Geres' side door. As he ate his ice cream, he thought he heard a slight commotion, then a muffled voice saying, "No!" It sounded like the daughter.

The Geres' screen door banged, and everything was quiet. "The idea of violence never entered my mind," Bonadore said later. "I figured she was having a few words with her parents. The dog didn't even bark."

He restarted his power mower. A few minutes later, he thought he heard a car pull into the Geres' driveway, but he couldn't be sure.

2

Elaine was routing phone calls for sixty employees and greeting visitors at the secure entrance to the FEMA building in Bothell, but she managed to make her regular checkup call around 3:00 P.M. She was a little concerned when Brenda didn't answer. She was probably in the yard with Kanga or in the bathroom or talking to a neighbor or . . . whatever. Brenda was dependable. She was her own best baby-sitter, and her brothers', too.

Elaine tried again at five after three, and a few minutes later. She suppressed an uneasy feeling. The boys would arrive home at three-thirty. Brenda could be involved in a zillion different things, none of them sinister. Maybe the phone line was down; it had happened before. Elaine always tried to avoid jumping to dire conclusions. Joe did enough of that for both of them.

The switchboard beeped, and for a while she was too busy to worry.

At 3:06 P.M., a Snohomish County deputy sheriff named Stan Breda was ordered by radio to check out a report of a suspicious man and vehicle near Thirty-fifth Avenue S.E. and Grannis Road. Breda's car was miles away and the drive took him fifteen minutes. The intersection was empty. He drove up and down the straight stretch of country road, looked into driveways, and saw nothing suspicious.

At three twenty-five, the road deputy drove up to Gordon Munson's house and reported, "The guy's not around."

"I suppose not," Munson said. He was plainly agitated. "It's been an awful long time. I mean, you guys are five minutes from here in every direction, and it took you an hour."

Breda explained that the substation was swamped, with kids just back in school and the roads crammed with drivers enjoying the gorgeous weather.

"I live here twenty-four hours a day," the angry Munson replied. "I know how *not* busy you are. There's four of you right down at the restaurant at May's Pond all the time, and that's two minutes from here. If you hadn't've told me to sit and wait for you, I would have driven down there and had everybody back in seven minutes flat."

The young deputy apologized for the delay—not an hour, as it had seemed to the upset Munson, but thirty minutes from the end of the 911 call to arrival. Citizens always felt that the police took too long, especially on calls to the boondocks. Every understaffed police department in the Northwest was accustomed to the complaint, and officers didn't take offense.

Breda wrote down a description of the walking stranger and his car, then cruised the area for another fifteen or twenty minutes before clearing the call.

Joey answered the phone at three thirty-five. "No, Mom," he said. "Brenda's not here."

"Is she riding the three-wheeler?"

"No, Mom."

"Okay. I'll call back."

Elaine still wasn't overly concerned. There could have been an unexpected delay at school. Or she could be with Annie. The two pals had been inseparable lately, and they might have stopped off at Annie's house. Later Elaine would be car-pooling the girls to soccer practice; they might already be waiting on Annie's front steps. Of course, that would mean Brenda had missed *General Hospital.* Well, it was possible. Kids' tastes changed. She hadn't been happy with her favorite show lately.

The harassed mother started to phone Annie's house but couldn't remember the number. Darn, she said to herself, I'm always calling them about the carpool. Wouldn't you think I'd remember their number by now?

The switchboard was quiet for a change. She flipped open the phone book and blanked on Annie's last name—Santos, DeAngelo, something like that. She was pretty sure it began with "De." Names had never been her long suit.

She buzzed a visitor through the security door and looked at her watch. Three forty-five. Her workday ended in fifteen minutes. No big deal, she assured herself. By the time I get home, Brenda'll be sitting on the front steps in her shinguards and soccer boots, telling me to hurry up. It's the kind of mix-up that happens when you start a new routine in a new neighborhood.

Gravel spurted from the wheels of her car as she drove up the long driveway. It was five after four, almost an hour and a half since Brenda should have arrived from school. Her three-wheeler was parked in its usual spot.

The boys were watching TV. "Where's Brenda?" Elaine asked.

Six-year-old Mikey raised his thin Magyar eyes and shrugged. Eleven-year-old Joey said, "We don't know. She wasn't here when we got home. We had to let Kanga in."

Elaine was surprised. It was clearly understood that the vizsla was Brenda's pet and she was in charge of admitting the dog to the house after school.

The first floor appeared undisturbed since Elaine's noontime visit. The mail was on the bar, which meant that Brenda had collected it from the rural box across Thirty-fifth and brought it inside, her daily custom.

Elaine ran up the stairs two at a time. Brenda's purse containing her $2 emergency fund was on the floor next to her bed. Her schoolbooks lay under an end table.

Elaine was relieved. Her daughter hadn't been in a bus accident or a landslide or plucked away by E.T. or some other space visitor. She'd reached home for sure. Now where the heck had she gone?

She looked up Annie's number in Brenda's address book. DeSantis, that was it. They were I-talian.

"Annie," she said when the child answered her call, "is Brenda there?"

"No," said her daughter's best friend. "Aren't you gonna take me to soccer today?"

"In a few minutes. Do you think she went to soccer some other way?"

"Not that I know of. The last I saw of her, she got off the bus and was walking home."

Elaine thanked the child and dialed Joe at the used-car lot. "Joe," she said, "we can't find Brenda anyplace. I'm just hoping she's at the soccer field."

"Get over there and check."

"Honey—"

"Now!"

Joe's tone was disturbing. She drove past the DeSantises' street before she remembered that she was supposed to pick up Annie. Brenda's best pal didn't complain about the oversight.

It was a twenty-minute drive to the field. The Daisies were stretching, and Elaine scanned the faces. "Where's Brenda?" she asked the coach.

"We don't know, Mrs. Gere," he said pleasantly. "It's not like her to miss."

"You haven't seen her?"

"Not since our last practice."

Elaine sped home and began calling neighbors and soccer mothers. In turn, they called others, and soon contacts were being made all around the Bothell and Clearview area, to friends old and new, asking about Brenda. No one had any idea where she was.

Elaine slipped through a gap in the hedge to the Bonadores' yard. "Is Brenda here?" she asked.

"No," Gretchen Bonadore said. "She hasn't been here."

"Well," Elaine said, her hands fluttering, "we don't know where she is."

Gretchen turned to her daughter. "Melanie, when did you see Brenda?"

"Walking home from the bus," the eighth-grader said, and added, "alone."

Elaine made an effort to compose herself. The boys were already upset, and she didn't think they should have to worry about their mother's mental state when they were already upset about their sister. Joey looked chalky. Little Mikey's breathing was shallow, a dangerous sign. It never took much stress to produce an allergic response and send him off to the nearest emergency room. Brenda's absence was a big enough problem for one day.

Elaine was back on the phone when the female Bonadores burst through the side door. "Tell Mrs. Gere what you just told me, Melanie," Gretchen ordered. "*Everything.*"

Elaine and the boys listened as the child described the huge man who'd been hanging around, how he'd blocked Wanda Munson from her own driveway, and how he'd been seen this very afternoon on Thirty-fifth, walking ahead of Brenda. Melanie said he resembled "Bluto on Popeye, without a beard."

Elaine turned away so her sons wouldn't see her expression.

The Bonadores stayed for moral support, and Elaine went back upstairs to look for a note or a clue. She wondered why Brenda's schoolbooks had been shoved under the table; she was usually neater than that. Otherwise the room looked undisturbed. A picture of her friend Karen Oberhelman was atop the night table. A low-powered microscope was on the dresser alongside a Duran Duran tape and an unfinished thank-you note to a former teacher. Her collection of stuffed animals was neatly arrayed on a shelf; four plastic horses marched in a row. The hi-fi was neatly covered with plastic. A crucifix and a collage of Mötley Crüe, Madonna and other rock stars were in place on the wall, alongside a set of rules Brenda had drawn up for the day she became queen of the world:

1. No smoking or will go to jail for 90 days.
2. No drinking or will go to jail for 90 days.
3. All people must have a horse.
4. All people must have a cocker spaniel or a yellow lab.
5. Dont pollute the ocean, rivers, lakes, streams or ponds.
6. Don't over fish.
7. Stay off wildlife reservation.
8. Must drive at a reasonable speed.
9. Respect mother & father.
10. Go out for pizza every Friday.
11. Have video games inhouse.
12. Cristmas must be fun.
13. Let off firecrackers on Cristmas.
14. You must respect these rules.

Nothing appeared to be disturbed. Except—

Elaine gasped. The rainbow comforter was gone.

"She's not at the soccer field," she told Joe on the phone. "She's not at Annie's. And . . . her comforter's gone."

Joe said, "Call the sheriff."

The idea hadn't entered her mind. Sheriffs were for violence, kidnap, murder. What connection could any of these have with Brenda? She was gone for a while, that was all. There'd been a mix-up.

A crisp female voice informed her that no search could be started for twenty-four hours. Elaine recognized standard police procedure; it was the same policy that Joe had observed in San Bernardino. He'd frequently spent his off-hours looking for missing kids, and sometimes he found them. But they were other people's children, not his own.

Elaine asked, "Can't you just send a car? It's—it's—my daughter. Brenda Sue Gere."

The dispatcher said that all units were busy and she couldn't send a car until the area unit cleared, and even then she couldn't promise.

"How long will it take?" Elaine asked.

"I wish I knew. Why don't you go ahead and give me a description, ma'am?"

Elaine tried to concentrate. She saw Brenda clearly in her mind but couldn't reduce the image to words. "Well," she said, "she's twelve, and she's—"

My God, she thought, I don't know my own daughter's height. It's been months since we measured. "Five-five," she guessed, "or— five-six. She's about ninety pounds." Wait, she thought, that was last year. "No, a hundred. Maybe . . . a hundred and ten."

"Hair?"

"It's light brown with, uh, blond highlights. Just put down brown. She has thin bangs to her eyebrows." Elaine paused to catch her breath. "Straight hair to her shoulders. Wears braces. And she has green—uh, blue—uh, hazel eyes." It was so confusing, describing your own child. It wasn't something you ever expected to have to do over the phone. To a cop.

"Little things can be helpful, ma'am," the operator said.

Elaine thought hard. Sometimes Brenda wore artificial fingernails, but she might have left them off. "Yes," she said, "she wore a clear plastic bracelet filled with water and glitter."

She called Joe and recounted the conversation. Her tongue felt heavy, her skin cold. She hugged herself and gripped the phone so hard that her hand hurt.

Joe arrived just after six-thirty, visibly angry with himself for being so late. He said he'd been closing a sale. "Have the police called back?" he asked.

"No," Elaine said.

"How long ago did you make the report?"

"Ten or fifteen minutes. Mr. Munson called them earlier, about a suspicious man out on Thirty-fifth. A deputy looked around and left."

"A suspicious man?" Joe said. "Jesus Christ, call 'em again."

The phone rang just as she started to pick it up. One of the sheriff's civilian employees reported that the area car was in the field on another call. Elaine put down the phone and told Joe, "They can't come for a while."

He asked about the suspicious man, and she repeated what she'd heard. "Oh, God," he said, "Brenda's done. She's gone." He mixed a drink of Kool-Aid, Jack Daniel's and ice.

After two or three gulps, he said, "Goddamn it, why're the cops fiddle-farting around?" He ordered Elaine to dial the sheriff's number and then grabbed the phone.

She listened as his voice hardened. "Look, don't try to program me. I'm a cop, too. . . . That's bullshit. . . . *Bullshit!* . . . Gimme the sheriff's home number. . . ."

After a pause, he slammed down the phone. "They're on the way," he said. The ice in his drink rattled against the sides of the glass.

3

Deputy Sheriff Bryce Siegel thought about another Brenda as he steered his police cruiser toward Clearview. He was thirty-one, college-educated, a self-described "Bible Christian" and a former state trooper who'd chauffeured the colorful Governor Dixy Lee Ray for two years before joining the sheriff's department.

Brenda Lee Jones had been stabbed seventeen times on her way to Lynnwood High School, a short drive from the Gere neighborhood, after she refused to enter a stranger's car. Like the tall, lean Siegel, she'd been a star athlete, clean-cut and popular. He'd worked the case and paid a price mentally. He had an unholy fear of becoming cynical and desensitized, "of starting to think that everybody's an asshole or a puke." The Brenda Lee Jones killer had put him to the test.

He hoped this new Brenda case would be different, but when he stepped into the log house he felt the chill that always came over him when children turned up missing. The father was throwing down drinks, but behind his alcoholic facade Siegel could tell that the tall, dark-haired man had an ex-deputy's instincts and smarts.

Joe Gere believed that his daughter had been abducted by the bulky stranger and probably murdered. He kept running his hand through a springy head of graying black hair and repeating, "I can't live with this."

The cool blond mother let her husband do the talking. When she was pressed for her own ideas, she insisted that her daughter was too precious to be murdered and even if she'd been kidnapped she was safe. Siegel didn't comment. It was often better to let people believe in their own denial, at least for a while.

He borrowed the Geres' phone and talked to the Bonadores and Gordon Munson. Then he called headquarters and asked for Search and Rescue.

As Siegel was walking out to his cruiser, Joe Gere caught up. He clutched the lawman's arm and said, "Please, deputy, find my baby girl. I swear, I'll never sleep or work till you do."

Siegel closed his eyes hard. This was the part of his job that disturbed him the most. He'd gone toe-to-toe with dopers and murderers and never felt much fear or discomfort. But informing a mother that her daughter was dead in a traffic accident, or a father that his only son had been killed in a drive-by, or dealing with a jaded ex-cop like Joe Gere who knew the odds against his daughter's survival as well as anyone and couldn't be jollied along . . . this, Siegel said to himself, is the worst. I'm sorry I got up this morning.

He didn't tell the shaken father that he agreed with his professional diagnosis. Everything pointed to foul play, especially the missing comforter. What good would it be to a kidnapper except to carry an unconscious or dead body?

Siegel made a practice of remaining detached, unemotional. But the Geres had shown him Brenda's picture—braces, silly bangs, innocent smile, such a sweet-looking child. He hoped they didn't show the picture to the sergeant on duty.

Tom Pszonka had just been promoted from the detective bureau and was on a personal crusade to jail every criminal in the Pacific Northwest. He'd already dispatched one with a single shot. The oversize cop looked tough enough to wrestle Sasquatches, but he had a weak spot for children. He had four of his own, and Bryce Siegel had two. Both were famous in the department for their softness toward kids.

After Pszonka ordered out Search and Rescue, he made a priority request for Deputy Stan Breda's report on the meandering giant in the off-white Toyota. As he read, the twenty-nine-year-old son of Polish immigrants felt sick. He'd overheard some of the radio chatter about the big stranger when he'd first come on duty at 3:00 P.M. At the time, he'd thought, Nothing unusual. The guy's just lost. Or drunk. Or high. Peculiar things happened in the backcountry of Snohomish County. But now a child was missing, and the events were too close in time and place.

Sergeant Pszonka lived a half mile from the Geres and had been preparing to drive home for dinner. He called his wife and said, "Honey, I can't make it." It was the third time this week that he'd had to cancel, but Karen was a cop's wife and required no explanation. "We got a problem right in our own backyard," he went on. "This looks—this looks bad."

Department of Motor Vehicles records showed that the white Toyota was registered to a Michael Kay Green of Mukilteo, a Puget Sound town a few miles south of Everett. Pszonka thought about the name Michael Kay. It was as though the guy had been named after both his parents, the same as male Hispanics with middle names like Maria and Carmen. A few years back, there'd been a Michael Kay Somebody on the University of Washington football team—a defensive lineman, Pszonka remembered. The sergeant had been a star lineman himself, at Southern Illinois University, after growing up in the tough Chicago suburb of Cicero, famous for Al Capone and other gangsters. He recalled that the football player was also named Green, or something close. Christ, he said to himself, are the Huskies turning out molesters these days?

Pszonka hauled his massive body from the chair and grabbed his work jacket. Bryce Siegel would be arriving from Clearview any minute. It was time for the two lawmen, five hundred pounds of power and muscle, to call on the wandering hulk.

After the deputy left, Elaine tried to maintain an air of normalcy on behalf of her sons. Joe was still raging up and down the living room—"If anybody touches my baby, I'll kill the son of a bitch. *Kill him with my bare hands!* I'll cut off his nuts. . . ."

Sometimes he subsided into quiet fits of despondency, flopping on the couch and rubbing at his eyes. Elaine heard him say, "Why wasn't I home? Why wasn't I *home?*" He blamed himself for moving his family into a house that was for sale and vulnerable to strangers. He cursed himself for going to work on his day off. He said they never should have left Fontana. "Everybody knew who I was down there. They were afraid of me, respected me. Nobody would mess with my family in Fontana. The scum of the earth hide in big cities. I should've thought of that when we came north."

It was plain to Elaine that whatever happened, he would always blame himself. That was his nature.

At nine, she told the boys to prepare for their baths. When Joey balked, she said, "You know the rules. You guys *never* miss your baths."

Mikey was six and half-filled the tub. He'd watched from corners all evening, frowning, listening, no one paying him much attention. At this stage, Elaine wasn't sure if he realized exactly what had happened.

"Mom," he said in his squeaky little-boy voice as she scrubbed his back, "I wish it was me instead of Brenda."

Elaine's instinct was to attack problems on her own, ask her family for help if necessary and use God for backup if all else failed. After a few murmured prayers, she phoned her ex-rowdy brother, Jim, now settled on an eighty-acre spread near Cheyenne, Wyoming, and living a conventional life with his wife and four kids.

"Listen to me, Jimmy," she said in the same bossy style she'd used when they were roaming the Jurupa Hills together. "Brenda's missing and some guy's probably taken her. The police aren't doing much."

"I'll be there," the welder said.

As Elaine put down the phone, she heard a bark and a howl from the driveway. She pulled the curtain aside and looked out the window. The first bloodhound had arrived.

4

Sergeant Tom Pszonka and Deputy Bryce Siegel, accompanied by an old hand named Jack Backus, left for the twenty-five-minute drive to the Mukilteo address just after 10:00 P.M. En route, Pszonka said to himself, Please, God, let the kid be inside the house, inside the trunk of the car, up the chimney, but *alive*. Let this be a kidnapping, a child taken against her will, not what it looks like.

Mukilteo perched like a Norwegian fishing village on the side of a low fjord. Third Street ran just above a wooden ferry slip, a lighthouse station with a cranberry roof, an asphalt parking lot that went by the nondescript name Mukilteo State Park, the narrow channel of tidewater between the mainland and Whidbey Island, and the main rail line between Seattle and British Columbia. A few miles away, Boeing manufactured 747 superjets in sheds the size of domed stadiums. The view from Mukilteo put Pszonka in mind of a children's picture book showing an airplane, dirigible, train, ship, ferry, bus, trucks and cars in a single spread. On any given day, he thought, you could see all of these from just about anyplace in Mukilteo. Except the dirigible.

The team of deputies spotted the off-white Toyota in the driveway of a traditional house landscaped in magnolias, roses and other shrubs and trees. Pszonka asked Backus to cover the outside while he and Siegel went to the door.

The woman who answered the door introduced herself as Sharon Pittman. Her surprised expression told Pszonka she had no idea what was going on.

He told her they were trying to find the owner of the Toyota. "Yes," the woman said pleasantly. "That's my son-in-law, Mike Green."

"Could we have a few minutes with him?" he asked.

The woman beckoned them into the kitchen. The house smelled like fresh bread. "What is this regarding?" she asked.

"Oh, just some robberies in the area," Pszonka said. "His car was seen. We just need a word with him."

The woman walked down the hall to a door and said, "Mike, the sheriff's department is here."

There was no response. Than a male voice said, "I'll be right out."

Mrs. Pittman returned to the kitchen, and the threesome made small talk. She seemed nervous. Yes, she said, she had children, five sons and one daughter. Most were grown. The Pittmans also took in troubled children. They were caring for two foster sons at the moment, a boy named Vincent and an Iranian boy with a name that sounded to the officers like "Cruise." She said her daughter Diana had been married to Mike Green since 1979. He was a weightlifter and former football star, between jobs at the moment.

The woman walked back down the hall and knocked again. The deputies heard a male voice grumble.

Ten more minutes passed. Pszonka thought, Why the hell doesn't the guy show? What's he doing in there? *Does he have the kid in there?*

Mrs. Pittman excused herself for a third time. "Mike," she called, "they're getting anxious. You better come out and talk."

A muffled voice came back, "Tell 'em I'm getting dressed."

When the stall approached the twenty-minute mark, Pszonka began to consider entering the room without permission. Brenda Gere could be gasping out the last few breaths of her life in there. Plainly she'd been abducted, and this joker was the prime suspect. Was that enough probable cause to justify busting into his room?

The big sergeant thought how simple police work could be if it weren't for technicalities. If this scene were being played on a commonsense basis, the door would be in splinters by now, the guy would be in cuffs and officers would be searching the room. Instead, Pszonka said to himself, I'm dicking around in this kitchen, talking about nasturtiums with this nice lady and worrying about the suspect's rights when I should be worrying about the victim's. And he's in there doing—what? Wiping off prints and stains? Flushing the comforter? *Getting ready to book?*

Mrs. Pittman walked down the hall, knocked, and disappeared into the room. After another short talk, the door opened and a large form darkened the opening. The man was bare-chested and barefooted, wearing only Speedo briefs. Dark brown ringlets framed a small face and what Pszonka later described as "sneaky little dark eyes."

To the big sergeant, the man looked carved from a redwood trunk. My God, he said to himself, this guy makes me look average. He himself stood six-three and was a little soft at two-ninety. This guy was just as tall, had a waist and a butt like a runway model, shoulders a yard across, arm and leg muscles that resembled sacks of grapefruits, and thick purplish veins that stood out like nightcrawlers. There wasn't a visible trace of fat, and yet the guy probably weighed ten pounds more than Pszonka. A single word leaped to the sergeant's mind: *steroids.*

The man was so big that his bare thighs made a chafing sound as he sauntered down the hall in a constipated rolling walk. Either he was sweating or he'd oiled his skin. The sergeant thought, Was that what took him so long? *Making up his body?*

"I'm Mike Green," the man said without smiling or offering his hand. "I was taking a shower. What's this about?"

The sergeant said, "A little girl is missing. We want to ask you some questions. First we'd like to read you your rights."

Mrs. Pittman looked perturbed and left the room. Pszonka said to himself, This son of a bitch has the girl. Not a goddamn doubt in the world. . . .

Bryce Siegel was thinking, If this guy makes a move on me, I'm gonna have to shoot him before he rips off my head.

Green acted flustered, made side-to-side eye movements, stumbled over his answers, backed and filled and looked at the floor. He seemed surprised and shocked that he'd been observed on Thirty-fifth Avenue. Apparently he thought of himself as nondescript.

It was obvious that he hadn't expected to be confronted so soon and hadn't had time to fine-tune his story. Siegel and Pszonka reached the same conclusion fast: the guy figured he'd done a great job hiding the child, and now he was thinking, Whoa, how'd they find her so fast? What'd I do wrong?

It was also clear to both officers that Green was " 'roided out.'' In their athletic careers, both had known plenty of users. This man was far gone. His eyes were dilated and he had the soft facial tissues of someone deep into anabolic steroids. Where else had he gotten those sharply defined muscles?

His story was as plastic as his looks. He spoke slowly and haltingly, as though adjusting the facts as he went along. He said he'd been on his way to an afternoon job interview at the Columbia Athletic Club in Mill Creek but changed his mind and dropped into a market for ice cream. Then he drove six miles out of his way to the corner of Thirty-Fifth Avenue S.E. and Grannis to take a walk because he'd often driven through the area and thought it was beautiful. Lately, he said, he'd been having severe headaches and "I had a pain in my temple and my back was sore." He said he walked around the car to relieve his pain and would have stretched out on the backseat, but a man on a riding lawn mower glared at him, so he left the area around two-thirty. He didn't remember approaching a residence, looking through windows, trying doors or seeing a school bus or children. He said he drove to Marysville, a small town to the north, and arrived home about five-thirty.

As the interview continued, other members of the Pittman family quietly entered the room and listened. Donne, the father, was introduced and signed a waiver for a search of the house. A young son sat quietly. Diana Pittman Green, a slender blonde, appeared, and Green asked her to confirm that the two of them had been sight-seeing in the Clearview neighborhood just the day before. At least twenty seconds of silence passed before the big man's wife backed him up.

Siegel asked what he'd been wearing this afternoon. "A T-shirt and slacks," Green answered.

"Could I have a look?" Siegel asked.

"Sure," Green said. He was beginning to sound impatient and a little arrogant. When he returned with the clothes, neatly cleaned and folded, he said, "This is what I wore."

A quizzical look crossed Sharon Pittman's face as she glanced at her deadpan husband Donne. She also looked frightened. All through the interview, nervous glances had passed within the group. Both Siegel and Pszonka realized they would have to call on the family out of Green's presence. You could almost feel the fear in the room.

Pszonka asked a few more questions but couldn't shake Green's story. Both officers realized they'd been hearing a hastily improvised alibi, but one that would take evidence to disprove. If they'd come to this waterfront house expecting a stammered confession or self-incrimination, they'd struck out.

After a silence, Siegel took a chance. "Uh, Mr. Green," he said in his best Columbo manner, "you don't mind if we look in your car, do you?" He added shyly, "Just to check things out?"

He knew he was pushing his luck, given that no body had been found and that no witness had come forward to put Green and Brenda together. He could stop answering their questions and order them out. They would have had more power with a warrant, but there hadn't been time to rouse a judge and argue the necessity.

They relaxed when Green granted permission. He seemed to be shifting into a superior mood, as though this confrontation was beneath the dignity of so important a personage.

The group assembled in the short driveway. Below the Pittmans' backyard, a freight train rattled down from Canada, and a green-and-white ferry churned the water with its thrust reversers, preparing to dock.

Pszonka, Siegel and Backus went to work with their long police flashlights. The car was antiseptically clean. They removed the back-seat, checked the glove box, looked under the floor mats and went over the empty trunk a square inch at a time. A single bloodstain would have provided justification for seizure of the car, perhaps even the arrest of Green, but they found nothing except unstained nap.

It was frustrating. Their instincts told them that six or eight hours earlier, a child had been in this vehicle, probably wrapped in a rainbow comforter. There *had* to be evidence.

The ratty little sedan looked as though it had been brushed out and vacuumed several times over, then detailed by a professional with Q-Tips and chamois cloths. If there was such a thing as cauterizing an automobile, this one had been through the process. To the deputies it was another sign of guilt, an "in-your-eye" by the big man, but a long way from hard evidence. This Green was no fool, even when he was caught unprepared and almost literally with his pants down. The first round was the bad guy's.

5

It was 11:00 P.M. when the sheriff's cruiser pulled into the Gere driveway and two deputies emerged. Elaine strained to look for Brenda, but the cops closed their doors on an empty car. "Did he admit anything?" she asked as they walked up.

The deputies shook their heads.

They went inside. Joe got up from the sofa, a wild look in his eyes. "Did you pick him up?" he asked.

"No," the big sergeant replied.

"Why not?"

"No probable cause, sir. It wasn't even close."

"Probable cause, my dick," Joe said.

The deputies explained that in Snohomish County, the rights of suspects were scrupulously observed, not out of a particular love for criminals, but out of a scrupulous prosecutor's reluctance to blow good cases on technical missteps. They told of an officer who stopped a driver for a bad taillight and found a body in the trunk. The murder case was thrown out for "unlawful search." There'd been similar disasters in the days before the tough new prosecutor, Seth Green, took over the office.

Joe said, "Are you watching the guy?"

The deputies said a tight surveillance was planned.

Elaine tried to follow the thread of the conversation, but all she could comprehend was that the deck was stacked for criminals. Under Washington law, the deputies explained, a defendant had to be tried within sixty to ninety days, and the clock started the day charges were brought. Lawmen were reluctant to take action unless they had solid evidence. The two cops told Joe they'd consulted a deputy prosecutor and he'd agreed that probable cause was absent.

Elaine recognized Joe's angry look. More and more these days, his personality soured as he drank. "The guy was following Brenda down the street," he said. "You don't consider that probable cause?"

"He was ahead of her," the deputy named Siegel pointed out. "A hundred yards, at least."

"Where is it written the guy can't turn around?" Joe said sarcastically. "Or stop till she catches up?"

"That's probably what he did," Sergeant Pszonka admitted. "But we can't bring charges on probabilities." His voice lowered. "Look, we just got started. As long as Green's walking, there's a chance he's gonna talk to somebody. He's gonna make a mistake. He's gonna book—"

"Book?" Elaine asked.

"Run. Or he's gonna try to hide the body."

Elaine winced. "I'm sorry, ma'am," Pszonka said. "I'm just considering every possibility. The important thing is, the pressure's on him."

She'd heard such discussions when Joe was a deputy, but this was the first time her own daughter's life had been involved. It seemed to her that as long as Brenda was missing, every legal technicality should be waived. What cold abstractions of law mattered as much as a child's life? She wished her little brother would arrive—Jimmy would pound the truth out of that Green, and the Washington laws could go to hell.

The deputies stayed for nearly an hour, trying to make themselves clear, advising Joe not to give up, repeating how sorry they were that they hadn't been able to throw Michael Green's muscle-bound ass into the county jail in Everett.

* * *

After they drove off, Search and Rescue teams began arriving, most in civilian clothes. Elaine felt as though the world were running on fast-forward. Flashlights lanced the darkness, and she heard thumps and bangs as tiles and boards were pulled loose so searchers could crawl under the house. Now and then she heard a bark, and neighbor dogs echoed the noise in the distance.

One of the searchers pointed out where three nails on a two-by-four back-porch rail had been knocked loose. He wondered if it might have something to do with the missing child. Elaine called Joe for a look. Neither was sure if the defect was old or new. Joe said it might mean that the kidnapper had bumped the rail while carrying Brenda out in her comforter. Elaine didn't want to think about that.

Just before midnight, she peeked out a window. The searchers had moved off, and the night seemed a shade or two darker than black. She turned and saw Joey and Mike peeking from their bedroom door. She shooed them back inside.

Joe was slumped on the couch. "She's gone," he said into his drink. "That's it." He shook his head hard, like someone trying to clear water from his ears. "No use looking. My baby's gone."

"No, honey!" Elaine insisted. "He wouldn't kill her, he'd *keep* her." Joe told her it was a crazy idea, and she insisted that nothing else made sense.

She dialed her Uncle Hank in Fontana and explained the situation. "Well, I don't know your system," the homicide detective told her, "but down here we'd hold the guy on suspicion for seventy-two hours. We'd go over his car with tweezers, lasers, ultraviolet, special chemicals to bring out stains and prints. You can't make a proper search with flashlights."

Elaine said, "They didn't have probable cause."

Hank said, "I guarantee you *we'd* find probable cause. What the hell, they got the guy's license number, his description, the car description. He's seen near Brenda and she turns up missing. What more probable cause could you want?"

Elaine asked, "Couldn't you come up and help the deputies, Uncle Hank?"

"Honey, I don't have jurisdiction," he said gently. "There'd just be trouble. They'd say here comes the guy from the big city. I'd be in the way."

She begged him to reconsider.

A man in a Seattle Police Department uniform knocked on the side door and asked for an article of Brenda's clothing. "For the dog," he explained. Elaine gave him a moccasin and followed him into the yard.

The dog took a sniff and wriggled through the hedge into the Bonadores' backyard. Then he began running in circles, his nose just above the grass. "Brenda was in that yard every day," Elaine pointed out.

The man said, "He's probably on an old trail." He explained that the Seattle PD dog was working his first case. Veteran animals would be along. Elaine trudged inside to tell Joe that the rookie dog had struck out.

He was on the phone in the kitchen. "I'm beggin' ya," he was saying. "Yeah. . . . Yeah. . . . As soon as you can." He sniffled. "We need help," he mumbled, then, "Thanks. Thanks."

Elaine asked, "Who was that?"

"Rick. He'll be here." Like other reformed rowdies in the family, Joe's youngest brother was now married, a father, and living a conventional life. "He'll be on the first plane," Joe told her, slurring his words.

"Did you call your dad?"

"Yeah. He said give it a day or two and he'll be up with his gun. I told him he'll have to get in line."

At two in the morning, Elaine helped her husband up the stairs. He flopped on the bed, muttering to himself. She put her ear by his mouth and heard him mention his heart.

"Your heart?" she said.

He said it felt as though someone had reached in and pulled out his heart. Just before he passed out, she heard him say, "I died today."

Well, said Elaine to herself, I didn't. My baby's out there, and if nobody else can find her, I will. She took Joe's three-cell police bonecrusher flashlight and looked around the yard. Bushes were trampled, and footprints covered footprints. She heard a soprano voice in the trees and had a momentary thrill that it was Brenda, on her way home after losing her way in the woods. Should she be spanked? No, hugged.

The soprano turned out to be a member of a search team, working outward from the house.

Elaine thought of a game the family had played with Kanga. Brenda would hide, and the others would say, "Go find Brenda. *Where's Brenda?*" Kanga would go from room to room till she sniffed out her best friend. They'd played the game dozens of times.

She let the dog out and said, "Go find Brenda!"

Kanga ran toward the Bonadores' house, then veered off toward the front yard and out on Thirty-fifth. The young Hungarian vizsla sniffed a few times and headed north with Elaine in pursuit. After fifty yards or so, the dog stopped.

"Go find Brenda!" she insisted. "Where's Brenda?"

Kanga turned and ran in the opposite direction, south toward the school bus stop. She kept her nose to the ground like an experienced tracker, stopping to sniff, then resuming her pace. "Go on!" Elaine encouraged her. "Find Brenda!"

About an eighth of a mile from the bus stop, Kanga stopped by the cornfield that had always frightened Brenda. After a few deep sniffs, the dog crossed the road and continued south. At the school bus stop, a quarter mile from the log house, she raised her snout, started off in one direction, reversed several times, and then trotted toward home.

It was four A.M. when Elaine finally took the dog inside. They hadn't accomplished a thing. She sat on the couch near the phone in case Brenda called. She pictured her lying by a roadside in her loud belt and her red stirrup pants.

"Thank you, God," she whispered, "for not making it cold out. Please help us find her. And . . . keep her warm."

She sat up for the rest of the night.

6

Six miles away, on the edge of the dark waters of Puget Sound, another woman tried to sleep. Sharon Pittman's side throbbed. She felt like someone who awakens from a nightmare to find that real life is worse. She kept going over every minute of the terrible day.

Late in the afternoon she and Diana had been finishing up their day's work as mortgage loan representatives in nearby Lynnwood when Mike phoned and asked to speak to his wife. To Sharon he sounded almost distraught.

"Mom," Diana said after she talked to him, "Mike can't pick me up. He's got a horrible headache."

Mother and daughter locked up the office and left for Mukilteo in Sharon's car. En route, Diana explained that Mike had been driving around Marysville and torn his pants in the crotch. There was nothing new about that; his abnormal musculature put such a strain on his clothing that something was always tearing loose.

Diana said he'd been feeling bad all day. There was nothing new about that, either. Sharon hoped he wasn't on the verge of a stroke or a heart attack from the steroids he took in his exalted effort to become Mr. America.

When mother and daughter reached home, Diana went straight to the master bedroom, which the elder Pittmans had given up for Diana and her weight-lifting husband.

"He's okay," Diana said as she hurried out of the room. "Just hungry. I'll make him a chicken."

Sharon hoped that one would suffice; sometimes he ate two. He refused to eat parts, explaining in his convoluted way that whole chickens weren't fed steroids. No one dared to ask him why he was willing to shoot steroids into his rear end but wouldn't risk eating the trace amounts in drumsticks and breasts. It was one of his many contradictions. He also insisted on brown eggs from free-range chickens, and he downed handfuls of amino acids, vitamins and minerals, all organic and expensive. He had no regular job.

Diana microwaved a chicken and prepared a green salad so big that it filled a serving bowl. She disappeared into the bedroom to set the meal up on a card table while her husband watched TV.

"He'll be okay, Mom," Diana said when she came out. "He has the sweats and a headache, but it's probably 'cause he's cutting back on steroids." Sharon certainly hoped so.

Diana left on an errand and said she would skip her own dinner. It seemed to Sharon that her daughter had been missing too many meals lately, but there was no point in flogging that dead horse. At twenty-six, Diana no longer solicited advice from her parents or listened when it was volunteered. Ever since the last beating in Arizona, she'd spun in her husband's orbit. And while Mr. America's clothes were splitting from avoirdupois, Diana was losing weight. Sharon had given up trying to understand the situation. It seemed to her that if events proceeded to their logical conclusion, Mike would become the Goodyear blimp and Diana would disappear altogether. It made no sense.

Sharon asked her husband, "Did you see Mike when he got home this afternoon?"

Donne said he'd first seen the son-in-law at five-thirty. "He just stepped out of the shower, said he wasn't feeling good. He went down and washed some clothes. He looked upset, real red in the face."

The rest of the evening had passed quietly till the deputies banged on the door around ten-thirty. Mike was watching a football game on TV when he finally let Sharon in after her third demand that he come out and talk. As she watched, he let a blanket slip from his shoulder. She was shocked; he'd appeared naked before her once or twice, but only by accident. His eyes were glazed and he appeared confused. She wondered if he'd just shot up.

Sharon had heard enough of the police interview to be disturbed. The questioning wasn't about burglaries; it was about a missing child, and Mike was telling lies. He *hadn't* been wearing the outfit that he turned over to the cops. When he'd gone to lunch with Donne earlier, he'd worn woolen slacks and a sweatshirt. The shirt he handed over to the deputies was much too small for his barrel chest and had been at the bottom of a pile in his dresser drawer. The route that he claimed he'd driven made no sense at all.

She remembered how the men had trooped outside to look at Mike's white Toyota, leaving Sharon and her daughter alone in the house. Without warning, Diana came up from behind and punched her in the kidney.

"From now on," she snarled, "you keep your fucking mouth shut. Don't say one word about anything!"

Sharon doubled over. She didn't understand. In twenty-six years, this child of Bible camps and piano lessons had never laid a hand on her. No mother had ever had a sweeter daughter or any husband a better wife. Why was she protecting Mike? Was he involved in the child's disappearance? *Was Diana?*

For a while Sharon sat alone, swallowing hard against the pain. The walls glowed and darkened from the lighthouse beam. When Diana was little, she used to sit in the living room, timing the pulses of light, "One-two. One-two." What a sweet child she'd been.

Sharon tiptoed to the washing machine. Freshly washed clothing clung to the inside. She lifted the soggy clump and recognized the shirt and black slacks that Mike had worn in the morning. The crotch was torn to the seat.

After the deputies left, the family gathered in the living room. "Those damn cops," Mike grumbled. "They're totally off their rockers."

Diana seemed angry, but not at the police. "They sure tracked your car fast," she said. "You had a job interview today in Mill Creek. What were you doing way over in Clearview?"

"I wasn't—"

"Mike, no more lies! They got your license number. You were there. *What were you doing?*"

"I got lost."

"How could you get lost on Thirty-fifth Avenue? You know how those streets run. It's simple."

Mike said he'd lost his way while trying to take a shortcut from his interview in Mill Creek to Howard's Bodybuilding in Marysville. When Diana looked dubious, he stood up and said, "I don't want to talk to you anymore, Diana."

"Well, I'm just trying to find out how they tracked you here so fast."

He made a crack about nosy people and said the cops should be spending their time on real criminals.

"Yeah?" Diana said contemptuously. "While you're out raping little twelve-year-olds?"

Sharon had seldom heard her daughter stand up to him this way. Mike lied constantly, persuasively, blatantly, and most of the time Diana just accepted it, except once or twice when he lied about his girlfriends. But tonight Diana was tenacious.

Sharon was curious about the damaged slacks. "Mike," she said, "how'd you rip your pants?"

He said he'd been climbing out of the car for the interview in Mill Creek when the crotch tore loose. That was what had kept him from going to the interview.

Diana jumped right in. "How could you rip your pants in Mill Creek and be seen walking around Clearview hours later?"

He stalked toward their bedroom. "We'll talk about it tomorrow," he said.

Diana called out, "We'll talk about it *now.*"

The door slammed hard.

7

Driving back to headquarters in Everett at midnight, Sergeant Tom Pszonka was positive that he and Bryce Siegel had just heard a collection of lies and that Brenda Gere had been hidden away, dead or alive, by Michael Kay Green.

"A logical person just doesn't drive around like that," he told his partner. "A logical person just doesn't go from point A to point B for no goddamn reason at all. Y'know, if he was gonna buy a house, well, *couples* buy houses. *Couples* look at houses together. He lives in Mukilteo; he has no reason to go toward Highway Nine. He says he was originally over on Five twenty-seven near the Safeway. None of it makes sense. One and one do *not* add up to two. He says he had a reason to be in the area? The reason sucks. Another thing—he looks like Man Mountain Dean, he's got this strange look about him, he's nervous and furtive. Remember how he was sweating? You could tell by his eye movement. This guy's done something to that kid.''

Siegel agreed.

At about the same time, Diana Pittman Green was prying a few more details from her husband in the privacy of their bedroom. Mike told her he'd driven past the log house on Thirty-fifth, noticed a FOR SALE sign, and realized that Diana would love the place.

"We could have a dog!" he told her excitedly. He said he walked up to the front door and found it open, called out, and left when no one answered. He didn't see a girl or anyone else, and he didn't go in. That was the whole truth.

When Diana started to cry, he told her not to worry; the police couldn't prove a thing, and they didn't even have a body. Of course, he said, he was innocent, but you never knew about the Snohomish County cops. . . .

Dan, the Pittmans' twenty-four-year-old, arrived home after midnight and heard about the evening's events from his mother and father, still mulling things over in the living room.

Preparing for bed, Dan heard noises. He peered outside and saw Mike standing like a sculptor's model while the family malamute Winter quartered the lawn. It looked as though Mike might be working out a show pose. Sometimes it seemed that he spent half his life grooming his body, examining himself, making his muscles jump in controlled little jerks and spasms.

Dan stepped into the yard. A soft yellowish glow showed in the little market at the ferry landing a hundred yards below. At intervals the lighthouse beam glistened on the mussels and seaweed that covered the pilings.

Mike seemed lost in his own thoughts. Dan wondered if his brother-in-law was stoned; along with his health food and steroid regimen, the big man smoked large amounts of marijuana, and he often toked in the yard or down by the tracks.

"Mike," Dan said. "You okay?" They were typical male in-laws: friendly and respectful, but not close.

The big man said he was fine. "I've got a lot to think about, Danny." He looked uptight, in a different zone.

"Tell me the truth," Dan said. "What do the cops have on you?"

"Nothing," Mike said. "I was over in Clearview, that's all."

"Mom said you went door-to-door."

"That's bullshit. Why would I go door-to-door?"

After a few minutes of stiff silence, Mike launched into a narrative of the day's events as though addressing a judge and jury. Dan didn't interrupt. It was plain that Mike was stuck with a bad alibi. Dan had never disliked his brother-in-law, but he had to admit the guy had a problem about truth and reality. And the bigger the lie, the more sincere he sounded. Maybe it was the steroids.

When Dan pointed out that he really hadn't explained why he'd been in Clearview, Mike began a rambling discourse on his life, his wrong turnings and bad breaks, ending with the curious statement "Man, the Snap-On Tools Company sure screwed up my life."

He'd been fired from his last regular job as credit sales manager at Snap-On Tools in Phoenix. The polite Pittmans didn't discuss the embarrassing details, nor was much said about his philanderings and his physical attacks on the frail Diana, who always forgave him in the generous family tradition.

In the same spirit, Dan felt sorry for the giant. The poor guy seemed lost, out of step with the world. "Freak" wasn't quite the right word, but it came close. Mike earned nothing from his bodybuilding efforts, but it only made him pump more iron, shoot up steroids, load carbs and health food. He'd sworn to make it to the top of the bodybuilding world by the time he was thirty, but he was only two years away now and losing ground. Dan thought, What a business—twitching your muscles for money! There can't be a dozen men in the world who earn a living that way, let alone make big bucks. No wonder the guy acts weird. And now he's suspected of kidnapping or rape, maybe murder. Who wouldn't be uptight?

Dan touched the big man's arm. "Ya know, Mike," he said gently, "it's not hard to get started again. You can turn things around. Especially when you've got somebody like Di."

Mike's big face turned chalky white in the lighthouse beam, and Dan saw that his eyes were wet. Dan committed a Pittmanesque act of mercy. He turned and went inside.

8

As the Friday dawn began to light the treetops in the woods behind her house, Elaine Gere huddled in a living-room chair. Brenda, Brenda, *Brenda*, she murmured to herself, where are you, honey? If you come home, you can boss me around all you want. . . .

She heard movement upstairs, then a sound as though something had fallen. Joe picked his way down the staircase, his big hair in tangles and spikes. She felt so sorry for him. He'd just enjoyed a few hours of peace. Now he had to face their loss all over again. And it would be the same every morning till Brenda came home.

Elaine had cried softly during the night, but she'd made up her mind that no one, not even Joe, would see her in tears. Crying was contagious, a self-indulgence. The boys hated to see her cry in any circumstances. They might cry a little themselves, but they needed stable adults around them. She didn't have the heart to awaken them for school.

"I'm gonna find Brenda," Joe muttered as he went out the side door in his jeans, short-sleeved shirt and slippers.

Elaine took extra pains with her hair and makeup. She started breakfast and on a hunch checked the knives and forks in the drawer. None appeared to be missing.

At seven o'clock, when the FEMA switchboard was turned on for the day, she phoned her boss and explained what was going on. Annie Daugherty told her to take as much time as she needed.

She steeled herself to break the news to her mother in Carson City, Nevada. Evelyn usually depended on Elaine, but the mother could stiffen up in a crisis, as when she'd thrown Big Ed out of the house in Fontana. She loved her granddaughter and deserved to know what was happening.

"Mom," Elaine said, "I didn't want to tell you last night, 'cause I knew you wouldn't be able to sleep. Brenda's disappeared."

"Oh, my God!" Evelyn said. A loud wail came over the phone line.

Elaine sketched the story, and her mother said, "Do you need me, honey?"

"Yes, Mom. I need you bad. And Beverly, too."

"We'll be on the next plane."

Her brother Jimmy called a few minutes later and said that he and Georgeann hadn't been able to get a flight out of Cheyenne. They were leaving home now in the family car and would arrive by midnight. Elaine was comforted. The Mayzsaks were accounted for. They shared one another's strength.

Around eight, Joe came back inside and slumped on the couch. Elaine turned away from the painful sight and went outside to check on a noise. A scruffy-looking red-bearded man sat atop a sleeping bag under a tree, surrounded by fifteen or sixteen others. He identified himself as Dick Cress, leader of a volunteer team that had been searching since midnight. Elaine thought how remarkable it was that total strangers were looking for a child they'd never met.

She asked Cress if he would like some breakfast. "Oh, hell, no," the little man said, lighting one cigarette from another. "I'm a survivalist."

Later Elaine learned that the survivalist's twelve-year-old son Patrick had gone roller-skating two years earlier and never returned. His bludgeoned and strangled body hadn't been found for eighteen days. The case remained unsolved, and Cress, a Purdue graduate in engineering, a mountaineer, first-aid instructor and ballistics and cryogenics expert, had been looking for other people's lost children ever since.

A vice principal's voice crackled over the PA system at Canyon Park Junior High School between second and third periods: "Good morning, students. I have an announcement. Our eighth-grader Brenda Gere did not return home last night and still has not been found. If anybody has information, please come to the principal's office."

The classrooms fell silent. Everyone from the principal to the custodian had been frightened by a recent abduction attempt at the school. Students whimpered and hugged one another. At lunchtime, trays went untouched. Crossing guards performed their tasks surrounded by knots of children whose wide eyes darted in every direction. No one was calm enough to misbehave.

Student Melanie Bonadore was proud of the way she'd stayed cool while the big man prowled her neighborhood, but something about the official announcement broke her composure, and she asked permission to go home. All she wanted to do was walk through the opening in the hedge and comfort the Geres. But when she arrived home, she became afraid that they would blame her: *You should've saved our daughter. . . . Why didn't you walk home with her? It should've been you, not her. . . .*

All afternoon she cried in her room.

Brenda's friend Crista Crownover tried to make it through her classes but ended up talking to a counselor. Walking home from her school bus stop, she heard a female voice calling from the woods: "Crista. *Crista!*" Then the voice said, "Crista, help me. *Help me. . . .*"

She ran home and hid. That night she asked her Ouija board for information about Brenda. The board told her that Brenda was being held captive in Anaheim, California, and was in good condition. It was a relief.

A few students said they had no intention of returning to school till Brenda turned up. A newspaper offered "Child Safety Tips," which served to frighten the children even more. Some tried to help police, but their information was limited. One reported that Brenda had acted nervous in the cafeteria the day before; maybe she was already being stalked. Teachers like Donald Halazon couldn't recall anything significant. "She seemed well-adjusted," he said, echoing his colleagues. He intended to join the search parties later.

Brenda's bus driver recalled nothing unusual on her route along Thirty-fifth Avenue S.E. Brenda had asked to be let off near Annie DeSantis's house, but that was an everyday request. She'd seemed her usual cheerful self on the bus, talking and giggling with her friends. She was new in the neighborhood, but everyone seemed to like her.

For a while, Elaine kept her resolve not to make matters worse by crying in front of the others. She was too busy. Someone had to talk to the media so that Brenda's picture would be published, and Joe was too upset.

"She was really happy," Elaine told the reporters who circled her on the front lawn just after 9:00 A.M. "I just can't believe she ran away." She described Brenda as "unique," "independent," and told how she'd outsmarted the two-man team of pedophiles when the family lived in Kent.

Detectives arrived at ten, and Joe pulled himself together for the police ritual known as a sit-down. "She's gone," he told Detective Joe Ward and Sergeant Clyde Foot. "You know the rule. If you don't find kids like this in the first twenty-four hours, they're dead."

To Elaine's distress, Ward, a handsome man of about thirty-five, didn't disagree.

"No, no!" she insisted. "He wouldn't kill her. She's too valuable. He's not working. He needs money. He would've sold her for porn films or something like that." She couldn't let the investigation proceed on the assumption that they were looking for a corpse.

She'd heard a rumor that a helicopter had landed in a nearby hayfield the day before. "Green passed her off to somebody in that helicopter," she went on, inspired by her own theory. "She's on her way to Iran by now, Iraq. What's that place? Uh—Saudi Arabia."

Ward looked at the wall and didn't comment. With his neat haircut and carefully knitted tie, he put her in mind of a high school science teacher. She couldn't imagine him in uniform.

Sergeant Foot accepted the offer of a cup of coffee and followed Elaine into the kitchen. "Listen, missus," the burly supervisor said, "Detective Ward's on your side. This is his case, and if anybody can find your daughter, it's him. The guy's a bull terrier."

Elaine felt reassured. Foot was an older deputy, heavyset and easygoing, a good ol' boy type who reminded her of Big Ed. She asked, "Are you watching this Green person?"

"Day and night," Foot answered.

"What do *you* think happened?" she asked. Joe had told her years ago that detectives always began an investigation with a scenario of their own, a theory, and some of them stuck with it too long and missed the obvious.

"I have to be honest with you, Mrs. Gere," Foot began.

"Please," Elaine interrupted. "Don't."

After the detectives left, Elaine went to her bedroom to lie down. "Shouldas" reeled through her mind: I shoulda locked the door . . . shoulda left Kanga inside . . . shoulda kept using a baby-sitter . . .

Then came the "if-onlys." If only we hadn't moved here . . . if only Joe hadn't gone to work on his day off . . . if only we'd respected Brenda's misgivings . . . if only . . . if only . . .

After a while she found herself in Brenda's room. A hand protruded from one of the cubbyholes. She lifted the fingers and saw the artificial nails. A clear plastic bracelet slid down the thin wrist, tiny specks of glitter swirling in the encapsulated water.

"Elaine!"

She awoke at the sound. It was Joe. "C'mon. We need help on the phones."

She blinked hard and looked at the clock. She'd slept for an hour. Joe said, "I'll be outside." She saw the outline of the pint in his pocket. She returned to her station at the phone and took shorthand notes on every suggestion, every lead. A man with a limp had been seen picking up a brown-haired girl at the Circle K the day before. A gray van had followed the school bus. An ox in street clothes had made a U-turn a mile down Thirty-fifth Avenue the day before Brenda vanished. A stranger had leered at women outside the Safeway. A volunteer fireman had been acting squirrelly. A girl had been approached at another school on Wednesday.

The panic seemed to ripple outward from the log house. Elaine took one call from a frightened mother in Anacortes, an oil refinery town forty miles away. For ten minutes, Elaine tried to calm the woman's fears. My God, she said to herself, I don't have time for this. We have to find Brenda.

Neighbor Wanda Munson almost fainted when a male stranger knocked on her door. "I mean, my legs felt like rubber," she told her husband later. "I couldn't even function. I said, 'Who is it?' and he said, 'Electric company,' and I said, 'Do you know what the hell is going on in this neighborhood?' He said, 'Yes, ma'am, I'm aware of it.' I said, 'God, you're picking a bad day to knock on people's doors.'"

Searchers borrowed the Gere phone to contact their families. Cops left messages and compared notes. Relatives and friends checked in from points east and south. Everything flowed through the skillful shorthand that Elaine had learned in Fontana High School.

By noon, Joe had downed so many drinks that he might as well have been speaking Hungarian. He would go outside and beat his way through thorns and brambles till his numbed hands and arms were laced with scratches, flop on the couch for twenty or thirty minutes, then return to the woods in the company of his bottle. It was painfully obvious that he was searching for a body.

Elaine didn't fault him for drinking; he was in terrible pain, blaming himself, mumbling his shouldas and if-onlys. "I never showed her how much I loved her," he mumbled into his Kool-Aid and whatever. "I never showed her she meant the most."

"You did, Joe, we both did," Elaine said, hugging his rigid body. "We gave her all the love she wanted."

He shook his head and turned away.

9

Elaine had controlled her tears all morning, but early in the afternoon she was struck by the realization that she might never see Brenda again. She rushed upstairs and covered her face with her pillow. Then she went into the bathroom and redid her face. Joe and the boys mustn't know she'd cried.

The phone summoned her downstairs. A coworker at FEMA informed her that they were rounding up a search team. Newspapers and newscasts were flashing Brenda's picture, and for a while it seemed as though everyone in the Northwest had seen the child or her abductor and wanted to discuss it on the phone. Elaine had just finished scribbling notes about a sighting in North Snohomish County when one of the searchers introduced herself as Linda Barker and gently lifted the pencil from her hand. "You've been transposing numbers, Mrs. Gere," she said.

"I *have?*"

"You're in shock and you don't know it. We called your last two numbers back, and they were wrong."

Elaine thought, Can it *be?* She'd been so careful. The phone was their only link to Brenda. Suppose the ransom call came in and she screwed up the details? She felt like a bad parent. Brenda could die because of her ineptness.

"I'll try harder," she promised.

"No, Elaine," the woman said. "You don't sit on this phone anymore. We'll take over."

"Who?"

"Our organization. Families and Friends of Missing Persons and Victims of Violent Crime. Just call us Families and Friends. That's what we are." It was the first Elaine had heard of them. "You get some rest," Linda Barker ordered.

Elaine gave up the phone but didn't take the advice. She had to straighten the rumpled house and feed Joe and the kids and make arrangements to pick up her mother and sister at Seatac Airport, twenty-five miles south.

When their plane arrived at 8:00 P.M., Beverly was calm, but Evelyn couldn't stop crying. As they entered the log house, she let out a wail. "Mom!" Elaine admonished her. "The boys, the boys!"

It took fifteen minutes to quiet her. Then she began to alternate between deep sobs and epithets about Michael Green. "That fuckin' bastard," she said. "Oh, excuse me, honey." Then she insisted on waking up her grandsons to greet them.

"Mom," Elaine said, "it's late. Can't it wait?"

Evelyn was already headed for the bedroom. She was in and out in a few minutes, wailing louder than before. A butcher knife glittered in her hand. "They're asleep," she said through sobs. "This was next to Mikey's pillow. He said it was . . . in case the man comes back."

10

ate on that Friday evening, Detective Joe Ward and a colleague returned to the log house in response to an irate demand for Michael Green's immediate arrest.

Ward explained to the raving Joe Gere that the prosecutor hadn't changed his position about probable cause. A surveillance was in place, but the big man hadn't been seen all day, and phone calls to the Mukilteo house were unanswered.

The lead investigator reported that Sharon Pittman had phoned headquarters several times to ask if Brenda had been found. In one conversation she'd hinted that her son-in-law had lied about his activities on the day of the disappearance. She would be reinterviewed in the morning.

Thus far, Ward went on, nothing had turned up in the fingerprint work except Gere family prints, but the FBI had promised to rush laser equipment. The polite detective said he was sorry about the lack of progress.

By the time the detectives got up to leave, Joe Gere was barely able to navigate. "He's anesthetizing himself," Ward observed to his partner. "Who can blame the guy?"

They drove straight to Mukilteo. A light scent drifted off the beach, as though someone was shucking clams. The channel between the mainland and Whidbey Island was awash in shades of purple and black. The Pittman house was even darker, and no one answered their knock. They performed a discreet walkaround and left.

In the Geres' neighborhood, a Washington state representative named Dick Vandyke was letting his sheepdog in for the night when he noticed fresh blood on the animal's head and leg. He found a slight cut on the tip of one ear and presumed it was the source of the stains. Snoopy didn't seem to want to turn in, and Vandyke didn't insist.

Early Saturday morning, some forty hours after the disappearance of Brenda Gere, Vandyke got up to find Snoopy lying in the carport, his head and shoulders slathered in blood and his feet muddy. Reddish swirls stained the floor. The usually frisky animal seemed lethargic. Vandyke wondered if he'd been hit by a car but found no injuries.

The state legislator was preoccupied with personal problems and didn't report it to police.

Like many of his jumpy neighbors, Gordon Munson had hardly slept in the two nights since he'd observed Michael Green on Thirty-fifth Avenue. He was a sensitive man, and he was haunted by the probabilities. Word had reached his house that some of Brenda's classmates were blaming him for the disappearance. Why hadn't he warned her? Why report a mysterious stranger to 911 and not point out that he was walking in front of a child?

Munson reworked the Thursday-afternoon incident in long exegeses with his wife and stepdaughter Michelle. He kept insisting that it wasn't out of negligence or stupidity or carelessness that he'd neglected Brenda. It was simply that he hadn't thought in terms of physical danger, hers or anyone else's. In a peaceful setting like Clearview, such ideas didn't spring to mind. At the time, he'd thought of driving up to the child and offering her a ride, but she hardly knew him and it seemed like an overreaction. Instead he'd rushed home and alerted 911. Whatever was going on—an overaggressive salesman, a lost motorist—the police would sort it out in minutes. That's why they had radios.

Now he consoled himself with the hope that Brenda had been kidnapped but not injured. Soon she would be home and everyone would begin to recover.

"We can't just sit around," he told his wife as she prepared breakfast. "We've got to help."

Gordon, Wanda and Michelle ate quickly, then went door-to-door, looking for information about the white Toyota and the stranger. They were surprised by the reaction of a neighbor who announced that they were acting silly. Go back home and enjoy your Saturday off, they were told. This kid's just another runaway.

Gordon wished with all his heart that the neighbor was right, but his stepdaughter had come to know Brenda well and said it was plain impossible. The new girl loved her parents, her brothers, her dog, her three-wheeler, and she was talking about getting a horse. She always had a pleasant smile, a friendly greeting. Michelle said she was the last child in Clearview who would ever run away.

Detective Joe Ward arrived at the sheriff's office early Saturday morning and digested the reports. A meticulous man who always wore the right socks with the right tie, he also made it a point to be fully prepared. In the detective business, surprises could be lethal.

At nine-thirty he discussed strategy with Sergeant Tom Pszonka and a captain. Pszonka kept emphasizing that Green had to be watched around the clock. "We've stirred him up," the big deputy said, "and now he's gonna book."

Ward agreed. He assumed that surveillance teams remained at the scene, but he couldn't be sure. To do the job properly, it would take a minimum of two units, one above the house and one below, working three shifts. Tying up a platoon of officers and two cars would put a heavy strain on the department, especially on a weekend.

He put in a call to the Mukilteo house and was surprised when Michael Green agreed to an interview.

Ward said he would arrive at the house in fifteen or twenty minutes.

"No," Green answered. "You guys've put my family through enough. Meet me at Lane Mortgage in Lynnwood."

At about the same hour of Saturday morning, Elaine heard a knock on the big Dutch doors and opened up to a crowd of familiar faces, fellow employees of the FEMA office in Bothell. Ever since her first government job at nineteen, she'd heard cracks about civil service workers—"That's good enough for government work" and other canards—and found them uniformly false. She'd seen a few idlers, but most of her colleagues worked hard for their pay.

Now here they were, three dozen strong, armed with portable radios and other search gear, giving up their weekend to hunt for Brenda. She was especially touched by the sight of the director, a middle-aged man with Parkinson's disease.

One member of the group suggested that Elaine drive Brenda's most recent picture into FEMA headquarters and run off a stack of color copies for distribution. The missing child's face belonged on every telephone pole in the Northwest.

As Elaine steered her car down the hill on Highway 214 toward Bothell, the sun peeked through a bank of clouds. She wondered how it could shine.

A brilliant arc of color connected one corner of the valley to the other. Elaine respected omens, especially when they told her what she wanted to hear. What could this rainbow mean except that Brenda was coming home? Rainbows were the child's favorite sight. Just a few days earlier, she'd told Elaine that she hoped the fall rains would start soon. "My goodness," asked the woman who'd grown up on the desert. "Why?"

In her slightly superior tone, as though she were talking to a lesser being, Brenda had answered, "Mom, it makes rainbows."

Elaine dropped off a set of flyers at the sheriff's office in the county seat of Everett, gave another sheaf to Dick Cress for his search teams, and handed more to parents and friends of Brenda's classmates who showed up to help.

The phone rang all day. A high-intensity female psychic from Oregon talked as though her information was fresh and firsthand, and Elaine scribbled in her steno pad: "B in Ore. W/man and woman. Dirty people. B not eating, sick."

The woman described a village outside Portland and said, "There's a little house on the northwest edge of town with a black stone chimney and a tan pickup truck with expired tags. Your daughter's there with a man and a woman with bad teeth."

Elaine phoned the sheriff's office in Clackamas County, Oregon. "Look, I'm not crazy," she said breathlessly. "My daughter's being held down there." She gave the description to a female deputy who sounded as convinced as Elaine.

An hour later the efficient deputy reported back. There was only one dwelling that came close to matching the description. A tan pickup was parked in the driveway, but it belonged to a respectable senior citizen.

When Joe returned from one of his wanderings through the woods, he chided her for wasting time on psychics. "They always come out of the woodwork," he reminded her. "Don't you remember Fontana?"

Elaine said this was different. Every lead had to be taken seriously, no matter how outlandish it seemed or how they felt about the supernatural. "Psychics aren't always wrong," she reminded him. "Strange things happen."

Joe shook his head.

11

Detectives Joe Ward and Barry Fagan pulled up in front of Lane Mortgage Company just as a bulky man emerged carrying two big trash cans as though they were salt shakers. He introduced himself as Mike Green and invited them inside. He explained that his wife Diana earned extra money by doing the weekend cleaning chores at her office, and sometimes he came in to help her out.

As lead investigator on a difficult case, Ward had made up his mind to keep his tone mild and his remarks light. This interview was voluntary and could end in an eyeblink. In all his years as a cop, he'd never faced a situation more delicate. Brenda Gere's life was at stake, and so was the case against this monster. They still had no physical evidence, and this interview might provide a key.

Green appeared affronted by the reading of his Miranda rights and wondered aloud why "you're questioning my intelligence." He signed the rights waiver with a flourish and then paced the office floor as he parried Ward's low-key questions.

It was an unsettling experience for the detective. "He would *not* look at me," Ward reported later. "I tried to make eye contact, but he stared through me or over my shoulder or off-center. It was as though he couldn't acknowledge I was there. He tried to convince me he was a better man than I was. It seemed important to him. I let him talk. I knew he wasn't gonna admit he took Brenda or tell where she was. I just wanted him to be comfortable enough to give me another shot later. I figured it would be an ongoing process."

The jittery Green emphasized that he could earn all the money he wanted in the banking and credit fields—"I made forty thousand a year in Phoenix"—but he'd dedicated himself to bodybuilding and health. He made it sound as though he'd taken monastic orders. He claimed that he had trouble with women who were attracted to his physique, "and it's affecting my relationship with Di and the family." And he slipped in the information that he had a bachelor's degree from the University of Washington, had starred on the Husky football team, and had been asked to play pro football.

Ward nodded and thought, How predictable. With these sociopaths, image is everything. They're better than you, they have more education, and they have to beat women off with a club.

It was hard to keep the big man on track about the events of Thursday; he kept returning to his curriculum vitae, his personal life, his overqualifications for jobs below the level of president or pope. Sometimes he seemed to engage in the verbal phenomenon known as "flight of ideas," an undisciplined switching from subject to subject that sometimes marks mental instability. Ward had learned about the concept in his own studies at the University of Washington. He'd also been exposed to the confusing subject of narcissism. It seemed that narcissists loved themselves because deep inside they hated themselves. They acted as though they were God's gift to the world because at a deeper level they considered themselves garbage. It was another of the paradoxes that kept psychiatrists in business.

As though sensing the detective's thoughts, Green said, "I've had a lot of headaches lately. And memory loss. I had a blackout five or six months ago."

How slick, Ward said to himself. And how stupid this dirtball baby-killer thinks we are. He's setting up an insanity defense in case his other bullshit doesn't wash. He might be flaky, but he's kept up on the latest trends. The insanity defense was popular these days. It almost never prevailed, but many criminal attorneys urged it on their clients when there was no other defense available.

It took fifteen or twenty minutes to maneuver Green into providing the latest version of his Thursday travelogue, and even then he had to be gently interrupted and redirected to the subject. He would pace to the far wall of the big office, spin around and return, like a caged bear. Ward had to remind himself not to get pushy. He couldn't afford to lose the man's cooperation until he'd exhausted the immediate possibilities and, at the least, talked him into signing a statement.

Green said he went to Mill Creek to pick up a job application, drove around the winding streets because he liked the upscale community and intended to live there someday, decided to work out at a gym in Marysville, and tried to allay the pain of a headache by stopping at the Safeway in Thrasher's Corner for an ice cream bar. After a visit to a gas station, Green said, he drove around waiting for the headache to subside. He took a stroll near Grannis Road to loosen up his sore back, but he hadn't walked up to any front doors or entered any houses.

Ward noticed that the itinerary was short on exact times, but he didn't take issue. The prosecutors could punch holes in the story later, on the witness stand, after Brenda had been found and charges brought. Green finally agreed to sign a statement. It was self-serving and unincriminating, but it was a start.

Around noon, Elaine heard another knock at the side door. The house was turning into a circus, with searchers checking in, neighbors arriving with casseroles, and police charging up and down the stairs with their evidence kits and dogs.

A short, slight, bespectacled man introduced himself as Reverend somebody and said he'd read about Brenda in the Everett newspaper. "Do you pray, Mrs. Gere?" he asked in a kindly voice.

Elaine invited him inside. "Oh, yes," she said. "I'm a Roman Catholic."

"And Mr. Gere?" the man asked. "Does he pray, too?"

"Uh—yes. At bedtime."

The preacher smiled beatifically and said, "Jesus wants you to pray together, Mrs. Gere. Picture a blue light around your daughter. Concentrate on that halo. It's Our Lord's love. It'll keep her safe."

Elaine thanked him for his comfort. She wasn't turning down any suggestions.

12

As soon as Mrs. Pittman answered the door, Sergeant Tom Pszonka knew that he was dealing with a woman on the edge. Her manicured fingertips trembled as she poured coffee, and a poached look in her eyes suggested that she'd slept poorly. But even in morning dishevelment, Sharon Pittman was a good-looking woman, chic, with gleaming reddish hair. Pszonka guessed she was close to fifty, judging by the ages of her children, but she didn't look matronly.

She shuffled ahead of him into the large living room and immediately launched into a recapitulation of the Pittmans' Thursday-night family circle after the deputies had departed. Her son-in-law, she emphasized, had lied both to family members and police. And the pants and shirt he'd turned over were *not* the clothes he'd worn the day the child disappeared.

Mrs. Pittman went into a back room and returned with a shirt and neatly folded black woolen slacks that still smelled of cleaning fluid. "These are the ones," she said. "He washed them as soon as he got home, and Diana took them to the dry cleaner's and had the pants mended. She's such a sweet person, always believes the best in people. That's the way we raised our kids. She says she's helping Mike 'cause he's not capable of hurting a child."

Pszonka commented that the situation seemed to have opened a rift between mother and daughter. "We argue about Mike all the time," Mrs. Pittman agreed. "It's the only thing we *ever* argue about. We used to have a peaceful home, but he has everybody intimidated. He beats up Diana and she comes back for more. He can be bright and funny and personable, but he's a habitual liar and a bully. Think about it. For six years, he's been pounding on a woman a third his size."

Mrs. Pittman said the young couple had stacks of unpaid bills, but Mike showed no interest in earning money. "Every cent Di makes goes into black-market steroids," the woman said. "I can show you the syringes."

She said he'd helped Diana with the weekend cleanup at Lane Mortgage to give the appearance of being a normal family man. It was his first time ever. He often disappeared for five or six hours and explained that he'd been applying for a job, but there were never any callbacks from the interviews.

Pszonka asked if he was still on steroids. "I think so," she said. "He's tried to quit. He's got a terrible temper, and withdrawal makes it worse." The cop recalled the phrase "'roid rage" from his own days at Southern Illinois University. You heard it all the time in college and pro sports.

The beefy sergeant drove away from the Pittmans' waterfront home convinced that he'd heard the truth, give or take a little fudging to protect Diana. In some ways, the long-suffering mother reminded him of Elaine Gere.

"I had to pry out some of her story," he told his wife when he returned home to complete an interrupted weekend job on a skylight. "She knew Diana won't be happy about some of the things she was saying. You can see she loves her daughter and doesn't want her hurt. She also wants to do the right thing. I think she's a decent woman caught in a bad situation."

Around suppertime, the decent woman took a call from a male who sounded a little drunk. "Please," he said, "I'm begging you. Where's Brenda?"

"I don't know anything about that," she said, trying to keep her tone level.

The man's tone hardened. "We can *make* you talk, ya know."

She wished she knew how to respond. She heard the anguish in the voice, but what was served by threats?

The dial tone resumed.

At seven that evening, the mother-hen side of Sharon's Nordic personality emerged. She hadn't minded cooperating with the police in the interests of justice, but she'd be damned if she would let them harass her family.

It was a cool twilight, a light breeze barely lifting the topmost leaves of her rhododendrons. Sharon and Donne were leaving for a concert with their oldest son and his wife when she noticed an unmarked sedan at the head of their driveway.

"Donne, there's a guy inside," she said. "Drive around the block. It might be Joe Gere. I think he called a while ago."

Her husband told her she was acting silly. Everyone admired Donne Pittman, but he was so easygoing and tolerant that she sometimes wondered what it would take to make him angry, short of a slur on the brownies he made at the bakery, regarded as the world's best, at least in the Pittman house.

"Please, Donne," she said. "Circle the block."

At the bottom of the hill she noticed a battered van in a far corner where the lighthouse beam just missed.

"If this is the Geres," she said, "we're not leaving here tonight."

She strode up to the van and banged her knuckles against the driver's door. The window lowered a few inches.

She said, "Are you guys from the sheriff's department?"

A man's face stared blankly.

She raised her voice. "What the hell do you think you're doing? Do you have my house staked out?"

The man said, "Hold on, ma'am." He rolled up the window and spoke into a microphone, then reopened the window and said, "Yes, ma'am. We're surveilling your house."

Sharon exploded. "*Without telling us?* For God's sake, I've got five boys inside! I don't know which of you guys might be trigger-happy. The least you could do is knock on my door and say you're here to watch Mike and allow me to get my kids out."

"Yes, ma'am," the officer responded.

She told Donne to drive them back up the hill to the house; she wouldn't feel comfortable at the concert. She rounded up her young sons and foster sons and drove them to her mother's house in Seattle to spend the night.

She was back in Mukilteo by eight-thirty. The police van was gone.

Jimmy Mayzsak and his wife Georgeann arrived just before midnight after a nearly nonstop drive from their home in Carlisle, Wyoming. Elaine hugged them both and stepped back for a good look at the brother she hadn't seen in two years. He seemed bigger in the chest than ever, and just as small elsewhere. His biceps showed through his cowboy shirt. More than ever he put her in mind of their father, except in the midsection, but she'd never seen Big Ed with a pistol on his hip. "Jim," she said, "what—?"

He unholstered a long-barreled pistol. "It's part of my gear," he explained.

Joe teetered down the stairs and slapped his old playmate on the shoulder. "Hey," he said, "where's your bike?"

"Why?" Jimmy asked, laughing. "Did you wanna break my ass again?"

The jocularity ended when the talk turned to Mike Green. Just before the Mayzsaks' arrival, a searcher named Lesley Caveness, an energetic dog handler and mother of Brenda's school friend Jennifer, had ferreted out the big man's address in Mukilteo by tracing the white Toyota's license number through a friend of a friend. It was illegal, but so was the abduction. Since the report from Lesley, Joe had been sipping his spiked Kool-Aid and planning a midnight attack.

Jimmy slapped his holster and said he'd ride shotgun.

"Have a drink first," Joe said. "You know you can't wear that thing here."

"It's legal in Wyoming."

"Tuck it in your belt."

"That makes it a concealed weapon."

"I'll never tell."

As the brothers-in-law laid their plans, Georgeann told Elaine, "I hope they don't ride tonight. Jimmy hasn't slept since we got your call."

"Joe's been drinking for two days," Elaine said. "It's the only way he can handle this."

Their husbands reminisced about a duck-hunting trip to the Salton Sea with Joe's brother Rick. Jimmy's lips began to go slack. He was still working on his first drink, but Joe had progressed to gulps. Elaine recognized the otherworldly stare and urged him gently to his feet.

"Whatever you're gonna do, it'll keep till morning," she whispered. "Let's try to sleep."

She was surprised when he didn't resist. *Too drunk, I guess,* she said to herself. She walked up the stairs behind him and noticed how his big body sagged. He was no longer the lean young man with the buggywhip shape and the long muscles. Alcohol and the sedentary life of a car salesman had softened him up. She realized that they had to find Brenda before he carried out his own death sentence drink by drink in front of searchers, relatives, friends and family. She'd given up trying to reach him with common sense and logic. She remembered his mother's final months, the bottles under the mattress, in her car, hidden in drawers at the day-care. Alcoholism was still the Gere disease.

Lying alongside Joe in their queen-size bed, she had a flash of pain and terror. My God, she thought, we might lose Brenda *and* Joe! We'll be alone. The boys and me . . .

"It's okay, honey," Joe said, drawing her close. She'd thought he was sleeping. "You can cry."

She sobbed out loud. Joe said, "You can't keep holding it in." Then he cried with her. "Oh, God, honey," he said in a choked voice, "she's gone."

In twenty years together, Elaine hadn't seen him cry, not even at his mother's funeral. It was disconcerting, but if they cried together, maybe he would start taking his comfort from her instead of Jack Daniel's.

He held her as she recounted the afternoon conversation with the minister. She prayed aloud for the blue light till Joe dropped off.

Around three in the morning, Elaine gave up on sleep. The words of one of the uniformed deputies had been going through her mind. He'd explained that Seattle was a center of child pornography where runaway children were lured into dope, prostitution and worse.

"They turn tricks all day and make films at night till they burn out," he'd said. "Then they're either thrown back on the street or just disappear. It's like a lost society. Some of the kids wind up in snuff films. In France, Japan, Denmark, they love those films. Kids getting killed during sex, women being strangled."

Elaine thought, We've got to find her before it's too late. She's not dead. She's being used by the pornographers. She's trussed up in a dingy apartment on Skid Road in Seattle, or maybe in a cabin back in the woods, where no one can hear her scream. There were groves so thick that the owls hooted till nine or ten in the morning, thinking it was still night. Maybe Brenda was being shot up with dope in one of those groves. She was too pretty just to be murdered, discarded. She was too valuable.

Elaine remembered something the search leader, Dick Cress, had said earlier, in between puffs on the cigarette that always hung from his lips: "These white slave ships wait offshore. It's a fact; I've talked to some detectives in Oregon. The police try to keep a watch on 'em, but it's tough. They've got the whole ocean to hide in. They take kids out there by small boat and ship 'em to the Middle East for white slavery."

Hours passed as she wrestled with her thoughts. It had been two days and three nights since the disappearance, and in that time she'd hardly slept. Well, so what? she asked herself. I'll be a long time dead. I can sleep in my grave.

13

At 6:00 A.M., Elaine was sitting at the kitchen table when she heard a footfall upstairs. All night long she'd listened to the snores and snorts of her extended family, ten Geres and Mayzsaks sprawled on beds and couches and quilts. At times it sounded as though every single sleeper were having nightmares, as though not a single one rested soundly or quietly in this Amityville house.

Now someone was up. She guessed it was Joey, missing Brenda so much that he couldn't get back to sleep. But it turned out to be Joe, looking remarkably clear-eyed for someone who'd been sleep-talking half the night.

"Honey," he said, "today's the day." For once, he didn't head straight for the Kool-Aid mix in the refrigerator.

She asked what he was talking about.

"I'm gonna make Green talk. Beat it out of him. Somebody's got to. I had a dream Brenda's still alive."

Elaine was dismayed. "Joe, the man weighs three hundred pounds. He makes the cops nervous. He's a weight lift—"

"Me and Jimmy can take him down. I'll shoot him in the leg if I have to. I'd kill the son of a bitch quicker'n I'd swat a fly."

"You'll wind up in jail."

"I'm in jail now."

He looked so pathetic and frustrated that she reached out and stroked his reddish-black hair, still fine and flossy twenty years after she'd first spotted him on the floor of the Cinnamon Cinder. The Geres were a handsome breed, and their hair was their best feature.

"Joe," she said, "we've gotta let the law take its course."

"When's it gonna start?" He sounded bitter. "She's not the law's kid, she's ours." He slammed one big fist into the other. "She could be *dying* out there."

It was a waste of breath to argue with him after he'd made up his mind, but she consoled herself with the knowledge that he couldn't do anything foolish for several hours. The detectives were due at ten for more gumshoeing around the house. Maybe Joe would wise up by then.

Shortly after eight, a shivering search team assembled at a Clearview grocery store to begin the third day of poking through the fields and woods. Some of the volunteers had never heard of Brenda, and some were family friends and teachers who'd become acquainted with the Geres in their meanderings in the suburbs of Seattle. Debbie Simmons, who'd taught Brenda in the fifth grade at Cedar River Elementary School, arrived with her husband Nate. He'd insisted on coming along. His supervisor at Boeing had promised that his workmates would share out his load.

Like many of Brenda's former teachers, the thirty-three-year-old Debbie had never lost contact with the bright child. She found the situation almost too painful to bear, "like watching a horror movie and suddenly realizing you're in it, and somewhere out there someone you love is lying dead. It shook me up something awful, not only that Brenda was gone, but that I might be the one who found her. And yet . . . I couldn't stop looking."

Dick Cress directed the search with professional skill. "We're gonna be looking for her bedspread," the leader announced calmly. "It's white, with a rainbow." He advised the volunteers to call for help if they spotted the child or any clues, and warned them not to disturb evidence.

Debbie shuddered as Cress added, "Look for fresh dirt, signs of digging. Remember, she might not look like the Brenda you knew. You've got to be ready for that."

The volunteers held hands at the edge of a snarl of Himalaya blackberries as Cress called out, "Okay, straight ahead!"

Debbie whispered to Nate, "How're we gonna *do* this?" He gave her a gentle tug and they walked into, over and under the stickers.

After they'd sloshed through a peat bog, they entered a thick stand of third-growth saplings and had to release hands. Poisonous toadstools as pimpled as some of her students pushed up through moldy leaves. Animal tracks crossed and recrossed. She saw pawprints so big that they might have been made by one of the cougars that wandered into Bothell every year or two.

She covered her ears against the clatter of a helicopter overhead. She was afraid she might faint on the spot, or waste the time of the searchers by losing her bearings and ending up missing. She'd been trying to visualize Brenda as lost in the woods, exhausted, smiling a wan sweet smile. But what had the leader said? Look for "fresh dirt."

She stumbled and fell against a spike of devil's club, thorny even to the backs of its leaves. She gulped and knelt alongside a cascara tree. No human life was visible in any direction. "Nate?" she called softly.

"I'm here, honey," he said. He sounded close, but she wished she could see him.

After a while, the fields and woods around the log house resounded with yips and barks and howls. Lop-eared bloodhounds shuffled toward every point of the compass, flushing quail and grouse, dickey birds, Steller's jays and an occasional varmint. King County contributed a cadaver dog, and the Snohomish County Sheriff's Department provided a jar of death scent.

Elaine was serving coffee and a slice of Katie Cress's bountiful supply of homemade peach pie to a famished searcher when a car rolled up the driveway and another bloodhound jumped out, huffing and shuddering and sniffing everything he could reach with his snout. It was a cold morning, and the dog's breath puffed out in little white hyphens.

The handler hugged Elaine, introduced herself as Annmarie

Kaighin, and said, "Tennessee and I'll do whatever it takes. I've got a daughter the same age as yours."

She said she needed an article of the suspect's clothing to start "Tenny" off. A sheriff's car delivered Green's sport shirt, sealed in a plastic bag to protect it from contamination. The bloodhound looked questioningly at his mistress. "Go find!" Kaighin snapped.

The dog started at the driveway, entered the long house via the side door, followed his drippy nose through the kitchen and living room, then stopped at the staircase and whined. The handler explained that Tenny hated to climb stairs—"He'll do anything to avoid it."

The bloodhound began a tentative climb, stopping to nuzzle each riser. At the top of the stairs he waddled down the hall, turned left into Brenda's bedroom, sat on his haunches, and howled.

Elaine exclaimed, "Green went up our stairs. That's our probable cause!"

Her exhilaration was short-lived. A deputy prosecutor reported that the bloodhound's tracking wouldn't be admissible in court. He explained to Elaine that it had something to do with search warrants and the fact that the Pittmans, not Michael Green himself, had supplied the shirt. Somehow it added up to a violation of his precious rights.

I might've known, Elaine said to herself. The law protects the Greens of this world. But it doesn't do much for the Brendas.

14

In midmorning, Elaine's sister Beverly and sister-in-law Georgeann drove to Mukilteo to reconnoiter the big house where Green resided with his in-laws. After a while, a slender woman opened the back door and peeked out. No males appeared.

The operatives snapped Polaroid pictures and tried to look like tourists admiring the lighthouse. They shot close-ups of three big footprints that ran from the railroad tracks into the Pittmans' back-yard.

If any police units were keeping watch, they weren't visible.

When the women returned to the log house, Joe Gere was in a detective's face. "Goddamn it, *make* the asshole talk!" he was saying. "If you don't, I will."

The officer responded in a calm voice, "Mr. Gere, we're asking you to be patient. Don't do anything out of line. You could jeopardize the case."

"*What* case?" Joe Gere answered. "Everybody knows who took Brenda. Why can't you just hook his ass up?"

The detective said that they were finally making some progress. Green had been caught in another lie. He'd claimed earlier that he'd used a gas station's rest room on the afternoon of Brenda's disappearance.

"What he stopped for wasn't the rest room," the detective related. "The toilet was out of order. He spent an hour washing and vacuuming his car. We checked this morning."

Joe snapped, "We already knew he was a liar."

"If we catch him in enough lies, we might have a case."

"Yeah. For lying. What the hell good's that gonna do Brenda?"

After the detective drove off, Elaine's brother came downstairs and asked for directions to the Pittmans' house in Mukilteo. "I wanna see the asshole for myself."

"Don't go, Jimmy," his mother said. "You'll be arrested." Elaine remembered how Evelyn had tried to keep Jimmy out of trouble as a teenager. He was as obedient now as he'd been then.

"I know what I'm doin', Mom," he said. He strapped on his holster and left.

An hour later he was back. "No Green, no cops, no nothin'," he reported.

Elaine was disappointed. "They gave me their word," she complained. "They were supposed to watch around the clock."

"Well, sis, they lied."

Elaine considered attending mass in Bothell, but the log house was full of relatives and searchers and her action list covered three pages of steno pad. God would understand.

She was catching up on the morning dishes when a priest arrived unannounced and said he was from St. Brandon's Church. Elaine's ears pricked up. St. *Brandon?*

She didn't usually deal with God through middlemen, but she was pleased by the visit. In the privacy of her bedroom, she made her confession. She told the priest that she shouldn't have allowed Brenda to stay home alone and shouldn't have let the regular baby-sitter go just to save a few dollars a day and she hadn't always been a good wife, a good mother, a good Catholic. She'd had evil thoughts about Michael Green and had been tempted to violate the Commandments.

The priest granted her absolution. After he left, she paged through one of her books of baby names. She'd guessed right. "Brandon" was a male form of "Brenda." Was that a message from God or what?

As the morning chill dissipated, more tracking dogs arrived in station wagons and vans. Chris Griffin brought "Sorrel," Sue Carpenter "Deacon," Sue and Gregg Perry "Clyde." Travis Stirek brought his basset hound, which resembled a bloodhound standing in a hole. All the animals seemed to find hot trails. Two went straight to the deep drainage trench that ran along Thirty-fifth Avenue in front of the log house, leading to a theory that Green might have wrapped Brenda in her comforter and hidden her in the ditch while he retrieved his car from the corner.

Another bloodhound crawled through the hedge to the Bona-dores' yard and yowled his way north on Thirty-fifth till he and his handler disappeared from sight. An hour later a sad-faced member of the search team drove up the gravel driveway in a Jeep and told Elaine, "We may've found her."

The searcher said the dog hadn't raised his nose for five and a half miles. Then he splashed into the cherry-colored water of an old log-pickling pond called Thomas Lake and began snapping at the surface. Another dog was brought to the pond and reacted similarly. "That's how bloodhounds taste for scent molecules," the helpful man explained.

He said a dive team and a Zodiac boat were on the way to grapple for the body. "I'm sorry, Mrs. Gere. I hope we're wrong."

Elaine knew they were wrong but didn't try to explain. This well-intended man, volunteering his Sunday to help strangers, would never understand. There were lines of communication between mothers and daughters that were unavailable to others. Elaine's logic was simple: Brenda wasn't dead because Brenda *couldn't* be dead. She might have been kidnapped, but she hadn't been murdered. She might be cold, or hurt, or tied up, or on her way to some sultan's harem, or drugged for a part in a porno film, but she was *not* dead. They could send an armada of Zodiac boats, a whole navy of divers, and a kennel of cadaver dogs. The child who loved horses and rock music and go-go boots would not be found at the bottom of a lake.

The searchers stuck to their belief. Dog expert Lesley Caveness had been at the scene when the two bloodhounds had padded into the water. "Elaine," she reported in her rapid-fire delivery, leaving out the punctuation as usual. "Those animals went nuts none of us ever saw 'em act like that before *something* happened at Thomas Lake if it's not Brenda it's something else."

The area was part swamp, part lake, part peat bog, surrounded by a squishy rim of rotting reeds and potholes. A deputy sank to the top of his hip boots and complained, "It's the goddamn Atchafalaya Marsh. There's more bulrushes than the Old Testament." One tractor had to be brought in to extricate another.

A Gere neighbor, master diver Sidney Christian, part Hawaiian and a distant ancestor of Fletcher Christian of *Mutiny on the Bounty*, searched Thomas Lake with a diving buddy. They came up sputtering and said the bottom was a tangle of tree trunks, logs, branches and other vegetation. A body could be trapped down there and never found.

While a police helicopter hovered a city block away to keep from whipping up the pond's surface, a four-man dive team from the Snohomish County Sheriff's Department swam to the bottom with high-powered lights. The divers confirmed Christian's findings; it was a waste of time and resources to search for Brenda or anyone else in Thomas Lake. Grappling hooks would hang up on snags and stumps that had been preserved in the cedar water for years. If the missing child was down there, and most of the searchers believed she was, the search was over.

15

Diana Pittman fervently wanted to believe in her husband's inno-cence, but she was having flickers of doubt. Her mother didn't help the situation, bitching about Mike's little inconsistencies and correcting his stories about what he'd worn. Di thought, Who cares if he got a few details wrong? Does Mom want her own son-in-law executed for murder?

On Sunday afternoon, the extended Pittman family piled into two cars and drove to nearby Mount Pilchuck for a long-planned outing. Donne and the kids took the family car, Mike and Diana their white Toyota. Diana was pleased that Sharon chose to stay home. At the moment, mother and daughter needed distancing. It was a familiar family dynamic: Diana and Sharon bickering about Mike. I don't know why she hates him so, Diana said to herself. He's always been nice to her. She just doesn't understand someone so different.

Atop the low mountain, Diana and Mike wandered off by them-selves. As soon as they were alone, Mike began complaining about being framed by the cops and the Geres. He said he was ashamed of "this whole mess I've brought down on you and everybody else."

As they walked and talked, he became more upset. "I need to be by myself," he begged. "I know how to solve this problem. This is the perfect place." It wasn't the first time he'd hinted at suicide. It seemed to come with the steroids, and especially with withdrawal.

As evening approached, she clung to his side. At last he calmed a little and they headed home.

In bed that night, he murmured, "Do you think it's possible I could've killed her during a blackout?"

Diana was stunned. Was this the beginning of a confession? She didn't answer. It was so hard to think straight, lying alongside a man who was suspected of murder, a man she deeply loved. She knew about his violence—she still bore the scars—but most of the time he was gentle. How could a man like that kill a child? How could *any* man?

She had a hard time falling asleep.

Deputy Bryce Siegel had spent his weekend sickened by the thought that he hadn't been able to slap the cuffs on Michael Green. There were frustrations in every cop's career, but this was the worst the cerebral deputy could remember.

He'd talked to Sergeant Tom Pszonka several times over the weekend, and Pszonka was suffering the same pangs. They both remembered Joe Gere's stammerings as they'd left the house: "I can't live with this. I can't do anything till I find my baby girl. You gotta find her. Please, *please*. Find my baby." It tore the deputies up.

On Monday morning, all hands were mustered for a strategy session at the sheriff's office in Everett. It didn't take long for Joe Ward and Siegel and the others to agree on the immediate problem. Brenda had been missing for four days and Michael Green was the only logical suspect, but there was no body, no proof that a crime had been committed, and no basis for an arrest. The guy didn't even have traffic warrants. There was no way around the law.

Back in his office after the latest busy waste of time, Siegel held a deep-think session with himself. It's obvious, he began, that whatever else is wrong with this guy, he's 'roided out of his skull. He's got a college degree, but he's not working and doesn't seem to care. He's on the outs with his mother-in-law and maybe his wife and other family members, and he's been driving around the country, looking for—what? Victims? *Kids?* I wouldn't be surprised if he got himself into trouble long before he showed up on Thirty-fifth Avenue.

Siegel began phoning police departments in surrounding areas and asking them to check for recent assaults or other violent behavior by a conspicuously large suspect. At noon he took a call from Keith Kingsbury, basketball coach at nearby Edmonds Community College, where Siegel's wife Shirley coached volleyball and Siegel shot hoops. Offhandedly, the detective asked his friend, "Did you ever see a great big guy, like maybe three hundred, three-ten, hanging out at your gym?"

"No," Kingsbury said, "but a couple of months ago a gal was

raped on our jogging trail, and she described the man as a Frigidaire with a head. I think the Lynnwood police worked up a sketch."

Siegel made the short drive to the Lynnwood police station and asked a duty sergeant, "Do you still have your composite on the jogging trail rapist?"

"Yeah," he replied. "It's on the board."

Siegel took a look. Michael Green stared back.

At sheriff's headquarters in Everett, a photo montage was prepared for the rape victim and rushed to the bank where she worked. She identified Green as the oversized man who'd wired her hands together at knifepoint, raped her, and apologized afterward. A Lynnwood detective named Brian Burkholder remembered Green as a suspicious person he'd stopped on the same jogging trail two days before the rape. The identifications were made easier by the fact that so few human organisms were shaped like refrigerators.

A second victim, a junior high school teacher, identified a picture of the former University of Washington tackle as the man who'd raped her at knifepoint on a different jogging trail not far from Edmonds Community College. The attack had taken place just five weeks before Brenda Gere's disappearance.

Joe Gere went out of his way to act comradely toward the Snohomish County detectives who reinterviewed him and assured him that they were doing everything possible to find Brenda. When the two plainclothesmen got up to leave, he shook their hands and said, "I'm sorry about this. I know it's tough on you guys."

As soon as they drove off, Joe huddled with his pistol-packin' brother-in-law Jimmy Mayzsak. The two old friends agreed that the last thing they wanted to do was kill Michael Green, at least as long as he held the key to Brenda's whereabouts. Somehow they had to make him talk. After they found Brenda, their strategy would change.

"We gotta make an impression," Joe said. "All it'll take is muscle and balls."

They were about to leave the house when there was a heavy knock on the front door. Joe's mother-in-law opened it and found herself staring at two fierce-looking men. Later Joe managed a rare grin over the encounter. "I'd barely opened my mouth when they knocked at the front door," he told Elaine. "There they were. Muscle and balls."

IBar Arrington, a retired heavyweight boxer who was known for his ability to take punishment and once remained conscious after a backhoe bucket dropped on his head, and his pal Dennis Mackey, an ex-Marine and Vietnam veteran, had arrived to assist. The cronies were as close as twins and combined muscle and strength with hearts of mush. "Between us," IBar liked to joke, "we make up one bright guy. And six tough guys." He was built along the lines of an ice cream cone.

Mackey had recognized Joe Gere on a morning TV news show. A onetime combat photographer with an alcohol problem, he was in the used-car profession himself and had met his fellow salesman in a bar. He remembered how Joe had droned on about being a cop in San Bernardino and getting sucker-punched in a street fight while trying to help a black guy put out a fire. Joe had seemed a little bitter, but after a few double shots he brightened up and told some great war stories.

Arrington and Mackey hadn't been sure where the Geres lived, but finding the house on Thirty-fifth Avenue S.E. proved easy. Vans from Seattle TV stations were lined up in front and reporters were buttonholing anyone who approached. IBar, a part-time security guard who worked unarmed and was known on the streets of Seattle's Chinatown as Robocop, recognized a few of the reporters from his boxing days.

The visitors had hardly entered the house when Joe Gere jumped up from the couch and said, "Dennis! I can't believe it! I've been looking for you guys."

Joe briefed the newcomers and explained that the cops knew that Michael Green had taken Brenda but were too chickenshit to hook him up and work him over. The raffish Dennis spoke up in his earthmoving voice. "IBar went ten rounds with Larry Holmes before

Holmes was champ. We can handle this pussy. What do you want us to do? Tear off his head and piss down his throat?"

"The guy's a weightlifter," Jimmy Mayzsak put in. "Weighs somewhere around three hundred."

In his mild voice, interrupted by sharp intakes of air that made him sound like a boxer working on the speed bag, IBar observed that he didn't care if the guy was the size of a Peterbilt. "He's just another steroid freak to me. I know about those, uh, jerks. No wind, can't take a punch. Your average, uh, nun, she hits harder."

"I guarantee you," Dennis told Joe, "Green will *not* be a problem. Where's he at?"

"Nobody knows."

IBar had a suggestion. "Let's just go out and, uh, beat up every three-hundred-pounder we find. How many can there be around here?"

Dennis explained to Joe, "IBar's basically cool, believe me. He just wants to be alone with the guy. In a street fight, he can beat anybody in the world."

IBar said, "I need two minutes with the asshole. I could do it faster, but I want to torture him first."

Joe seemed cheered by their attitude and said, "Let's drive over and see if he's home."

Elaine told a friend later that when the three men walked out the side door, they looked like bouncers leaving a club.

At Mukilteo, the scouting party drove around the block three or four times but saw no sign of Green or the Pittmans. A stubby ferry blew two longs and a short and eased into its slip, but otherwise the harborside village was quiet. Later they figured they'd missed their quarry by an hour.

They took a spin past the Lake Goodwin area home of a Pittman relative with ties to Saudi Arabia, one of the exotic places where some thought Brenda might be secreted in a harem. The house looked vacant. They reconnoitered Thomas Lake and other search venues, then dropped into a Bothell bar for a nightcap.

"Michael Green?" the bartender said in answer to their query. "Yeah, he comes in. Drinks the same drink as you, IBar: orange juice. Always by himself, doesn't interact, ripples the muscles. Hits the rest room six, eight times a night, struts across the floor like the *Nimitz* arriving.''

En route home after midnight, Dennis and IBar held their own council of war. "We decided that whatever it took, we had to have a frank exchange of views with this Michael Green," Dennis said later. "IBar would conduct the interview as he saw fit. I was gonna referee and Joe Gere would be the commissioner. The three-knockdown rule is waived. A fighter cannot be saved by the bell. We didn't really intend to kill him, 'cause we wanted to know where Brenda was. *Then* we'd kill him.''

17

Michael Green was so depressed at lunch Monday that Diana could hardly hear his mumblings. He nibbled at his restaurant food and sat slump-shouldered, bemoaning the trouble he'd caused her family and casting more self-pitying hints about suicide. Diana told him to stop being stupid. "If you didn't do anything, what's there to worry about?''

"The cops," he whispered. "You don't know how they operate.''

He paid the check, drove her back to work in their little white Toyota, and said he had to go somewhere to pay a bill.

As Diana stepped into her office, the phone was ringing.

Elaine could never explain exactly why she called Diana Pittman Green at work. "It was simple frustration, I guess. Brenda was still gone. The police weren't getting anywhere. Jimmy and my husband were talking crazy. Somebody had to make a move, even if it was wrong.''

She recounted the conversation:

"I started out asking for help, cooperation. I didn't want her to hang up. I asked her, couldn't she just talk Mike into taking us to Brenda?

"Diana said she didn't know what I was talking about. Mike hadn't done anything. He would *never* harm a child.

"I got a little mad. I said, 'Listen, your husband took my daughter and I want you to find out what he did with her.'

"She said no he didn't and it was a waste of time to talk about it. I said, 'Yes he did! We have hair samples, we have his fingerprints.' I was making it up as I went along. 'He was in our house. We can prove it! We *have* him. *He took her!*'

"She just kept saying, 'Oh, no. Oh, no.'

"I thought about Dennis Mackey and IBar Arrington and some of the other people that were helping us. 'Look,' I said, 'we've got friends a lot bigger than your husband. Tougher, too. Ex-Marines, Green Berets, cops. If your husband doesn't bring Brenda back or tell us where she is, we're coming after you. Every darn one of you! We'll have you taken care of.' "

An hour after the threatening conversation, a Snohomish deputy phoned and said, "Elaine, I know you're upset. But—you can't do that!"

She didn't feel ashamed. Brenda could be lying in a ditch, freezing, dying. She could be locked in a dungeon, tortured, cigarettes sizzling against her skin. There wasn't time to be fair, to keep everything legal and proper.

"I just wanted to put the fear in both of them that something could happen to them," she explained to the deputy. "I know it was wrong. But if it brings back Brenda . . ."

"Please," he said, "let us handle it. Okay?"

She said she hoped they would get started.

By midafternoon on Monday, TV journalists like KOMO's Connie Thompson and KIRO's Linda Coldiron headed back to Seattle to prepare reports that would air at five o'clock and again at eleven, the first comprehensive TV pieces on the search. At the last moment, the media learned that an arrest warrant was being issued for a former University of Washington defensive tackle named Michael Green, but it hadn't yet been served.

That night, Green didn't show up for dinner. The Pittmans were concerned; he seldom missed a meal. Around seven he phoned and asked for Diana. "I'm sorry about the mess I got us in," he began, reprising his luncheon theme.

"Mike, where *are* you?" she asked. She told him the police wanted to talk to him again.

"What for?" he asked.

"I don't know."

"I don't know either." He was quiet for a few seconds, then told her it didn't matter. No one in Snohomish County would ever see him again. "I'm trying to steal a car so I can leave the Toyota for you."

She told him to drive straight home. "Only guilty people run."

He said he would tell her where to collect the car when he got where he was going.

"Where on earth is *that*?" she asked. He said he wouldn't know till he got there. Then he hung up.

18

At twenty-five, Krista Marie Klawa laughed so often and so hard and sometimes so unexpectedly—raucous guffaws and bellows that ended in a breathless sigh—that friends figured it was just her way to cope. Now she was headed home in her gold Accord and still giggling to herself about a question someone had asked a few hours earlier at the Navy warehouse where she drove a forklift. Krista worked a forty-hour week, took night courses at a community college, studied computer engineering at the University of Washington, attended Bible-study classes several times a week and Christian Church on Sunday, worked out daily and never missed aerobics class, and someone at work had asked, "What do you do in your spare time?"

As she turned into the parking lot of her apartment in Seattle's University District, she was still thinking how funny that was. Yeah, she said to herself, in my spare time I'm an astronaut.

She was exhausted, a familiar state. It was nearly 9:00 P.M. and she'd just finished buying books for her fall courses. All she wanted to do was park her '78 Honda and go inside. The rats would resume their race at 5:00 A.M.

She headed for her assigned parking spot next to apartment manager Patrick Oliveri's and noticed that a light shone from his window. It was always reassuring to know that the manager was a holler away when she entered the three-story building after dark.

As she drove slowly, a blocky silhouette appeared in the darkness about thirty feet ahead of her. Something told her not to stop and get out. This neighborhood was full of creeps. What was the guy up to? She knew most of the residents by sight, and she'd never seen this man before. He was a little on the slovenly side, wearing a jacket and a backpack, and he was *large*. As he turned to watch her approach, it occurred to her that God was telling her to be somewhere else.

Then she thought, I *live* here. I'm tired, it's nine o'clock and I want to go to bed. I can make it to the inside staircase before he can even reach me.

She'd barely locked her car and stepped toward the entrance when the hulk appeared alongside, asking her what street was at the end of the block. "Just bushes," she said. "It's a dead end."

In his purple jacket with gold bands around the arms, he looked like a Husky football player. He carried a small dark-colored bag. She wondered if he was looking for the Burke Gilman hiking path. She told him he could reach the popular trail via a ladder on the far side of the parking lot.

Suddenly a hard forearm circled her neck. A sharp point pushed against her throat and a voice snapped, "Shut up."

She thought about letting out the scream of her life. But then she remembered this is a fraternity district. Nobody would pay any attention. She thought, These are my last seconds. . . .

The man whispered, "I'll kill you if you make a sound."

Her next thought was that she *had* to survive. She'd lost her father to a heart attack two years earlier; he'd just turned fifty, never been sick. As the knife pressed harder against her throat, she thought, Mom and the family, they could never deal with another death. *I can't die!*

"Unlock the car," the man ordered.

She fumbled in her purse for her key. The dome light blinked on as the door opened. He grabbed the handle and nudged her inward, but she resisted. If I get in, she said to herself, I'm dead. If he intends to kill me, let it be right here, not in some faraway place where they'll never find my body.

The metal blade tilted sideways and she realized that the dull edge was against her throat. She grabbed at the blade and screamed, "Patrick! *Patrick!*"

She found herself in midair, flying over a retaining wall. She rolled to a stop at the bottom of a fifteen-foot embankment. Blood welled from a gashed finger and stained her clothes. "Patrick!" she yelled. "Oh, please, Patrick! Call the cops!"

Two brothers on the top floor rushed down the stairs with a baseball bat, and Patrick Oliveri ran out the front door. A big man called out, "What's going on back there? Sounds like a crazy lady. You better check." Then he was gone.

The young manager called the police and drove Krista to nearby University Hospital. A doctor took seven stitches in the L-shaped cut in her left index finger and treated abrasions on her cheek and neck. She couldn't think of anything to laugh about, but at least she was alive.

19

At eight the next morning, Tuesday, September 24, a huge man who looked as though he'd been evicted from a Salvation Army shelter approached a woman as she stepped from her car at a parking lot in Bellevue, a ten-minute drive west of Seattle. "Excuse me, ma'am," he said courteously, "do you know what time it is?"

She was raising her wrist to check her watch when the giant smashed her in the face and knocked her down. She screamed and he fled on foot.

A description was flashed to local police agencies: "WMA, 35 yrs., 6'2"–3", 240 lbs., large athletic build, standard length dark brown wavy hair, 2 days' growth beard, wearing a bright yellow rain slicker, carrying a duffel-type bag."

Less than an hour later, a florist in the Cascade foothills town of Issaquah was setting out her flowers and plants when a man in a light-colored sweatshirt entered and explained, "I had an argument with my wife last night and I'd like to get her a gift."

She kept an eye on him as he browsed for eight or ten minutes, picking up an occasional pot or vase. He couldn't seem to make up his mind. "What do *you* think?" he asked in a friendly voice.

"Would you prefer fresh flowers or silk flowers?"

"Gee, I don't know."

The florist removed her till money from a paper bag and counted out bills. As she was opening up the second cash register, the man clutched her left shoulder and said, "Be quiet and give me all the money."

A knife flashed blade-up in his free hand. He grabbed the white sack. "Is there any more?" he asked. She shook her head and he shoved her toward the rear of the shop. "I don't want to hear anything out of you," he said. "Just stay quiet."

She watched as he emptied the cash register. "Be quiet!" he warned. Then he ducked out the front door, almost bumping into the transom, and turned left toward the Safeway parking lot.

She told the investigating officer that the man was about six-three, 280 pounds, had brown hair, hazel eyes, and "a bodybuilder-type build." His total take was $50.

At 10:00 A.M., a quartet of lawmen converged on the Pittman rambler in Mukilteo to serve arrest and search warrants. Lynnwood detectives Neil Knight and David Ivers, who'd worked the Edmonds jogging trail rapes, joined Snohomish detectives Joe Ward and Rick Bart. They'd hardly stepped inside the big house before Diana Green informed them that Michael was gone.

"We don't know where he is," she said, her pretty face drawn. "He didn't come home last night. We're afraid he's . . . dead."

Ward asked, "Does he often stay out all night?"

She hesitated, then answered, "No." She said that some of the Pittmans were in the Mount Pilchuck area, searching for his body.

When the detectives asked if she'd heard from her husband at all, she said she'd had one hurried phone call and didn't know where it originated. Mike had apologized for the trouble he was causing but hadn't said much else.

Ward pressed her. "Are you sure you're not in touch?"

"Oh, God," she said, "I wish."

The lawmen collected some lint from the clothes dryer, a coil of copper wire that looked similar to the wire used on one of the rape victims, some oversized clothing, and various other oddments, none very promising as hard evidence in the Gere case. They radioed a request for a helicopter to search the Mount Pilchuck recreation area for a very large man with dark hair and a twelve-year-old girl in a rainbow comforter. It wasn't much to go on.

When they returned to the sheriff's office in Everett, Ward checked the Seattle phone book for the phone number of Delbert Green, Michael's father. The senior Green said that the family hadn't heard from Michael Kay in years. He gave the impression that the Green residence in Seattle was the last place Michael would go if he was on the run.

Joe Ward called the log house. "We're getting there," he told Elaine.

She said, "You arrested Green?"

"Green's missing. But we've linked him to some rapes."

Elaine said, "I thought you were watching him every minute."

"Don't worry. A guy his size won't get far."

Elaine's fingers trembled as she put in a call to Michael Magee, the assistant prosecuting attorney who'd been shadowing the case. He remembered later that "she blistered me pretty good. I understood. What could I say? She was out of her mind with grief."

"I was mad," Elaine said. "How were we gonna find Brenda if they let Green get away? I told Mr. Magee, 'You coulda picked him up on circumstantial. You were supposed to be watching him. You guys lied to me.'

"He told me his hands were tied without hard evidence. He said if he arrested Michael Green and it turned out that Brenda was a runaway or had amnesia or something, Michael Green would own Snohomish County. He said if he moved too fast, he could lose the case down the road. I said I didn't care about down the road. All I wanted was Brenda."

Elaine fell deeper into the doldrums at the news that the sheriff's office was calling off the official hunt for Brenda. A spokesman said, "Unless we develop more leads, we feel no reason to conduct any further ground search at this time." They'd made twelve official searches, employed twelve dogs and six divers, and racked up 290 man-hours. As one of the deputies explained, "We pretty near busted our budget for the year."

Elaine complained to her husband, back on his spiked-Kool-Aid diet, and Joe consulted Dick Cress, leader of the volunteer searchers. The man who'd lost his own son to a sex killer told him not to worry. The county was quitting, but "that'll just make the rest of us work harder."

Joe asked, "How much longer can you guys go on?"

"Whatever it takes," said the tireless engineer who'd pitched his tent on the front lawn the morning after Brenda vanished.

Joe led Cress into the kitchen and confided in a slurred voice, "I'm bringing in some extra help."

"Who?"

"Some guys from California."

Cress was puzzled. He couldn't imagine recruiting searchers from two states away when so many were available locally. "You don't want to know who," Joe added in a conspiratorial whisper. He draped his arm across the shorter man's shoulders. "I'm gonna have to sleep with the devil."

Cress hoped Joe's brain wasn't softening. Elaine and the boys had suffered enough.

IBar Arrington was also worried about Joe. "Half the time he's off the wall," IBar confided to a friend. "He tells me and Dennis, 'I got some big men coming in from California. They're gonna take care of Green.' He has a few drinks and pretty soon he's not making sense. He says, 'Don't worry, IBar. This'll all be taken care of.' And I'm thinking, How, Joe? By passing out on the sofa every night?"

Sergeant Tom Pszonka was working the phones Tuesday night when a call came in from State Representative Dick Vandyke. The big sergeant didn't catch the import of the politician's words— something about his dog coming home covered with blood the previous Saturday.

Pszonka scribbled notes as Vandyke rambled on about Snoopy leaving bloodstains in the carport, and how the sheepdog was usually loaded with personality, but lately he'd been acting depressed, indifferent. For Christ's sake, Pszonka said to himself, why don't you take him to a shrink?

He wondered where the steroid freak was hiding out. Maybe his poisoned tissues were killing bugs and slugs under a log in the woods. Maybe he was at the bottom of Thomas Lake along with Brenda. Maybe he'd stashed her in some secret spot and was doing his thing. He was a rapist, and some of those perverts preferred children. Pszonka hated to think about it.

He promised the politician that he would look into the problem. "What's your address, Mr. Vandyke?" he asked.

The state representative gave a street number in Clearview. Pszonka considered it for a few seconds and then realized that Vandyke lived right down the street from the Gere house. He straightened out of his slouch and asked the man to stay on the line. My God, Pszonka said to himself, that neurotic sheepdog might've found Brenda.

As lead investigator on the case, Detective Joe Ward visited Vandyke in his pleasant home. Three days after they'd first appeared on Saturday, the bloodstains remained visible on the carport cement. To Ward, they looked as though they could be of human origin. On the other hand, most of Snohomish County was rural, and animals from llamas to voles roamed the fields and woods. Maybe Snoopy had bumbled on a deer carcass and was teasing his taste buds with an occasional snack of venison, reverting to his lupine ancestry. In this Gere case, nothing would be surprising.

Vandyke told Ward that the gloppy liquid had covered the top of Snoopy's head, with a smaller smear on his chest. It looked as though he'd been rooting into something. "I don't know what the hell's wrong with him," the politician said. "His whole disposition's changed."

Ward was baffled. What could a country sheepdog have seen that would affect him so profoundly? Dogs licked their crotches and rolled in their own crap. Since when had they become such sensitive creatures?

The meticulous detective opened his trunk and pulled out a camera and an evidence kit. He snapped flash pictures from all angles and made two sets of swabs of both bloodstains.

He returned to headquarters, labeled each set, and sent one to the Washington State Crime Laboratory and one to the FBI. Such redundancy was frowned on by forensic labs; sometimes it produced contradictory results and subsequent problems in court. But Ward had to be sure. Brenda had been missing since the previous Thursday, and it seemed as though everyone in the Northwest was following the case. Mistakes had been made, and he didn't want to be responsible for another.

With each package of swabs he included specific instructions. He asked the FBI for complete tests, including blood typing and DNA. In his note to the state lab, he wrote, "Tell me if this blood is human or nonhuman. I need to know fast."

The Pittmans of Mukilteo were aware that they were being observed as they searched in the dark under the blackberry bushes, in the brush along the railroad right-of-way, in alcoves and crannies and crawl spaces big enough to conceal a bodybuilder's bulk. The yellow cones from their flashlights danced across the lawn while the Mukilteo light chalked their faces in its old pattern: one-two, one-two. Every day of their lives the Pittmans heard the same background noises and barely noticed them anymore: seagulls wheeling over stern wash from the ferries, switch engines rumbling, sea lions barking, cars and trucks grinding up the hill from the landing.

When they found no trace of Mike, they lifted the cap on the well that provided the family's water. "God, I hope he's not in here," Donne told his son Dan. Of all the Pittmans, the father had always been the most solicitous of the son-in-law.

Dan shone his flashlight into the dank pool and said it was empty.

20

Lesley Caveness, mother of four, veterinarian's assistant, and Gere family friend, arrived at the log house early Wednesday morning and heard the news about Snoopy. She was known for her enthusiastic assistance on searches and for her rapid-fire speech. ("It's familial. When my sister and I get together people think we're speaking a foreign language.") She was also known for a medical miracle that had made the papers a few years back. Her right forearm had been wrenched off at the elbow by a laundromat's rug-washing machine. A team of surgeons had reattached it in an eighteen-hour procedure. If the hand and arm weren't quite as good as new, they were at least usable, and the injury hadn't slowed her. She'd carried a pistol ever since a man had snatched a woman from a nearby hospital and kept her in a box for three days. "Excuse me that ain't happenin' to me," she explained in her brisk staccato.

When the Geres informed her about Ward's visit to Dick Vandyke, she was puzzled. "Blood on the top of the dog's *head*?" she asked. "But not on his cheeks?"

"That's what they said," Elaine reported.

Lesley frowned. "Gee," she said, thinking aloud, "do you suppose it dripped from above? Maybe from a tree?" My God, she thought, was Brenda . . . hanged? Killed by a predator? Some of the African cats dragged their kills into treetops. Did mountain lions do the same?

Elaine had just finished reading a copy of a report from a well-known psychic who sometimes worked with police. He'd advised the Snohomish deputies that Brenda was buried in a shallow grave under an eleven-foot log on the downslope of a hill. Maybe Snoopy had found the log.

"I don't know what you've got in mind," Elaine told Lesley, "but whatever it is—go for it."

Within an hour, Lesley received permission from Representative Vandyke to search his property and the surrounding woods. She spent the rest of the morning under bushes and trees. Nothing turned up. She planned to continue the search tomorrow.

On that same Wednesday, Joe Ward took a call from one of the forensic chemists at the state crime lab. They'd completed his priority tests. The substance on the swabs was blood, but not of human origin.

He told himself that he should've known. Somebody's cow must have died and Snoopy had been dining from the inside out. Another lead gone.

He discarded his photographs of the bloodstains.

At the Pittman home in Mukilteo, a note arrived from a staffer at the Washington Park Arboretum, a public nursery not far from the University of Washington campus and just off one of the main roads leading east out of Seattle. The note was addressed to Michael Green:

> Dear Mr. Green:
>   A blue shoulder bag was found at the Arboretum yesterday. It contained a wallet with your driver's license. You may stop by to pick it up between 10 A.M. and 4 P.M. Monday through Friday at the Arboretum office.

The note cleared up the question of where the wanted man had overnighted Monday. He'd slept in the arboretum area and abandoned his blue shoulder bag before driving east over the Lake Washington bridge Tuesday morning to attack one woman and rob another. After that . . . the trail died.

The team of IBar Arrington and Dennis Mackey chased down one lead after another.

Elaine Gere passed them a psychic's tip that Green was holed up in a shack near a power line in the Granite Falls area. Just after dark Wednesday, the warriors made a running assault, hit a chest-high string of barbed wire, and went sprawling. They broke through the door and found marijuana plants under grow lights.

Some of their work proved more useful. They helped to flush a pedophile who'd been sitting in his pickup outside an elementary school and making overtures to children. The students were already on edge over the Gere case. Most were convinced that Brenda had been sold into white slavery.

The degenerate was about sixty, with a round, pleasant face and a Santa Claus beard. "Hi," he would tell a little girl. "I'm just a grandpa. It's okay to get in my truck. I've got candy." Then he would reach for her crotch.

Lesley Caveness learned the lurker's address by checking his license number through her private contacts. It proved to be in an upscale neighborhood of Seattle. Dennis and IBar drove past the house and spotted the truck in front.

IBar dialed the man's phone from a booth. "What the fuck are you doing at that school, old man? Bothering little kids? I see you again, pervert, I'll feed you your dick for breakfast."

The man stammered, and IBar hung up. He dialed the number every day for a week with the same simple message, "Soon, old man. Soon." The pickup didn't reappear at the school.

21

On Wednesday evening, Dick Cress learned what Joe Gere had meant when he spoke of sleeping with the devil. Cress and Lesley Caveness were in the Geres' kitchen preparing box lunches for the next morning's searchers when a black Lincoln Town Car slid to a stop in the driveway and four men in topcoats emerged, neatly arranging their hats and ties as they walked up the back steps. A detective who'd been conferring with Joe said, "Jesus Christ, I can't be here for this," and hurried away.

Joe opened the door for his visitors and said, "Lou! Thanks for comin'." He ushered the visitors into the other room.

In her usual machine-gun style, Lesley asked Cress, "You know who those guys are don'tcha?"

Cress said that they looked like extras from *The Godfather*. He peeked into the living room. The two older men lit cigars as the two younger ones dipped into the hors d'oeuvres that were kept on a long table to sustain family and troops.

Holy Jesus, Cress thought, Lesley's right. They have that sinister aura. You can see they're something special—or think they are. Something malevolent, too. He wondered if these John Gotti wannabes were aware of how banal they looked in their $600 suits. Did they really want to stand out in a part of the country where a dress outfit consisted of a wool work shirt from Eddie Bauer, holey jeans and worn moccasins? Maybe, he thought, the evil persona was deliberate, part of their act, their threat, making things easier when they shook down store owners and shylocked their loans. He was glad that such characters had never had a foothold in the Pacific Northwest.

The living-room session was sotto voce and short, and Joe ushered the men out. When Elaine drifted into the kitchen to help with the sandwiches, the irrepressible Lesley asked, "Were those guys who I think they were?"

"They're friends from California," Elaine said, and quickly corrected herself: "Friends of the family. Uh, friends of friends. Like . . . distant acquaintances."

"They're the mob," Lesley said. "They're crooks." Euphemisms had never been her style.

"No," Elaine said abruptly.

"All they need is shoulder holsters."

"They're wearin' 'em."

Linda Barker, the local ramrod at Families and Friends of Missing Persons and Victims of Violent Crime, was outraged when Cress recounted the events of the evening and ordered him to call off the organization's participation in the search. Cress promised to comply, but his fingers were crossed. The police search had already ended. If the others quit, no one would be looking for Brenda. What the hell do we care, he asked himself, if a few criminals help out? I'd cut a deal with the devil himself if it would help me find the SOB who killed my son. Who can blame the Geres for seeking help?

On the other hand, Joe's drinking and desperation were turning him into a problem. He talked to his brother-in-law Jimmy about hanging Green from a meathook. Other fantasy solutions were under discussion daily in the Gere living room. Cress thought, Who wouldn't be losing touch with reality on two bottles a day?

He decided to move the search headquarters from the Gere house to Fire District Seven in Clearview, where there were multiple phone lines, scanners, blackboards, pulldown maps and bottomless cups of coffee provided by Chief Rick Eastman. They would move in the morning. Cress sliced off some Monterey jack, opened a jar of mayo, and made another sandwich.

Later the search leader and his colleagues learned what the underworld figures reported to Joe. No one involved in the case—Michael Green, Diana, the Pittmans, the gym owners where Green worked out, his former employers and Diana's present employer—was connected to any Mafia family or activities. Brenda wasn't in the hands of a mob porno ring, nor had she been sold into white slavery, nor was she part of an organized ransom plot. The Mafia despised sex offenders. They gave criminals a bad name.

22

In the second week of the search, the Geres logged some unsolicited help. A bewhiskered biker informed Joe that his club was searching the back roads every night for Green. "If we find the asshole, he's toast." The man explained that the Fontana chapter of Hell's Angels had sent word that the missing child belonged to a bikers' friend named Gere.

In a Seattle bar, Joe ran into an African-American drug dealer he'd sent to prison in California. The man bore no grudge and seemed fascinated by the details of Green's flight. When Joe finished relating the story, the ex-con said, "We got a simple problem here, Deputy Joe. We cut off the mothuhfuckuh's head and put an apple in his mouth. Gimme a call. Glad to help."

The former blood enemies exchanged phone numbers.

* * *

Dennis Mackey promised Elaine that he wouldn't rest till they caught the steroid freak and found Brenda. "Vietnam was my war," he told her. "This is yours. We're foxhole buddies."

His comrade IBar Arrington, the teetotaling former heavyweight boxer, had been suffering from bad dreams. He saw pretty little Brenda being dragged from the house by her hair, flung in the trunk of Green's car, then chained and gagged in a basement.

On their search missions into the countryside, the two friends were sometimes joined by Julio DeSantis, West Point '65, a transplanted New Yorker, former Army Ranger and father of Brenda's friend Annie, and by Dale Caveness, once a sergeant in the Green Berets and husband of the busy searcher Lesley. DeSantis and Caveness recruited a few of their neighbors, including a former Marine "tunnel rat" in Vietnam who enjoyed shooting and eating raccoons.

"Any one of us can take down this punk," Dennis observed optimistically. "Together we'll make him into chicken parts."

The team checked out a tip that Green was hiding in a house about five miles south of the Geres, and Elaine volunteered to go along. IBar hyperventilated on the half-hour drive and Dennis nipped from a pint. They parked in front of the house and Dennis ran around to cover the rear. A man in the driveway stopped him cold with a .38 revolver.

"Wait!" Dennis yelled. "Put the gun down, man. Put—the—gun—down!"

The man said, "Who the hell are you?"

"We're looking for Michael Green, the guy that took the little girl in Clearview."

"That's why I'm here," the man said, holstering his weapon. He was a neighbor and had received the same tip.

A few days later, Dennis, IBar and Elaine sped to a house in Maple Valley on a rumor that Green had been observed at a front window. A burglar alarm went off when they stepped inside, and a short, skinny man catapulted out a side door and jumped into a car.

"Duck!" IBar shouted, and heaved a rock the size of a grenade. It missed the target but almost hit Dennis. The car left a trail of smoking rubber as it wheeled around the corner.

"I guess we got the wrong place," IBar said.

Elaine Mayzsak in South Fontana, age ten.

Big Ed Mayzsak, Evelyn and acres of doomed turkeys.

Adonis of the checkout line—
Joe Gere at seventeen.

(Right) Cheerleader Elaine at
sixteen in the Christmas
parade.

(Below) Elaine with her first
Corvette.

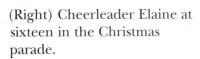

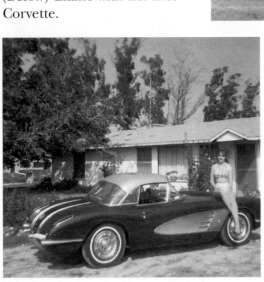

(Above) Members of the wedding—Reva Gere and Joe Sr., Elaine and Joe, Linda, Bob and Rick. (Below) Big Ed, Evelyn and Jimmy Mayzsak at the wedding party.

The bad-tempered officer candidate Joe Gere.

The best times—Deputy Joe just before the mob assault.

Baby Brenda with her parents.

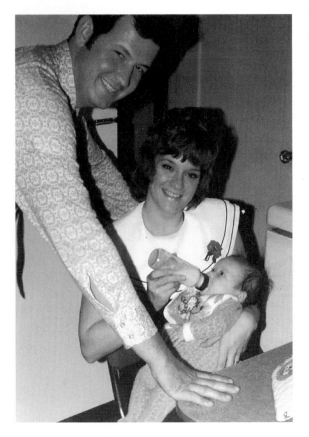

Pals forever—Joe and Brenda.

Brenda, age seven, discovering the joys of sunfishing.

Family portrait—Michael (left), Joe Jr. and Brenda.

Brenda and her dog Kanga.

(Left) The Gere log house. Murderer and victim exited left.

(Below) Easter tragedy—suicide house in Idaho.

Newly svelte for the jury—power lifter and football star Michael Green.

Elaine Gere at forty-nine, indomitable, still making plans.

Back at the Geres' house, the posse members agreed with IBar: "We gotta go to the streets and the bars." They began to call friends and friends of friends. A contact advised them that Green was tight with a former University of Washington football player named Jim Champagne. IBar got on one phone and Dennis another as they played their roles of good cop and bad cop.

Champagne acknowledged that he'd once been friendly with Green but hadn't seen him in years.

"We'd sure like to know where he is," said Dennis, the good cop.

Champagne said he wished he could be helpful.

IBar, the bad cop, said, "If we find out someone's lying to us, man, we're gonna be very unhappy."

Then they were tipped that Green was hiding out in an abandoned cabin not far from the Gere home. They smashed in the door and burst inside. The place was empty.

A deputy pulled up and said, "You guys can help us more by staying the hell home."

23

The Pittmans of Mukilteo wondered how long they would be the subject of pointing fingers, leering faces and snide remarks for sheltering a monstrous pedophile. The picture of the smiling child with braces and bangs had touched hearts south to Oregon and west to Idaho and Montana, and gawkers streamed past the big frame house. When reporters weren't banging on the door or tying up the phone, the cops were hinting that the Pittmans knew more about Michael's whereabouts than they were letting on, and if they didn't cooperate, they could end up in jail as accessories. And there was always that damn car with the Wyoming plates, parked below or circling the block. It was like living in a habitat group at the Seattle zoo.

The pressure began to set one family member against another.

Sharon's husband Donne and daughter Diana lined up on the side of Michael's innocence, while Sharon and son Dan were doubtful. Her side still sore from her daughter's sucker punch, Sharon told her husband, "Di will do anything to get Michael off the hook. *Anything.* She doesn't believe he did the rapes and she thinks the cops are being unfair. I wish I was as sure."

Diana couldn't forgive her mother for talking to the police, and the relations between the two high-strung women became so volatile that Di's attorney instructed her not to speak to Sharon at all, since anything she said might end up in the prosecutor's files. At the lawyer's suggestion, Diana moved a few miles away to the Lynnwood home of her aunt, Sandy Bain, Sharon's sister. It meant that Mike might have trouble reaching her by phone, but at least she would get some peace and quiet.

Instead, Green made a collect call to his former football teammate Jim Champagne, the Seattle real estate broker, and began sputtering into the phone that the cops were after him and he didn't know where to turn. He said he'd tried to reach his wife at her office but couldn't get past the answering machine. He wondered if his old teammate would try to put them in touch.

Champagne asked what the problem was, and Green told him, "Never mind. I'm in deep shit."

"Where are you?"

Green said he was gone from Seattle.

The next day, Friday, September 27, eight days after Brenda Gere had disappeared and five days after Michael Green had "booked," Diana accepted his collect call to her office and warned him not to talk—the phone might be tapped. They agreed to a telephone rendezvous that evening at her Aunt Sandy's. The police didn't know she'd changed addresses and she thought the phone was safe.

That evening, as Sandra Bain listened on an extension, Diana accepted the charges from the operator. Her mother sat on the bed; they were still feuding, but Sharon had learned about the planned discussion and insisted on being at her daughter's side when Mike called.

Diana said later that he talked so fast he sounded as though he were in the middle of a footrace. He told her he'd run out of gas and needed money right away.

She asked why he'd left town, and he repeated his lament about visiting shame on the family. She told him it was better to face whatever he'd done than run like a guilty man.

"I didn't do *anything*," he said. "I was just in the wrong place at the wrong time."

"What about the rapes?" she asked.

"Rapes?" He sounded surprised.

She told him that the police had a warrant for his arrest and had searched the house.

"That's ridiculous," he said. "If they can't get me on one thing, they make up another."

"Mike," said, "you have to come home. I'll do everything I can to help you. You've got to get yourself out of this."

He rambled on about crooked cops. How could a private citizen fight the Snohomish County machine? It would be better to do away with himself than bring more shame on his family. "This is the end of the line," he whined. "I don't even have money for food."

He said he was in Idaho, but refused to be more specific. He told her he loved her and would never do anything to hurt her or the Pittmans.

She said, "Look, Mike, I'm not sending you any money. You've got to get back here and face up to this." She asked him point-blank, "Were you in that house or not?" According to Elaine Gere, the police had the proof.

"Absolutely not!" he said. "I was on the porch, yeah, but not inside. I already told you, Di."

She whispered to her mother on the bed, "He says he wasn't in the house."

Sharon replied in a voice loud enough to carry over the phone, "Well, he better hope to God they didn't find his fingerprints."

Diana repeated the statement to her husband. There was a silence. "Okay," he admitted. "The place was for sale. The door was open and I went inside. But only to see if anybody was home. Then I left."

Diana waved her mother toward the door. "Please, Mom," she said. "This is . . . private."

Sharon stepped into the room where her sister was listening in. A shocked Sandra Bain cupped her hand over the phone and whispered, "He admits he was in the house."

Sharon had known her daughter's charming husband as a wife-beater, philanderer and liar. She doubted that he was a rapist; she was already annoyed at the Snohomish detectives, and she suspected they'd fabricated the charge. But there was no longer the slightest doubt that he was involved in whatever had happened to Brenda Gere. Only a fool or a wife could possibly believe otherwise. She wondered how long it would take her upset daughter to see the truth. In Sharon's opinion, Di wasn't far from the breaking point.

When the phone conversation was over, her aunt told Diana, "You better play this straight. This is no game."

Joe Ward and his colleagues were working late at headquarters that night, as they had every night since the disappearance. The lead investigator felt doubly frustrated at not being able to find either Green or Brenda. He'd given up hope that the child was alive. He would never admit it to the Geres, but at this point he would settle for a body. Then, at least, the shadow of the gallows would fall across Michael Green.

Deputy Bryce Siegel figured that the best way to attack the case was to work on Diana Green. "I interviewed her on my own," he recalled. "I used every tool I had, the whole nine yards. The first time was at the mortgage company. I was in uniform, and I said, 'Come on out to my car for just a minute.' I tried to appeal to her humanity. I said, 'Look, Diana, Joe Gere can't live without knowing where his baby girl is, and I know he's serious.'

"She got in the car and just lost it, broke down completely. She said, 'Please, please, give me a day or two.'

"I didn't realize at the time; that was her pattern. Put you off and put you off. I don't think she knew her own mind.

"I talked to her at her apartment later, and I could see she was thinking about cooperating. She was close. Then she says, 'No, no, no, no. You better go now. Let me think about it.'

"Each time I'd leave she'd hear from Green on the phone and get strong for him again. The typical battered wife. I thought that deep down she was a good person. But she was married to an abuser—say no more.

"I was ready to approach her again when the sheriff got a call from her lawyer. 'One of your deputies is bothering Diana Green. Don't you dare talk to her without me present. And don't harass her.'

"I was shut down. In some ways it was aggravating and in some ways it was just another day in the law enforcement business. You get used to being shut down by lawyers."

Joe Ward had also noticed that Michael Green seemed to exert a strong power over his wife, even in absentia. Ward knew that Michael had abused her, but he couldn't get her to admit it. In Diana's loving eyes, her husband was a red-blooded American boy who'd caught a few bad breaks. When he came home, he would explain everything.

Ward was perusing incoming police teletypes when he noticed that an oversized hulk with dark curly hair had hit adjacent shops in Pocatello, Idaho, on the morning of Thursday, September 26, robbing female clerks at a florist and an apparel shop. His threatening note was written on a paper towel and didn't sound much like the work of a college graduate in English: "Open your till and empty it—or I will blow off your fucking head—any noise and your dead!!"

Ward flashed information about the bodybuilder to the Ada County sheriff in Idaho and added, "Suspect possibly traveling western states." The FBI backed up the teletype with a warrant for Green's arrest on charges of unlawful flight to avoid prosecution, a federal offense. A description of Green was dispatched to eleven western states and the U.S. Border Patrol. The FBI message warned, "Approach with caution. Subject is known to be armed with a knife and reportedly has suicidal tendencies."

Then the authorities in Bountiful, Utah, reported that a knife-wielding man with a football player's physique had just robbed a female real estate agent. The robbery spree continued in an eastbound direction.

Details of her son-in-law's latest felonies reached Sharon Pittman, and she couldn't resist telling Diana, "Have you noticed that every crime he's committed was against women? He's too chickenshit to tackle men."

Diana said she didn't want to discuss the subject.

24

The letter to Diana was written in pencil on a paper towel, post-marked Salt Lake City, and dated September 27, the day after the Pocatello and Bountiful robberies. It bore a dramatic title in stark black underlines, "*My Darkest Hours*," as though it were part letter and part writing assignment.

Michael Green opened on a light note: "Diana my love, what do you think of my writing paper? Its not so bad. Jack Keroac wrote 'On the Road' on a roll of toilet paper."

In his sometimes clumsy style, Green wrote that he might never see her again and how crushing it was to suffer such a "cruel twist of fate." He expanded on his alibi:

> All I did was walk into an unlocked house that was up for sale. God, Di! The front door was wide open. Sure, I would've taken some money if I found some. I looked into a purse it was empty. I did not take anything. It was very scary and I really could not handle it. I am so sorry. It was very stupid and I cannot believe I did it. My head hurts so bad. I felt so desperate and so low. I guess the police were on me so much because somebody must have seen mee go in. Then a local girl disappears at the same time. Obviously who ever is up there looking out after Saint Diana wanted me out of her life. . . .

As always when he was in trouble and needed his wife's support, he rhapsodized about their love:

> In a strange way I feel at peace now. I found out that the love that I crave so badly was surrounding me. The sun was warm because of you . . . the flowers alive

because of you. My smile because you made me special—
you really did. . . . Yes, because of you I had somebody
who took pride in me. God, my insides ache for you!
Just to hold you once more. To gaze into eyes just once ·
more. Diana, go to church. Believe in Jesus Christ.
Because there is a hell. I know—its a personal thing.
My hell is going through eternity without your touch,
your love.

He wrote that he was tired and hungry and "I am no criminal."
He'd gone into a Mexican restaurant and couldn't eat because the
lettuce and tomatoes reminded him of her. He offered some advice.
"God. these fucking tears. . . . You will quit smoking. Meet a man
you can take pride who can give you all those things you deserve.
Promise, Di—hate me and love yourself. Love your family. See them
through this humiliation I have given us. . . . I feel with my parting
you can know true peace and start to find happiness again in all
things."
   He quoted a passage from Elton John's "Indian Sunset": "Now
there seems no reason why I should carry on. . . ."
   The letter ended, "And love you, Di—I always will."

Joe Gere had spent another day poking in the woods for Brenda's
body, turning over leaves and brush, following animal signs and
looking in caves and digs, and just sitting on fallen logs and shaking
his head from side to side. Every few hours he would come home,
gasping and sweating, his hands black with dirt, and throw down
two or three long drinks. He looked pale, shaky, on the brink of
the DTs or exhaustion. Elaine figured that was probably his aim. If
he didn't drive himself till he was ready to drop, he couldn't sleep.
   In bed that Saturday night, nine days after the disappearance, she
was surprised when he stroked her cheek with the back of his hand.
He'd gone to the Kool-Aid pitcher a little less often than usual this
evening, had sat quietly, his face almost pensive as she rushed around
attending to houseguests.
   Joe had always been a gentle, considerate lover, uninterested
unless she was interested. Since their loss, she hadn't felt like sex,
and neither had he.

"Honey," he said softly, "me and you, we gotta be closer than ever."

"I know," she said, lifting his fingertips in her hand.

"Something like, uh, Brenda—it can be hard on a marriage." He fell silent, as though the very name had frozen his tongue. "When I was a cop I saw people go through things like this. First they draw together, then they pull apart. They love each other more, then love each other less. Pretty soon . . . it's over."

She'd never thought about it, but he was right. She could remember any number of marriages that had collapsed under the stress of business setbacks, injury, illness, death. She thought, Look at all the celebrity relationships that can't survive money and fame. Modern marriages were fragile. Theirs, of course, was for life.

"Not us, Joe," she murmured. "Not ever."

"We have to make an effort," he said, turning on his side toward her. "I mean . . . our sex life." Sex had never been his favorite subject of discussion. She figured it was part of being Hungarian. Their sex life wasn't something they'd had to work on.

They made love for the first time in weeks. When it was over, she felt the tears on his face.

25

In the lead investigator's words, "Day after day after day we just kept on being snake-bit." Hardly had Joe Ward found out that the blood on Snoopy wasn't human when the second rape victim failed to select Green in a photo lineup. She was "pretty sure" but not positive.

Then a big break fell through the ceiling. A community leader phoned to say that she'd been nailing up a Brenda poster in a Bothell market when an old man started a conversation.

"You know," he said in a shaky voice, "I was driving past the Gere house the afternoon the little girl disappeared, and I saw a great big guy carrying something over his shoulder. Looked like a rolled-up carpet.''

The woman asked if the package could have been big enough to conceal a twelve-year-old child. The man's rheumy eyes opened wide, and he said, ''Oh, my, yes.''

She asked if he could specify the time, and he said it had been about three o'clock.

She advised him to contact police. This was hard evidence, exactly what the prosecutor needed. There were eight eyewitnesses to Green's movements along Thirty-fifth Avenue, including some who'd seen him trying doors and windows, but no one had observed him with a package. Obviously it had been Brenda's rainbow comforter, with the child inside, dead or dying.

The old man had left the store before the woman realized that she hadn't asked his name. Nor had the storekeeper. They decided it didn't matter. Police would find out when the man got in touch.

He never did.

That was what Joe Ward meant by ''snake-bit.''

Another volunteer, an energetic grandmother, observed a man carrying a naked child into a small house in Edmonds, a Puget Sound community a few miles south of Mukilteo. The girl appeared to be ten or eleven. The man wasn't being gentle.

The investigation was put on hold while police entered the house with drawn pistols. The child, now fully clothed, turned out to be four. Her daddy had neglected to kiss her good-bye, so she'd dashed out to his car at the curb.

Some of the more imaginative searchers refused to let go of the incident. A rumor spread that the Edmonds address was really a ''safe house'' where kidnapped children were chained in cells before being transferred by fishing boat to tramp steamers offshore and thence to Asian ports. The theory gained such momentum that a report was made to the FBI. A few days later, some of the volunteer searchers paid an unauthorized call on the house and found it empty.

Then someone intercepted a CB message to the effect that a man about the size of Michael Green had been seen dumping a large package into a ditch near Thomas Lake. Lesley Caveness tracked the report to a trucker who said he'd heard it from a group of men and women at Alexander's Restaurant in Bothell. A meeting was set up at the bar.

"I brought my German shepherd and my .38 Chief's Special," the speed-talking Lesley said. "I also brought Dick Cress and his wife Kate. She was a nervous wreck 'cause she never went into bars and she thought these people were dangerous. At the last minute Joe and Elaine came along. They were all excited.

"The people we met were from another planet. Three or four guys with some slimy broad—tall, thin, looked like a hooker. Then we noticed she's holding a Bible that's covered with upside-down 666s.

"They started to tell us how Brenda was safe on the sixth planetoid, they'd wrestled her out of the arms of Satan, some such crap. Joe and Elaine hung on every word. Kate's little face turned purple and I thought she was gonna pass out. Dick mouthed a word to me— 'wackos'—and we got the hell out.

"The next day I was in the log house when a police car arrived and a couple of detectives rushed upstairs with Joe. It was all hush-hush. I thought, Oh, my God, they found her! They'd grappled up a pillow slip at a nearby lake and thought it was Brenda's. It wasn't."

Lead investigator Joe Ward warned the Geres not to waste more money on psychics and other information hustlers, but Elaine refused to listen. "It's not his child that's missing," she explained to Lesley.

"We're spread awful thin," her friend cautioned.

"I'll run down leads myself," Elaine said. "And if I can't, Joe will."

A self-described *bruja* shuffled up the driveway with a sheaf of testimonials to her dark powers and asked to be shown the missing child's bedroom. Elaine was glad to comply. The Hispanic woman stroked Brenda's dolls, closed her eyes tightly, and announced, "I see her with a greasy black-haired curly-haired man. Dark skin. I see them driving out of Washington into Oregon."

The witch reported other news "that I heard on the wind." A few days before the disappearance, the woman said, Brenda had confided a premonition of danger to a friend. When the woman couldn't produce a name or initials, Elaine phoned Annie DeSantis, Melanie Bonadore, Michelle Hickey, Jennifer Caveness and several of Brenda's other schoolmates. She learned that Brenda's previously unbeaten soccer team had lost two straight, but nothing about a premonition. Crista Crownover recalled that Brenda had seemed a little down while waiting in the lunch line at school. When Crista had asked what was wrong, she'd replied, "Oh, nothing."

Elaine took this as verification of the psychic's information and sent a sheaf of flyers to police in northern Oregon with a request to display them in Hispanic areas. "My attitude is I don't question anything," she explained to Dick Cress. "I'm gonna get help wherever I can."

Cress understood. A man of science, he'd taken the same approach when his own child turned up missing.

A Nevada psychic wrote that Brenda was being held in a "white clapboard house near power lines and a chemical smell." Elaine asked around, and a firefighter called with the address of an abandoned house that fit the description.

The search party consisted of Brenda's former schoolteacher Debbie Simmons, Lesley Caveness, Elaine and a team of firemen with search equipment. The boarded-up house was under a set of power lines not far from a factory that made fiberglass hot tubs and stank up the area. "This is it!" Elaine cried. "This can't be a coincidence."

She walked up the steps and yanked at one of the boards that had been nailed across the door. "You can't do that!" a fire lieutenant yelled. "That's breaking and entering."

Debbie and Lesley came to Elaine's assistance, and soon they removed the last board. As they took their first steps into the black hole of a house, they noticed that the men had backed out of sight. Flashlights illuminated nothing but junk and scrap. A dark hole seemed to lead into a basement, and Debbie was the only one tiny enough to enter. "I don't want to do this," she yelped as she slid into the opening.

Two greenish sparks shone in her flashlight beam. The animal was too big to be a rat, but she didn't wait to find out. It certainly wasn't Brenda.

Joe Gere's younger brother Bob, a stocker at the Kaiser mill in Fontana till he'd cut off several toes, was staying at the log house with youngest brother Rick to help Joe and his vigilantes pound the truth out of Michael Green. Joe had warned them both, "It's gonna take all three of us."

"No problem," Rick had said. He'd always been willing to do whatever his big brother suggested. "When do we start?"

Bob, who shared the family's drinking problem, was disgusted with psychics and disturbed at Elaine's refusal to turn them away. Joe felt the same, but he was usually off in the woods looking for Brenda when the seers phoned or arrived. He told Elaine, "Honey, these people are horseshit."

Elaine refused to be dissuaded. In press and broadcast interviews, she enlisted public aid in looking for a white van with the word "sound" on the side—on advice from a psychic.

An old man who said he lived nearby called excitedly and said, "Your daughter's alive! She's being held hostage by two guys in a shack! It's right near my house!"

"How do you know?" Elaine asked.

"It's the second time I dreamed it."

Joe and his brother Bob talked her out of rushing to the scene. "Cases don't get solved by dreams," Joe explained as he poured himself a drink.

Elaine said she didn't care if the case was solved with a Ouija board or a fortune cookie or a lucky guess: "I just want Brenda." She poked at her eyes as Joe held her close.

Her spirits reached bottom when she learned that Green had phoned and asked his wife for money. If he'd sold Brenda off, he would be flush. It was the worst blow yet.

She sat up all night, thinking about the monster who'd stolen their daughter and their peace of mind. Half asleep, she saw herself staking out the Mukilteo house and drawing on Green when he drove back home. *I'll make him get out and lay on the ground. I'll shoot his kneecaps off, just to keep him alive. I'll castrate him and skin him alive till he tells me where he put Brenda. I could do it. It wouldn't be as hard as dressing out a steer. . . .*

When she repeated her fantasy to Dennis Mackey, the big ex-Marine said, "Leave that violent shit to me and IBar. We're better at it."

IBar said, "I promise you, Elaine. When we find Green, I'll bring you his heart in my hands. Okay?"

Elaine said it would be a pleasant sight.

26

On Monday, September 30, the eleventh day of Brenda's absence, the Geres made a grasp at normalcy by sending their sons to school and returning to their jobs.

Elaine cried on the drive to the FEMA offices and struggled through her first day by running to the bathroom and locking herself in whenever she thought of Brenda. Her fellow workers didn't mind picking up the slack; many were still searching for the child in their off-time.

Joe lasted a few hours on the used-car lot and then went home. His boss, Will Rohrich, explained, "He wasn't any good to us or to himself. Sat there like a zombie. Couldn't work, couldn't eat, couldn't talk. We knew he had bottles stashed around. No one could sell in that condition."

In a way, Elaine didn't mind Joe's drinking. She was afraid that, without the steady anesthesia, he would already be dead.

"He was turning into a shell," she recalled. "When people came over to ask how we were doing, I would feel comforted, but Joe would run to the refrigerator. And when they left he'd tell me he didn't want 'em back, ever. I'd say, 'What'd they do wrong?' He wouldn't answer, but I already knew. *They mentioned Brenda!* Nobody could mention her around Joe, not even me. So we were denied the comfort of a man and wife sharing their grief."

The boys mirrored their father's silence. Now and then Joey would ask why the police hadn't thrown Michael Green in jail and made him talk, but he hardly ever mentioned his missing sister and closest friend. "Mom," he said as she was tucking him in bed, "I feel really bad about something. Brenda and me had a big argument and I said, 'I wish you were dead.'"

"When was that?" Elaine asked.

"Two years ago. In Maple Valley. Do you think that's why . . . she left?" He started to cry.

She held his bony body close and said, "No, no, Joey. You mustn't think like that. People say things in arguments. It doesn't mean nothin'. Brenda knows you love her."

"How do you know?" he asked in his soft voice.

"Why, she *told* me!" Elaine lied. Brenda was no more demonstrative about love than their dad. But a little white lie might help Joey sleep.

After that scene, she started giving short pep talks at bedtime. "We gotta remember the good memories of Brenda," she would tell the boys. "As long as we have the good memories, we'll have her in our hearts, and she'll never die."

27

By Monday morning September 30, Michael Green had been on the run for a week, and his wife Diana received a collect call from Colorado. By now they'd talked several times on a public phone near her office at Lane Mortgage.

This time he sounded even more forlorn and desperate. Once again she begged him to turn himself in, and once again he was indecisive. He said he was afraid of what Joe Ward would do to him if he returned.

They agreed to another phone rendezvous at noon.

Then Jim Champagne took a call from his former college teammate and offered the same advice for the third or fourth time. If Mike was innocent, the only sensible thing to do was to come home and stand up for himself. No one his size and shape could dodge the law for long, and it was a senseless course anyway. What kind of a life would he have as a fugitive?

In the afternoon Diana talked Green into taking part in a conference call with Joe Ward, attorney David Leen and herself. After each appealed to him to surrender, Green promised to give himself up to the FBI. He said he would call later and tell them where to meet him.

The final call came the next afternoon, Tuesday, his eighth day at large. Green told his lawyer and an FBI agent that he would be in his white Toyota that night at a phone booth in Moraine Park Campground in Rocky Mountain National Park. As proof of his sincerity, he provided the Colorado phone number: 303-586-9995.

He was arrested just before midnight on an unlawful flight warrant. FBI agents found a bodybuilder's belt in the back of the car and wondered if he'd used it to tie up Brenda. The lawmen were impressed by his size and docility. He wore baggy sweats, a puffed-out jacket and surprisingly small running shoes. On the twisting fifty-mile drive from the mountains to the Denver City Police Jail, he volunteered that he'd spent most of the last week in the ski town of Vail and on the University of Colorado campus in Boulder. He said he knew nothing about any crimes in Pocatello, Bountiful, Issaquah or Seattle. As the FBI reported later, he'd fled because "the police in Washington state were trying to frame him for something he did not do."

Elaine Gere took the call from Joe Ward. "Green just surrendered in Denver," he said.

"Thank you, Lord," Elaine exclaimed.

She shook her husband, slumped on the couch, his long legs angling to the floor. "They got Green."

He mumbled, "Great, honey, great." She wasn't sure he understood. She would tell him again in the morning.

She awoke the boys, huddled together in their bed, and told them the news. Little Mikey still slept with the butcher knife under his pillow. Even in broad daylight, the boys were scared to leave Elaine or the house.

Eleven-year-old Joey asked, "Will he give back Brenda?"

"We'll see, honey. We'll see."

She realized that her sons were victims, too, and in all the confusion and strain, they hadn't been getting the attention they needed. Every night they climbed into their double bed in the downstairs room and asked the same question: "Mom, are the doors locked?" If she didn't double-check, they would lie awake.

28

Dick Steiner and John Boren, Seattle PD detectives and family men with a special abhorrence of pedophiles, welcomed the assignment to fly to Denver and return Michael Green to the Northwest. Neither of the middle-aged cops was prepared for the sight that greeted them when the fugitive was led from his cell for a late-night interview.

"He was as big as both of us put together, a good-looking guy, well-groomed, carried himself like the All-American jock," Boren said in a voice and style reminiscent of Sergeant Joe Friday of *Dragnet.* "Short dark curly hair, no neck, massive shoulders, a slightly blown-out look like the Michelin tire ad. When he sat, his thigh muscles wanted to pop through his pants. He acted tense, but he didn't have that watery-eyed look you see in addicts.

"After we gave him his rights, he started mumbling. He says, 'I'm pretty sick. I can't talk straight. Been having kidney problems from taking steroids. Pissin' blood. Makes me ornery.' "

Steiner, a bulky six-footer himself, said, "Michael, we wanted to ask you about some rapes."

Green looked surprised. "I don't know what you're talking about," he said. "I'm not a rapist." He paused, then added, "My attorney told me to say I don't understand my rights and not to talk to you guys."

Both Boren and Steiner realized that they'd heard the key word. They could talk all night to a willing subject, but as soon as the word "attorney" was spoken, they had to be ultracareful.

Green seemed glad to talk with someone from his hometown, but also wary about saying too much. He was obsessed with the idea that Joe Ward was out to get him—not the Snohomish County prosecutor or the Geres or the authorities in other venues where he'd committed serious crimes, just the demonic Ward. "He's been telling my wife stuff about me," Green complained. "None of it's true. He's trying to come between us and ruin my life. He threatened to expose me to the media.''

The officers tried not to look judgmental. Surely Michael Green had bigger worries than being exposed in the media? Such as . . . the gallows?

"That damn Ward made me run," Green was saying. He admitted he'd committed a few misdeeds en route to Denver, but "I was scared and broke." Diana and his new lawyer had restored his optimism. He seemed to think he could square his interstate crimes with apologies and restitution.

He barely mentioned the Gere case, except to say, "Ward's after me on that one, too. I wish I knew where the hell he gets his ideas. I was seen in that area the day she disappeared, but so were a lot of people. I had nothing to do with it."

The next morning, a phalanx of Denver lawmen helped to escort the fugitive to the gate at Stapleton Airport. Muscle-bound guards cleared the way through the lobby. Ankle and belly chains forced the handcuffed Green to take short steps, the links clinking in a syncopated rhythm. When a good-looking woman passed, Green's cavernous chest seemed to grow even larger and his face took on a cocky look. Airport visitors backed against the walls and gawked. One asked if they were shooting a movie.

The two Seattle detectives were practiced in the art of escorting prisoners. Steiner had a simple technique: "You look 'em right straight in the eye and let 'em know who's boss. If they think you're weak or apprehensive, you're in trouble."

Green's size and strength were a problem, and Steiner spoke bluntly. "Michael," he said, "you're under arrest for some very serious felonies. If you make one wrong move, if you even *look* like it, I'm gonna kill ya. Do you understand that?"

Green said, "Okay, okay, I understand. I won't try anything." For a homicide suspect, he seemed uncommonly meek. Word had trickled down from his Denver jailers that the behemoth seemed intimidated by men of any shape or size but was aggressive with women. Still, it wouldn't be wise to take chances.

Protocol called for the senior pilot to choose the prisoner's restraints and to decide whether to disarm the officers. At high altitude, one wild bullet could cause a fatal depressurization. Some pilots were easygoing and allowed criminals to travel unrestrained or handcuffed to an escort.

The Continental Airlines pilot glanced at Green and said, "You can take off the ankle chains, but I want the other stuff kept on. And please—keep your weapons."

The threesome boarded before other passengers and shuffled to the last row of the two-by-two seating. John Boren was blessed with the same trim shape as his alter ego on *Dragnet* and took the aisle seat next to Green. Steiner squeezed into the seat across the aisle.

Attendants interrupted their preflight duties to gape. "We can feed you guys," one said, "but we can't give him utensils."

"No problem," Steiner said. Green shielded his face and stared out the window.

At cruising altitude, John Boren sensed a restlessness in his traveling companion. Neither man had spoken. The handcuffs had been removed long enough for Green to eat a sandwich, then snapped back on. Now Green seemed to be straining at the links.

Boren took a look. The big man's eyes were moist and red. His tanned skin glistened like wet mahogany. Oh, my God, Boren thought, if this guy flips out at thirty thousand feet, we're in the shit.

He'd heard of handcuffs being snapped by exceptionally strong prisoners who used one link as leverage against the other. It had never happened to Boren, but he had no experience with three-hundred-pound bodybuilders.

He decided to treat Green as he would a fractious mare. "Michael," he said soothingly, "is something bothering you? Anything I can do for you?"

Green turned his head slowly, and Boren could see that he'd been crying. "I think I fucked up," he said. "I think I did something awful stupid."

"What was that, Michael?"

"You know about that little girl that's missing up in Snohomish County? I was in a house there, the day she came up missing." He lowered his head to wipe his eyes on his shirtsleeve. "I made a hell of a mistake."

Boren was thinking, Hoo, boy, here we go. He's gonna spill. Let's make sure it's legal.

"Wait a minute, Michael," he said, a little more sharply. "Do you remember your rights? You don't have to say a word about this, you know."

"I know my rights," Green said. "I think they're gonna find my fingerprints inside her house."

"How's that?" Boren asked.

"The day she came up missing, I was driving around that neighborhood, killing time, waiting for my wife to get off work. It's a nice area. I like to walk around there."

He said he entered the driveway to turn around. A car pulled in and the driver appeared angry when she had to back up to let him out. "I told her, 'Look, lady, I'm just turning around.' Then I saw this house next door with a for-sale sign, by appointment only. I drove into the driveway and saw the front door standing open. I thought it was an open house, so I walked right in and hollered hello a couple of times."

"What'd the place look like?"

"It's got a basement, and second-floor bedrooms. The guy's a hunter. I was afraid he'd come home and shoot me."

"How d'ya know he's a hunter?"

"There's shotguns and rifles in the upstairs closet. And a bow and arrow on the wall. There was a dog in back, looked like a Doberman. He didn't bark."

Boren waited silently for more words. Voluntary admissions were admissible in court, but as soon as an interrogator began to push and plead, delicate legal considerations came into play. It was best not to prompt.

Green turned to look out the window and tugged on his handcuffs like a man shooting his French cuffs. The detective concluded it was a nervous tic rather than an escape technique. Where would the guy go at thirty thousand feet?

Green sounded more controlled as he continued his story. "So I'm upstairs, I'm thinking, Mike, you idiot! Get the hell outta here. There's no real estate agent in this house. Somebody's gonna find you in here and you're in trouble."

Boren said, "About what time was all this?"

"Between two-thirty and three-thirty."

"Was it the same house the missing girl lived in?"

"I don't know," Green said. "It was a log house, about seventy-five yards back from the road. Big Dutch doors in front."

He said he panicked and left. As he was pulling out of the driveway he saw a boy staring at him from the front window of the house next door. "I thought, Oh, God, he's seen me."

Boren asked if he remembered the assault on Krista Klawa, a crime that fell under the jurisdiction of the two Seattle detectives. Green said he'd talked to Detective Ward on the telephone before deciding to flee Seattle, then hung around the University District for a few hours trying to steal a car so he could leave the Toyota for his wife.

"But I didn't know how to hot-wire or pick a lock. I didn't mean to hurt the lady. I panicked when she screamed and I pushed her away."

Boren waited for him to mention the fifteen-foot embankment, but he left out the part about throwing the woman over. "I could've snapped her neck if I wanted to," he went on, as though to show his compassion. "I had my arm around her. With my strength, it would've been no problem."

He said he drove to the arboretum and wrote a suicide note after giving up on the Klawa car. That was where he'd abandoned the backpack that was found later. Boren asked, "What made you change your mind about killing yourself?"

Green said he didn't know. In the morning, he'd driven east to put more distance between himself and the relentless Ward. He said he couldn't discuss the incidents on the road; "My lawyer's taking care of those."

After a few minutes of silence, he seemed to become agitated again. "Hey, tell me about the little girl," he said as Steiner leaned across the aisle to listen in. "What kind of girl was she? Do you know what she was wearing?"

When Boren admitted that he didn't know the details of the Snohomish case, Green said, "Well, everybody's making her out to be such a little angel. How do you know she didn't go into the woods to smoke a joint or maybe she was meeting some guy in the woods for sex? She might have been a bitch instead of a nice girl like everybody else is saying."

Steiner caught the remark from his seat across the aisle. These sociopathic killers, he said to himself. They'll talk for hours about how gentle they are and how they didn't mean to do anything to anybody and it was all just a big misunderstanding. But sooner or later they'll lift off the top of their skulls and give you a peek inside. *She might have been a bitch.* . . . Wasn't that a lovely remark to make about somebody's missing child?

When the delegation arrived at the King County Jail in downtown Seattle, the dinner carts had come and gone. A helpful officer went out to buy the newcomer a deli sandwich and a carton of milk. After Green ate, he was allowed to call his wife and lawyer and assigned a cell.

Boren and Steiner couldn't wait to brief Joe Ward. The lead investigator sounded relieved and excited at the fugitive's description of the log house. "He's nailed it exactly," Ward said over the phone. "That son of a bitch was *inside!*"

Now, he told the Seattle detectives, there might be enough evidence to justify an indictment—provided, of course, that they found Brenda. Or her body.

After Ward informed Elaine about Green's crucial admission, she told her husband, "Remember when I phoned his wife and told her we had proof he was inside the house? Fingerprints and all? I bet she gave him the word, and now he's designing his alibi to fit. Otherwise he wouldn't've admitted a thing."

Joe told her she would have made a hell of a cop.

29

On the morning after Green's return to Seattle, Joe Ward picked up his phone to hear an excited voice saying that she'd just opened a newspaper and spotted a picture of the man who had raped and assaulted her and a girlfriend six years earlier when they were in the sixth grade.

Ward realized that she was talking about the Westside Explorer School rapes. He remembered the case well; he'd worked it as a cop and a young detective. Just about every hand in the department had been involved at one time or another.

He made arrangements for the young woman to look at Green in a lineup and then perused the old files. The two twelve-year-old girls had been walking to school when they were approached by a leviathan with curly medium-length brown hair, a beard, mustache, mild acne and an automatic pistol. He shunted them into the woods, made them remove clothes and shoelaces, slapped one and knocked her down, tied her spread-eagled to a pair of small trees and raped her repeatedly. The other child wasn't violated. The assailant tied their hands behind their backs with the shoelaces, then ran off. The girls walked to a nearby golf course, where two foursomes observed their dishevelment, giggled and played through. The victims continued on to school and made a report.

A police composite sketch of the suspect fluttered from the old folder. The drawing resembled Michael Green with facial foliage added. The bodybuilder had never been a suspect in the unsolved case.

Ward sent for the physical evidence, including the rape kit with dried scrapings from the victim's vagina and other specimens. At a minimum, the semen would divulge the rapist's blood type, and new forensic techniques in DNA testing might connect Green directly to the crime.

Ward was told that the material had been discarded. A deputy prosecutor advised that the case was dead; the five-year statute of limitations had expired a few months earlier.

In the conversation, both the prosecutor and the detective came to a painful realization. The judicial clock had started running when the rapes were reported, but a peculiarity of the law allowed a restart if the suspect left the state. The object, of course, was to keep criminals from absenting themselves till the statute of limitations ran out, then returning home immune to prosecution. By now both men knew that Green had left Mukilteo a few years back to work for Snap-On Tools Corporation in Arizona. The clock could have been restarted on his return, the case reactivated and prosecuted. But the physical evidence had been destroyed.

The two victims positively identified the bodybuilder and insisted on pressing charges. It bothered Ward to have to break the bad news. These sensitive young women had been assaulted, kidnapped, humiliated and abused, made the victims of a crime that would trouble their minds for the rest of their time on Earth. They deserved satisfaction. Sometimes the justice system was itself unjust. Detectives learned to understand that. Rape victims didn't.

The next sign that the Brenda Gere investigation remained star-crossed came a few days later in the form of a hot-line call from the FBI crime lab in Washington. A serologist wanted to know, "What's the deal with this blood you sent?"

"What blood?" Ward asked.

"This human blood you sent for kerotyping."

Ward felt as though he'd been punched in the face. The blood specimens from Dick Vandyke's sheepdog Snoopy were *human?* But the Washington State Crime Laboratory had reported weeks ago that the blood came from a nonhuman source, and photographs of the bloodstains had been discarded.

He held the phone against his ear while the FBI chemist explained why the complex tests had taken so long. As far as Ward could follow the polysyllabic phrases, the chemist was saying that the sample had been difficult to analyze because it consisted of human blood mixed with dog saliva.

The lead investigator shook his head dolefully. The Snoopy lead was dead.

When Elaine Gere found out what had happened, she fired off a letter to U.S. Senator Slade Gorton, accusing the state crime lab of blowing a call that might have led them to her missing daughter and spared the family anguish.

She didn't expect any heavy reaction from the other Washington, but she wanted her complaint on the record. A pro forma reply said that the senator had checked the case and "the police did all they could do."

30

By mid-October, the hunt for Brenda Gere was winding down, but the news that Michael Green was stubbornly refusing to talk revitalized the effort. Citizens were annoyed, enraged, puzzled, insulted, but mostly challenged. They took Green's silence as a personal affront, a gratuitous cruelty of a piece with his others. Mass empathy for the Geres swept the area; Brenda became the child that everyone had lost or feared lost or never had.

Neither Dick Cress nor any of the other search veterans had ever seen such a reaction. Volunteers converged on the log house, the Clearview fire station, and the old rallying point at Thrasher's Corner shopping center. Local newspapers and broadcast stations kept the story in the public eye.

Phone lines hummed with tips and information, some from as far away as Florida. Many calls were collect, and the Geres saw to it that charges were always accepted. Although the official search was over, off-duty deputies and city cops from Everett, Lynnwood, Edmonds and other towns pitched in with Snohomish County Sheriff Bob Dodge, Sergeant Tom Pszonka and his wife and children and other police families to hunt for Brenda.

"We're so limited financially," the sheriff explained to Julio DeSantis as the two of them hacked their way through a maze of vine maples. "We don't have a large tax base. But I'll be damned if I'm gonna quit on this case."

Deputy Bryce Siegel, searching on his day off, told the Geres that the sheriff's office was taking dozens of calls from angry residents. "They say, 'If you can't convict that Green of taking Brenda, turn him loose out here at One-eightieth and Thirty-fifth Avenue and *we'll* convict him.' I only wish we could."

* * *

Elaine Gere stoked the publicity fire with frequent media interviews. A team of searchers arrived from Vancouver, British Columbia, followed by Explorer Scouts from Tacoma and elsewhere. The commanding general at Fort Lewis, sixty miles south of Clearview, dispatched helicopters equipped with "sniffers," and for days the searchers worked to the snarling sounds of the blades.

The renewed search took on some of the aspects of a business, with planning sessions, tables of organization, printed instruction books, flowcharts, spreadsheets, grids. Teams consisted of baggers, scratchers, beaters, dragliners, bulldozer operators, pumpers (to drain swampy areas), loggers (to clear stumps and undergrowth) and worker bees preparing coffee and field rations. Lesley Caveness manned the phones at her own home and at the search headquarters, scribbling at top speed with the hand that had once accompanied her to the hospital in a box. She wrote on anything handy: notepads, napkins, pages ripped from phone books, doilies, cereal boxes, menus, coasters, legal pads and index cards. Sightings were logged from Woodstock, Illinois, and Woodstock, New York, Corpus Christi, Sacramento, Phoenix, both Kansas Cities, San Antonio, Los Angeles, and Greenup, Kentucky, and other sightings were reported on the National Hotline for Missing Children.

The paperwork mushroomed into tall stacks leaning against one another in an anteroom of the fire station headquarters. Dick Cress's field orders were Xeroxed daily, along with advice and instructions from other search leaders: "Canvass this neighborhood again. . . . Watch for nosy neighbors. Might know more than they're telling. . . . Look for breaks in symmetry—people telling two different stories. . . ."

A Green River Killer task force detective addressed the searchers on the latest techniques for finding human remains. At the talk, Lesley Caveness learned a useful acronym, GOYBKOD, and began adding it to all search correspondence. It stood for "Get off your butt and knock on doors." Lesley suspected that the original version was GOYAKOD, much easier to pronounce.

By the third week after the disappearance, the number of processed tips had reached three hundred, and not a hair or fingernail from Brenda Gere had turned up. "We were still working a lot of nonsense leads," said Julio DeSantis. "Elaine wouldn't let us ignore any of 'em. Sometimes we'd go out with a dog and lose the dog. Most of us were businessmen, a little soft, and the damn hounds outran us. IBar Arrington was the only guy the dogs couldn't shake. He said it was like doing roadwork.

"On one stupid tip from one stupid psychic, I went into an abandoned cabin and got the hell out when I heard a growl. The psychic didn't mention the black bear. We turned up a wild man living alone in the woods, dope stashes, marijuana patches. We came across a stolen motorcycle north of Everett and a cache of stolen electronic equipment at an abandoned cemetery. We kept checking *every* lead. It was like throwing mud at a wall and seeing what stuck."

A thousand posters were nailed up and twice as many handed out at schools, theaters, markets, malls and other public places. The workers scratched out the word "missing" and substituted "abducted" with their Magic Markers. The number of "specific searched scenes" passed forty. Toilet paper marked the searched areas, hanging from stately maples, spruces and cedars and garnishing the rhododendrons and rose bushes in formal gardens.

Like many of the searchers, DeSantis found his personal life affected by the pressure-cooker atmosphere. "My wife and I were hollering at each other all the time. I put my insurance business on ice. Clients would call to talk about buying a policy and I'd say, 'I'll get back to you when I get back to you. Our Annie's friend is missing.' Bills went unpaid while I was on my knees digging up animal parts. I left eleven pounds in those damn woods, and most of it was bone. We were bughouse, obsessed. Goddamn it, we were gonna find Brenda!"

The Caveness family briefly lost cohesion, but Lesley found it hard to give up the search. "You can't imagine the intensity," she said. "We were like, My God, this *can't* be happening in our neighborhood. This did *not* happen to one of our kids. We gotta find Brenda! That search was a hot flame. It burned families and kids, disrupted relationships that had lasted for years.

"Our children felt abandoned, and they were right. Dozens of kids went into counseling, even boys. My junior high daughter put on black clothes and blackened her nails and her hair, sort of a subtle mourning. She could have used some counseling, but I was too busy looking for Brenda. We couldn't stop. We were like compulsive gamblers in Las Vegas. *We didn't hit the jackpot this week or last week, but Brenda'll show up around this bend or under that log or at the end of this trail....*

"Good God, the excitement, the vitality! In its own odd way it was an exalting experience, people working together, crying together, shivering and shuddering, falling down and helping each other up.

"Helpers came from everywhere. A man named Langlois arrived, I think from Canada. Had this funny little French accent. He claimed he'd perfected a device that could locate buried bones, like a water witch. He was an engineer, college degrees up to here. He showed me this thing with wires and dials, and I thought, How do I get rid of this crackpot? We drove him up to Thomas Lake, and he really found bones! I took 'em to the animal hospital where I worked. The vet said they were from deer."

Total strangers bypassed the sign-in rules established by search leader Dick Cress, wandered through yards and woods and mingled with search teams, adding to the general paranoia. Whole shifts were wasted on anonymous phone tips from pranksters. "The little Gere girl? She's eating a sundae at Baskin-Robbins . . . walking through Alderwood Mall . . . just came in and ordered a Big Mac . . . riding the Edmonds ferry with a man."

A detailed map of Brenda's whereabouts appeared one morning in the Gere mailbox. It was marked with a big X and a childish scrawl: "Mom and Dad. I am HERE."

Cress, a former pilot, pored over the map with Joe Gere, Dale Caveness, Julio DeSantis and other military veterans with a knowledge of cartography. It took three or four brainstorming sessions and several trips into the bush to conclude that they'd been hoaxed again.

Suspicion began to fall on innocent neighbors—the Bonadores, the Munsons, an elderly woman down the street, even on the Geres themselves. For a while, Dennis Mackey and IBar Arrington wondered about their fellow Clearview commando. After a few drinks at the Geres' living-room bar one night, Dennis asked offhandedly, "By the way, Julio, where were you when Brenda disappeared?"

"Up in Bow, feeding some cows I own," DeSantis replied.

"Weren't you supposed to drive Brenda to soccer?"

"Yeah."

"Well, why the hell didn't you?"

Julio frowned and said, "Gee, I don't remember, Dennis. Something came up. Why?"

"Oh, nothing," Dennis said. He was thinking, This fucking Rambo could be dirty. It's possible. Why's he always picking our brains? One thing for sure, his cows won't alibi him out of this one.

The next morning, the ex-Marine awoke with a clearer head and realized he'd been confused. Julio had been breaking his ass to find Brenda. If anyone was beyond suspicion, it was Julio.

Dennis berated himself. "Booze and Brenda and that shitheel Green," he mumbled, "they're making me crazy." He knew he had to shorten his drinking sessions, especially with Joe Gere and his brothers. Too many wild ideas flew around the log house. The latest plan involved punching a cop, getting thrown into the Snohomish County Jail, where Green was now ensconced, following him into the shower, and squeezing his nuts till he turned soprano or told the truth.

It had sounded like such a good idea at the time.

31

As the search entered its second month, the frustrations produced an occasional sharp exchange. Armed parents escorted their children to bus stops and derided police. Letters to the sheriff's department complained about official inaction. The raffish Mackey referred to the unsuccessful bloodhounds as "those buffoon dogs," enraging handlers who'd spent hundreds of hours in the woods without pay. Every stranger became an object of suspicion. A taciturn man in high-top sneakers and a scarred leather jacket was asked why he was hanging out at search headquarters. He turned out to be a teacher from one of Brenda's grade schools. She hadn't attended his classes, but he'd read about the case and wanted to help.

The field expeditions ended abruptly for one of Brenda's teachers, Don Halazon, when he stepped into a pit at Thomas Lake, fell six feet, and tore nerves and tendons in his arm so severely that doctors warned he might never be able to raise his hand above his shoulder again, ending his days at the blackboard.

Charlene Richardson, Brenda's sixth-grade teacher at Canyon Creek Elementary, found herself driving a daily giro around Snohomish County, tacking up missing-child posters and replacing the old ones when she wasn't thrashing through the woods. She still turned teary when she thought about the first word of Brenda's disappearance, how she'd tried to explain the situation to her sixth-graders and ended up making everyone cry, including herself.

Some of her students were in counseling, terrified that the monster man would return, and the teacher herself never failed to check her closets and bathtub for intruders before going to bed at night.

Making her rounds with the Brenda posters, she had little patience with reluctant store owners who thought the displays were bad publicity or relegated them to a far corner of the store. "This child comes from *this* neighborhood," she would tell a merchant in emphatic tones, as though he were hard of hearing. "I'm sure your *customers* will appreciate your help."

At night Debbie Simmons and her husband Nate drove the back roads of Bothell and Clearview, looking for places where bodies might have been thrown into the brush.

"I had the strongest feeling Brenda was in a little glade not far from her house," the teacher recalled. "Dick Cress told me the whole woods had been searched by dogs, but I went in anyway and found some small vertebrae that looked human. I took 'em to a veterinary clinic and they didn't want to get involved. Doctors at a medical clinic acted like I was unstable. I called Joe Ward and he told me to bring 'em in. The crime lab said they were from a raccoon."

Early one evening the Simmonses sifted the wrack on the beach below the Pittman house in Mukilteo. Whitecaps punctuated the water surface like commas. The sun set behind Whidbey Island, producing its customary late-summer streaks of chrome and flamingo.

Nate's theory was that Green had tossed Brenda's body into the sound on an outgoing tide, and sooner or later it would wash up. They found crab shells, a dead squid, seaweed, and some bottles.

Driving home, Debbie flashed on an idea. "If Green's in-laws knew what kind of kid Brenda was," she told Nate over coffee, "they'd help us, I'm sure. She's just a name to them, a nothing. Let's drive back and see if they'll talk."

Nate was reluctant. "Don't you think they've been bothered enough? They're not responsible for Michael Green."

"Diana married him."

Her husband's sour expression showed what he thought of that line of reasoning.

Debbie pleaded, "Couldn't we just drive by? Maybe somebody'll be in the yard. I could say I'm Brenda's sister. I'll walk up and say, 'We understand you're upset about this, but could you maybe give us a little information?'"

Her enthusiasm prevailed. When they drove down the long hill toward the water and reached the turnoff to the Pittman house, Nate said, "I really don't think we should do this."

"I'll go up," she said. "I'm not intimidating."

"Debbie—"

"Nate, I have to do it."

The big house lay in gray-black shadow. She walked up to a large door, knocked softly, then harder. The door was slightly ajar, and she peeped inside. Atop a small table, a gun pointed square at her face.

They got away fast. Nate said the Pittmans had probably positioned the gun as a warning. Debbie gasped, "They made—their point—with me."

Sharon Pittman was fed up with the anonymous letters, the gawkers and strollers, the policemen who slowed as they drove past and peered inside as though expecting to spot a criminal act through the drapes. She wasn't surprised when a friendly deputy told her about the Simmonses' pistol sighting. She explained that in three decades of marriage, she and her husband had never allowed a weapon in the house, not even a .22 rifle or a .410 shotgun. The "dangerous weapon" on the table had been a paint-pellet gun. The boys yelled "You're dead!" and spattered one another with gobs of washable paint.

Sharon was also fed up with Joe Gere and his bumptious cronies and relatives. She suspected that most of the threatening phone calls were from Joe himself because the wording was similar. The threats usually came at night, when her husband Donne was away at his baking job. In the same thick voice, the man would say, "We know where you live, where your kids go to school. We'll pick 'em off one by one."

She tried to reason, but the man didn't seem to hear. In desperation, she called Joe Ward. "Look," she said, "Joe Gere's gotta stop harassing us. He's got us terrified. I know he's upset, but who knows what a guy like that'll do when he's drinking?"

The lead investigator promised to make a phone call. The threats stopped.

32

With Christmas approaching, Elaine couldn't decide who was closer to the edge, her husband or her sons. Mikey, Joe and Joey moped around, woke up sweating, had trouble concentrating. The boys sat in front of the TV for hours, lost their capacity for joy and play. They no longer slept in their first-floor bedroom; it was too frightening to be in the back of the house. Instead they pitched sleeping bags in the living room.

Lesley Caveness eased matters by inviting the Gere boys to her home for overnights with her ten-year-old son, Andrew. They rented movies, downed pepperoni pizza with double cheese, traded baseball cards and comic books, converted their plastic Transformers into imaginative shapes, and chattered endlessly about Brenda and Michael Green and what might have happened the day Brenda picked up the mail and disappeared.

"We can't talk about that kinda stuff at home," Joey explained. Lesley saw that the conversations were therapeutic. The boys had to confront the tragedy sooner or later; why not now, when they were closest to Brenda's loss and still hurting?

Sometimes Andrew Caveness slept on the Geres' floor in his own sleeping bag. There were difficult moments. One morning at breakfast he gave a little gasp when he noticed that his plate bore the name "Brenda" in a childish scrawl.

"Brenda made that plate at school," the father explained.

"Yeah?" Andrew said, looking down. When he raised his head, he saw that Mrs. Gere and the boys were trying not to cry, and Mr. Gere was gone.

At night the father would lie on the couch, sipping at his Kool-Aid. Lesley thoroughly disapproved but said nothing to her friend Elaine.

"I can sympathize with alcoholics," she told her husband Dale, "but you don't lay there on the couch hour after hour with your body half on the floor for your children to see. Come on! I can't forgive Joe. He leaves *everything* to Elaine. My God, Dale, she suffers, too! Joe's not the only one who lost Brenda. How long can she last?"

Joe took another crack at his job in Bothell but sold few cars. His income added up to less than he spent on vodka, Jack Daniel's, VO and rounds of drinks for his barroom friends. Dennis Mackey, who worked part-time on the same lot, sometimes drank with him but seemed more resistant to alcohol. One night the ex-Marine philosophized to Elaine about the situation:

"Selling cars is an attitude. Your head's gotta be right. It's not like digging a hole with a shovel. Joe's head is way off somewhere. When he's not drinking, he's staring into space. I opened the door of a demo car the other day and a pint of VO fell out. Found another bottle hidden behind the Dumpster. Joe's into full-blown acute alcoholism. His liver's shot. It's drip drip drip—whiskey, vodka, beer, anything. He might as well mainline it, shoot it up." He shook his head. "What a way to mourn your kid."

Elaine insisted that Joe's problem went beyond the loss of Brenda. "It's the way he was raised, Dennis. Drinking was a tradition in Fontana. Joe might've broken out, but after he was beat up he got the idea he wasn't a man anymore. He'd say, 'Hon, I have to drink for the pain.' His mom used the same excuse."

Elaine almost cried when one of the salesmen told her about a scene at the car dealership a few days later. Joe had posted Brenda's pictures around the lot so that her smile and braces were visible in any direction. "We didn't think it was a good idea," the salesman said, "but if it helped Joe—what the hell."

He'd been in the greeting stage of a sale when the customer caught sight of one of the pictures and said. "That's the missing girl, isn't it?"

"Yeah," Joe said. "She's my daughter. She's—"

Joe turned and walked off the lot. No one had the heart to call him back.

His commissions continued to shrink. Before September 19, he'd racked up ten to fifteen sales a month; now he was down to three or four, some shared with his colleagues.

In early November, Elaine took a call at her office from Will Rohrich, owner of E.A.L. Motors. "You better get over here," he said. "There's something wrong with Joe."

"What's the matter?" she asked.

"He's just sitting here shaking. Can't walk, can't talk. I don't know what the hell it is."

Elaine caught the smell as soon as she entered the overheated office. Joe gave her a wan smile. She grabbed him under the arms and announced they were going to detox.

"I don't know why we didn't help her take Joe to her car," Dennis Mackey said later. "We were just stunned by the sight of this woman dragging this two-hundred-pound guy and haulin' ass. You could still hear her tires when she was a block away."

In a week and a half, Joe dried out, but his morale stayed low. One of the therapists briefed Elaine: "We can't do any more with him. He balks at the step where you tell the group about your excess baggage so you can get rid of it. Mr. Gere won't cooperate."

Elaine recognized a lifelong problem. "He's too proud," she explained.

The therapist said that Joe was having a negative effect on the other patients and required psychiatric treatment that was beyond the small clinic's capacity.

On the drive home, Joe griped, "I don't know why you can't solve an alcohol problem without telling your whole goddamn life to a bunch of strangers."

There it is again, she said to herself. That darn tight-ass old-world Hungarian syndrome. *That's my business. . . . That's personal. . . .*

Another kamikaze drinker thought he understood Joe's problem. "He's just one big seething mass of anger," Dennis told IBar on one of their midnight patrols. "Anger at Green, anger at losing Brenda, anger at Mother Theresa, everything, everybody. The only thing that'll shape him up is finding Brenda and killing Green. Or total lockup in a padded cell for six or eight months. Any other treatment is Band-Aids and bullshit." IBar said he was certainly glad he didn't drink or smoke.

After a few days at home, Joe returned to E.A.L. Motors and a gelid reception. "I just couldn't have him working here no more," the plainspoken Will Rohrich explained later. "He wasn't fired, but he woulda been. Joe was a great guy, our best salesman. He was an ex-GI and I was a Marine machine-gunner in Vietnam. We had a lot of things in common. But booze wasn't one."

With Joe out of work again, the family had to make do on Elaine's salary at FEMA and the disability pension from San Bernardino. Their twin Corvettes were distant memories; Elaine had bought a used Chevette to save on gas, and Rohrich allowed Joe to drive a demo truck till he found another job.

But Joe wasn't looking for work. He'd replaced his whiskey, vodka and Kool-Aid cocktails with light wine but seemed to drink more than ever. "That'll never work," Dennis told Elaine. "He'll just drink more and more till he reaches the same level. You watch."

Soon Joe was up to a quart and a half of fortified wine a day and arguing for more credit at the deli and liquor store. The family's living costs remained high; long-distance collect calls still arrived, usually from psychics offering charts and maps showing Brenda's precise whereabouts, or from airy theorists who'd examined the case logically and had answers for every question—except the most important.

Lesley Caveness arrived at the log house on a chilly November morning and found the two sons shivering in front of the fireplace. "Hey, you lazy guys," she joked, "why don't you start a fire?"

Joey said they'd run out of firewood and wouldn't have money for more until the next disability check from California.

"When'll that be?" Lesley asked. The weatherman had predicted a long, cold winter.

"Dunno," little Mikey piped up. "Mom said awhile."

The boys said their mom was at work and their dad was sleeping. "Did you guys have a good breakfast?" Lesley asked.

"Oh, yeah!" the boys chorused. Lesley didn't doubt it. Elaine and Joe would go hungry before they would skimp on the boys' meals. She wondered why Elaine hadn't mentioned the firewood shortage and the obvious financial crush. That damn Gere pride, she said to herself. They'll freeze first. They must be paying five hundred bucks a month in phone bills, and who knows how much Elaine gives those psychics?

Lesley returned home and filled the back of her van with firewood. "Forget about it," she told Joe when he asked how much he owed. "Wood we got. We live in a forest."

Dale, her husband, was driving for Frito-Lay at the time, and he brought home a load of discontinued beef jerky and smoked sausages. Lesley dropped the meat off at the log house a bag or two at a time so the charity wouldn't be noticed.

One day Joe called and asked if they had more. When Lesley delivered another box, Joe said they could use some firewood. Lesley thought about the change in the Geres' lifestyle since Brenda's disappearance. Begging food and wood. What a fall.

When word of the financial crisis reached Dennis and IBar, the big-hearted musclemen decided to run a surprise benefit and scheduled it for December 2 so the Geres would have cash to spend on Christmas. For years the two cronies had successfully arranged private parties, sports events and other moneymaking promotions. Between IBar's boxing career and Dennis's career as a salesman and barroom bon vivant, they figured they'd met half the citizens of Snohomish County.

They printed posters and tickets, placed radio and newspaper ads, hired a hall and a live band, and applied pressure to friends, acquaintances and enemies to buy tickets "so we can help Elaine and Joe bring their daughter home."

A high-pressure center swirled down from Alaska in the last hours of November, and the benefit was held on the coldest night of the year. Starting at dawn, radio and TV news programs had advised citizens to stay home. Salt trucks parked on shoulders, ready to begin de-icing. Shopkeepers lowered their shutters early and hurried home with their collars turned up.

The Brenda Gere benefit turned a profit of $104. Joe Gere accepted the money despite what Elaine said was his "total humiliation." He drank it up in a week.

For Christmas, Joe bought Elaine a pair of white denim jeans and she bought him a hunting knife and a goose call. The boys received a set of plastic He-Man figures from the Sears catalog and some Transformers. Dozens of hand-inscribed cards and small presents arrived from Brenda's schoolmates, and Charlene Richardson's sixth-graders sent a festive box of individually signed cards and a purse full of cash collected door-to-door.

Elaine decorated the windows as she did every year, trying to maintain the holiday spirits, and the boys helped her dress a small tree. Brenda looked back at her from every piece of tinsel.

Dick Cress and a few stubborn searchers drove up to the log house to exchange season's greetings on their way to the latest sighting. Elaine was raking leaves in the front yard. She usually looked made-up and coiffed, the perennially youthful California beach blonde, but today she showed her forty-one years. "Dick," she said, "you've been through this. When does the pain let up?"

"I don't know, Elaine," he said, squeezing her hand. "We lost Patrick two years ago, and it hasn't let up yet."

VII

LIMBO

1

The New Year blew in cold and damp, and Elaine found herself in a losing battle to keep up the family spirits. Most of the searchers were inactive, but old hands like Dick, Lesley, Debbie and Nate, Dennis and IBar were still hacking at underbrush and lifting up logs. There were phones to answer, posters to tack up, new leads and tips to collect and pass to Joe Ward.

Elaine found her husband of little help to her or himself. She served him nourishing meals, stayed out of his way, and tried to keep the boys from disturbing his moods. He still refused to discuss Brenda with those who'd loved her most. It was up to the boys and Elaine to keep her memory fresh.

Now and then he roused himself for a short perambulation in the woods behind the house, but most of his time was spent on the couch, brooding or watching TV with heavy-lidded eyes.

Elaine warmed herself at her sons' childish innocence and resilience, finding comfort in helping them handle their fears and despair. "I saw what was happening to Joe," she said later, "and I thought, What am I gonna do? Collapse like him? What'll become of Joey and Mikey? They were looking to me for strength and they had nobody to turn to. When you lose a child, you have to be careful you don't lose a whole family."

She began to realize that she needed her boys as much as they needed her. "They helped me get through the days. They were my support, I was their support, we were *our* support. Staying busy for my boys—that was the best therapy. After a while, they began to talk to me about Brenda. I thought it would hurt, and it did, but it also helped. One night at bedtime, Joey said, 'Brenda's gone for good, Mom. She's dead in the woods.'

"I wanted to put the best face on things, so I said, 'Remember how Brenda said she never wanted to leave the Northwest? Maybe she got her wish.' Joey agreed that was a good way to look at it. Nobody cried. That's when I realized we might get through this thing. . . ."

She prepared the boys for a different kind of tragedy. "Your dad," she said hesitantly. "This drinking is like a cancer. Do you understand what I mean?"

Wide eyes stared up from the bed. Eight-year-old Mikey said in his little voice, "We know, Mom. We been talking about it."

Joey asked what they could do to help their dad stay alive. Elaine said she wished she knew.

She was working overtime at the FEMA office in Bothell, trying to earn extra cash, and taking calls all day long from psychics, detectives and others about Brenda. She served as a steno-receptionist, telephonist, payroll clerk and computer operator, wherever she was needed. She was under the impression that she was doing her usual good job, drawing the same high ratings she'd earned as a civil service employee for twenty years, but one of her supervisors put her on notice that she was becoming a little scatterbrained. Just that morning, the boss said, she'd misrouted some incoming messages.

Elaine was baffled. She knew she'd been taking on too much, but she didn't think it had been noticeable.

Joe became concerned about her mental state, when he was sober enough to notice. "Hon," he said when she arrived home from work one night, "did you drop my suit at the cleaners?"

She said she was sorry; she'd been forgetting things lately.

"It's not like you," Joe said. "Why don't you see a doctor?"

The family physician advised a complete checkup, including mental tests. When the results were in, he said, "Elaine, you're suffering from delayed shock. I'm amazed you're functioning at all. Don't worry, it'll pass. If you forget a few things, so what? You need a little rest, maybe a change of scene. Otherwise you're normal."

He suggested sleeping pills or tranquilizers. No, thanks, she said.

Like Mikey, she considered herself allergic to the world and stuck to the same safe diet year after year. The doctor said, ''A little drink wouldn't hurt now and then.''

Elaine said she couldn't handle alcohol. Joe drank enough for both of them. She made herself busier than ever, taking on extra assignments at the office, cleaning at home, dusting, vacuuming, doing yardwork, fixing lunches, chauffeuring the boys, keeping up the daily logs on incoming tips and events. She tried to become so tired that she would flop into bed and fall into such a deep sleep that she wouldn't dream.

Toward the end of January, she began to realize that the plan wasn't working. ''I saw Brenda around corners, behind trees, on the three-wheeler. I saw her in the window of every school bus. I saw her on TV, in every song, every book. My nightmares were more vivid than life. She came to me one morning just before the alarm went off. It was black outside, cold, dead of winter. The days are only eight or nine hours long at that time of year.

''I put my arms around her and we sat together and talked. I was so relieved. I said, 'Honey, what happened? Where have you *been*?'

''She said, 'It didn't hurt, Mom. I just felt a little tingle in my neck.'

''I reached out to hug her and woke up. I was so upset I grabbed Joe and told him. He said it must've been Brenda 'cause that's exactly how a broken neck would feel, just a tingle.''

That evening Elaine recounted the dream to a visitor from Families and Friends.

''It's strange,'' the woman said when Elaine was finished, ''but missing kids find ways to tell their parents what happened to them. The message might come from a little bird, an insight, a dream. I think Brenda found a way.''

2

Elaine dreaded the arrival of Saturday, February 8, 1986, Brenda's thirteenth birthday. She asked for a mass at a nearby Catholic church and talked her agnostic husband into attending, along with the boys and a few dozen of Brenda's classmates and friends. The priest began. "This mass is said in honor of Brenda Gere," and continued the ritual in Latin and English without another mention of her name.

Joe walked out midway. When Elaine and the boys joined him in the parking lot, he said, "I thought this was supposed to be for Brenda."

She touched his arm with her gloved hand. "That's the way priests do it, honey. They don't give a long sermon. They just say the mass is for so-and-so and get on with it. The comfort is supposed to be in the ritual."

"He didn't say a goddamn word about Brenda," Joe repeated. The boys sat quietly in the backseat.

When they got home, Elaine let Kanga out of her backyard pen for a romp. The vizsla hadn't been the same since the disappearance. She'd been wearing a groove in the dirt, pacing up and down, spinning around at the slightest intrusion as though she were expecting Brenda.

The dog began quartering the lawn, sniffing at bushes, running along the front edge of the yard and stopping by the deep drainage ditch that paralleled the road. God, how I wish she could talk, Elaine said to herself. This is the second time she's gone straight to that spot. Something must've happened to Brenda there, but only Kanga knows.

A few hours later a neighbor ran in to report that Kanga had been hit by a car. Elaine thought, Brenda will never forgive us. She rushed the pet to the veterinary clinic where Lesley Caveness worked and was told Kanga had serious injuries but would survive. Elaine breathed a prayer of thanks and wondered what was next.

At work in the morning, she found out. A supervisor told her, "Elaine, you've always been one of our best people." She seemed hesitant, and Elaine steeled herself. She'd misrouted some mail on Thursday and again on Friday, and she knew it had caused problems. The supervisor went on, "This just isn't working out."

Elaine thought, We need this income. I *can't* lose this job. I've *never* lost a job. Joe's pension barely covers the rent, and he can't work.

She stammered a few words about trying harder, then left, biting back tears. She reflected on her civil service career: her first job at Mira Loma AFB, her thirteen colonels at Norton, the inspector general's office at Fort Leonard Wood, the IRS in San Bernardino, the U.S. Forest Service in Bonners Ferry, the VA, FEMA, other agencies. She'd always had a high efficiency rating, despite the skipping around. She couldn't risk losing it now.

Joe was talking about returning to Idaho. "We gotta get out of this house," he complained. "The boys are scared to death. We need to make a new start."

Elaine hated to leave and hated to stay. Brenda occupied every inch of the log house. Up until a few weeks earlier, Elaine had sometimes sat on her bed, feeling her daughter's presence, but lately she'd found it too painful. She could hardly bear to look at Brenda's dog.

She wondered when her pain would ease. Wasn't time supposed to be the great healer? Dick Cress was still hurting after all these years. Maybe the only way to heal was to get away. That was what she and Joe had always done in the past. But this time it would mean leaving Brenda forever, giving up hope. Elaine wasn't sure she was ready.

Joe had worked up to a gallon of fortified wine every two days, then reverted to his lethal Kool-Aid concoction. He picked at his food and seldom joined the others at the table. His flesh hung, his complexion turned pale, his eyes sank deeper in his skull. In her nightmares, Elaine saw him laid out in a funeral parlor, as she'd seen so many of her relatives and friends in Fontana. What would she and the boys do without Joe?

Friends offered useless advice. No one could understand why a man with so much ability seemed to be killing himself by ounces. "Any normal father would be devastated by losing a child," Debbie Simmons said in the Gere kitchen one night. "But with Joe—it's like he's totally given up."

Elaine explained that he was suffering from guilt, loss and alcoholism, intermixed, one worsening the other. "But why so much guilt?" Lesley Caveness asked. "Joe was a good father. He didn't take Brenda away. Michael Green did."

"Joe went in to work on his day off," Elaine said. "He blames himself for not being here."

Everyone agreed that a crisis was coming, but no one knew how to head it off. Elaine tried a transparent bluff. "Listen, Joe," she said, squaring off with her hands on her hips, "if you don't quit drinking, I'm gonna take the boys and leave."

"If you do," he said coldly, "I'll kill myself." She knew he meant it.

She kept preparing her sons. "Boys," she told them, "we've got to make every minute with your dad mean something. Take every day and make it count. Unless he quits drinking, he's gonna die."

She consulted Julio DeSantis, by now a close family friend, about life insurance. He sold her a $50,000 universal life insurance policy and waived his commission. She and the boys were beneficiaries.

She stuck the certificate under Joe's nose. "See this?" she said sharply. "I've taken this out because if you don't straighten up you're gonna be dead and we won't have nothin'. I'll have to raise these boys."

His dark eyes opened wide. "Wow!" he said. "Am I getting that bad?"

He reached for his Kool-Aid, walked into the kitchen, and poured it into the sink.

For a few weeks no one saw him take a drink. Then another bottle of Thunderbird appeared in the refrigerator, but only for sipping at meals. Color returned to his cheeks and he resumed his excursions into the woods.

One day he came home and told Elaine, "I gave it a try, honey, but it's no use. We gotta go. Brenda was right. This is the Amityville house."

She'd never objected to his peripatetic ways, even matched them with some bedouin attitudes of her own. Flux had become their way of life. She wondered if leaving the house would be an affront to Brenda. Her empty bedroom seemed like a cavern, the walls expanded by her absence. Orange tape was still stretched across the entrance—POLICE LINE—DO NOT CROSS. It would remain in place until the FBI arrived with its newest laser equipment, already a month overdue. There were smudges of fingerprint powder, black on light surfaces, silvery white on dark.

Her sons were growing up afraid, huddling together instead of playing with other boys, scared to walk to the bus stop without an escort. It took a major selling job to talk them into crossing Thirty-fifth Avenue to pick up the mail, even on days when the sun warmed the fields and traffic buzzed up and down the rural road. They maintained a nervous vigil for "the boogeyman," their name for Michael Green, and acted as though he were around every corner.

Elaine thought about Idaho and the life that they'd sampled in the past. Three hundred miles from the boogeyman, she said to herself, we might become normal again.

Joe placed a call to Jim Nash in Bonners Ferry. His old hunting partner offered a free acre of bottomland between his small home and the barn that he'd stuffed with World War II artifacts. The effusive Nash said it was worth the value of an acre to have the Geres nearby. He was a well-fed, blustery man, hard of hearing and large of heart, with a voice that rattled the phone lines. "*We got plenty land here, Joe, more'n we know what to do with! Edna and me, we know what you folks been through!*"

It was mid-February, rainy, windy, the weather as unsettled as the family's future. Joe said he didn't see any reason to hang around the log house a minute longer. Elaine gave FEMA notice. They weren't sure what to do about Kanga. Without Brenda, the vizsla had become broody, snappy, a poor playmate for the frightened boys.

"Kanga was Brenda's dog all the way," Elaine explained later, "and it hurt us too much to have her around." They decided to put her up for sale to an owner who offered space and love. Brenda would approve.

* * *

A few nights later, two of the Geres' friends topped off a movie date by dropping into a tavern for a nightcap. They were escorted to a dark corner booth by a flashy waitress, thirty going on fifty, wearing bright makeup and a skirt that rode up her rear end.

They'd barely ordered drinks when a tall man with big hair walked through the front door and headed straight for the end of the bar. The waitress kissed him on the lips, and they huddled together for a few minutes of conversation.

"Oh my God," the wife said. "We *can't* let him see us!"

The couple slipped out the back door. Pulling away in their station wagon, the husband said, "Remember what Elaine said? 'He's dying of guilt'? Maybe this is why."

Later someone asked Will Rohrich, owner of E.A.L. Motors, if Joe Gere played around. The ex-Marine was plainly uncomfortable with the question. "Women liked Joe," he said after a hesitation. "They came on to him in the bars. What the hell, he was good-looking, a great talker. Everybody liked Joe, not just women."

Was it possible that on September 19 Joe had driven into Bothell on his day off to engage in what is known among the sexually sophisticated as "a matinee," and not to sell cars?

Rohrich said he had no idea. There were matters a gentleman didn't discuss.

The night before the exodus to Idaho, Lesley and Dale Caveness joined Julio and Judy DeSantis and some of their children in helping the Geres load their rental truck. Everyone tried to stay upbeat, but Elaine kept running to the bathroom and Joe downed a carafe of wine. Joe and Julio ended up sprawled in front of the TV, watching a commando movie, and it was after midnight when Joe drove his friend home. The insurance salesman and West Point graduate was still upset when he told his wife about the short trip:

"We were driving along in the car, and Joe said, 'Ya know, Julio, I really appreciate everything you did. It's just totally frustrating, what we've been through. I've lost my baby. I've lost my little girl.'

"I didn't talk. What the hell d'you say? We pulled up in front. I got out and so did Joe. He walked around the car and hugged me. It was so unexpected. He put his head on my shoulder and burst out crying. I felt a little uncomfortable, but, ya know, I just let the guy cry till I felt my shirt getting wet, maybe five or six minutes. It was sad, heart-wrenching. It was total resignation that he wasn't gonna ever see her again.

"I said, 'Hey, Joe, I know how you feel.'

"He said, 'Nobody knows, Julio. Not till they lose a kid.'

"I said, 'I'm sorry, Joe.' I patted him on the back. I said, 'Hey, I'll call you guys in Idaho.' He wiped his eyes. You could see he was embarrassed. He said, 'Yeah, man, we'll keep in touch,' and then drove off."

Julio told his wife, "I've got a feeling we'll see Elaine and the boys again. But we won't see Joe." He'd never been more certain.

3

The Geres planned to move into a rental house, work hard, and save enough money to park a double-wide on their acre, but they'd hardly entered the city limits of Bonners Ferry before Joe resumed his heavy drinking. As always, Elaine sought advice from her mother in Carson City, Nevada. Evelyn promised to discuss the problem with her Gypsy fortune-teller.

Two nights later, she phoned in tears: "It's bad news, honey. Joe's gonna get in a terrible fight with his best friend. And he's not gonna be with us much longer."

Elaine thought, Joe's only got one real good friend in Bonners Ferry, and that's Jim Nash, and he's the sweetest guy in the world. She didn't worry about the prediction. If one half of the crystal ball was cracked, the other half was probably cracked, too.

By April 1, two months after their latest move, neither Joe nor Elaine had found work. Joe bought an old wreck of a Ford truck for $800 and began chopping and hauling firewood in competition with every drifter in town. He claimed to be weaning himself off hard liquor, but the rental house was small and Elaine came across his stashes without trying. There was no more VO, Wild Turkey or Stolichnaya; he was reduced to drinking blended whiskey from Canada, the stomach solvent that flowed south from Creston and Cranbrook after midnight.

His moods seemed to fluctuate with the phases of the moon or some other occult pattern. Every few days he phoned the Snohomish County detectives or they phoned him, but there were no signs of Brenda, alive or dead. Whenever an unidentified body was mentioned in the newspapers or on TV, Joe would call long-distance to provide a description of Brenda, her go-go boots, her braces. He kept asking Joe Ward and the other Snohomish officers when Michael Green would be charged with the abduction, and was told that the prosecutor was waiting for more evidence. Green was scheduled to go to trial in July for the jogging-trail rapes and was still playing dumb.

Joe would hang up the phone and stomp around the house cursing Green and the Pittmans, Diana, the cops, the prosecutor, even the governor. Then he would visit one of the cowboy bars for an hour or two. Elaine gave him credit for trying. At least he was *pretending* to kick hard liquor. Back in the log house, there'd been no pretense, just nonstop consumption in front of the world.

Nowadays he was acting a little more like a father, taking the boys hiking when he wasn't hungover, trying to help them readjust to another setting. Joey turned twelve in March, a tall boy whose feet reached the pedals of Elaine's blue Chevette. Joe taught him how to shift gears and steer on the old dirt logging roads. He made both boys display their homework and went over every essay, every equation, every journal entry. Listening to him explain how to diagram a sentence and when to say who and whom, Elaine was reminded of the brilliant man she'd married.

When Joey complained that the homework sessions were interfering with TV, Joe grabbed the skinny boy by the shirtfront and said, "You listen to me, buster! You're gonna sit here and do your homework and you're not gonna watch any goddamn TV till you're done."

A few nights later he came home from the woods reeking of booze, slung a videocassette across the coffee table, and squinted at a monster movie with his sons while sipping from his bottle.

Elaine kept quiet. The way she saw it, this battle was between Joe and booze. If he pulled off a miracle and recovered some idea of his own reality, his own self-worth, he would never need alcohol again. If not . . .

He had to win the fight on his own, not through the ministrations of a henpecking wife or a circle of fellow addicts. A detox psychologist had told her that Joe was "oppositional"; such people were reluctant to take advice and often had trouble in groups. Outside interference might only delay his recovery.

Two months after the return to Idaho, Joe was drinking openly, teetering home from the forests behind his personal cloud of boozy breath. Sometimes he went hunting with Jim Nash and returned with venison, elk, bear, partridge, pheasant, grouse. The two companions developed reputations as successful hunters, but Elaine knew from Edna Nash that Joe did most of the shooting and Jim most of the hitting. Back in Southern California, Joe had plunked rising grouse with a .22, but the eye that had been injured in San Bernardino was half-blind now, although he would never admit it, and his hands were palsied. He had less than 50 percent hearing in his left ear.

"The main reason he went hunting," the gentlemanly Nash said later in his megaphonic voice, "was to get out there and set with his bottle. I found a deer for him on Mission Crick, standing in brush fifty feet away. I whispered, 'Yours.' He says, 'What? Where is it?'

"Well, you don't set and talk about where a deer is—it's gonna be gone. I had *no* intention of shooting that deer. I found it for Joe. He needed to do something good for himself and his family needed the meat. He says, 'I can't find it,' and starts waving his thirty-ought-six.

"I says, 'Whoa, boy, I already been shot once!' By that time the deer was out of range. It was a downright scary experience. After that, I was afraid to hunt with him."

Elaine also worried that Joe might kill someone, perhaps himself. Sometimes he could barely walk when he came home, and his rifle would be scuffed and dirty, as though he'd dropped it or used it as a cane. He would clean the gun when he sobered up, ashamed of himself. He'd always shown an ex-sniper's pride in his weaponry, but it seemed to be dissolving in alcohol.

Elaine realized that his self-control was almost gone. Periods of abstinence grew shorter and shorter, and in some ways they were harder on the family than the periods of heavy drinking. He'd always been demanding of Joey, expected too much of him in the tradition of fathers and firstborn sons, but now he was becoming overbearing. The boy was having minor problems in school, and the hypercritical Joe made him keep at the homework till he approved every word, sometimes till after midnight. Elaine thought the seventh-grade boy would do better work if he had an occasional break, a touch of playtime, but she yielded to the family scholar.

Tensions grew between father and son. Joey trembled when his father gave him an order. Little Mikey, the sickly one, was spared. Elaine couldn't tell if Joe loved Mikey less or had given up on him because of his physical problems.

One Saturday afternoon a squabble broke out between the two boys after Mikey appropriated one of Joey's Transformers.

Joe was in the second day of his latest period of abstinence, acting surly and put-upon. He yelled at Joey, "Let the little guy play with your toys! *I've had it with you!*"

He crushed the plastic Transformer under his boot and punched his son in the face.

Elaine rushed in from the kitchen. Never before had Joe raised a hand to her children. He was already contrite, but in his own fashion. He put on a sickly grin, slapped Joey on the shoulder and said in a mock-cheerful voice, "See, Joey, you'll never have to be afraid of anybody in this world. You just proved you can take care of yourself. Look, somebody twice your size gave you his best shot, and you didn't even go down!"

The boy accepted a high five and looked wanly proud. Joe had always had the ability to make people think they felt better than they did. Now he was acting as though his outburst had been a test of manhood, a bonding experience between father and son. Elaine knew otherwise. It was an outburst of uncontrollable temper, fueled by his need for drink.

But at least he'd issued some sort of constipated Hungarian apology. It was a rare event in their lives.

The family was scheduled to pose for pictures at Joey's school the next evening. "You take him," Joe told Elaine as she applied pancake makeup to the boy's black eye.

"No, Joe," she said. "We'll go as a family. We may not be together again for a picture like this."

His hazel eyes narrowed. "What's that supposed to mean?"

She didn't want to admit that every time he left the house she halfway expected to hear from the coroner. "Oh, nothing," she said. "It's just . . . we never took a family picture with Brenda, and, like, she's gone now."

His jaw dropped, and he left the room. "Brenda" was still a name he didn't want to hear. He posed with his family for the last time.

A few nights later he stomped into the living room and said, "What'd you do with my whiskey?"

"Nothing," Elaine said. "I don't touch your whiskey, honey." It was true. She was faithful to her policy of noninterference. It didn't seem to be working, but she couldn't think of another approach.

"Goddamn it," he raged, "you took my goddamn whiskey!"

She told him that he'd probably lost track. He grabbed his .22 pistol off the mantel. "Goddamn it," he said as he pointed it at her temple, "I oughta blow your fucking head off!"

"Go ahead," she said. She wondered why she wasn't afraid, and thought, It's because I'm impervious, I don't care anymore. Death would be an improvement. "Put me out of my misery," she said calmly. "Go ahead! It's no big deal."

"You're right," he snarled. "It's no big deal."

She turned toward the kitchen. She heard a shot, jerked her head, wondered why she felt no pain. Then she heard the front door slam shut.

A wisp of smoke curled up from the charred edges of a neat round hole in the hardwood floor. She heard the engine on Joe's rattly old pickup and looked out the front window to see the taillights receding in a tunnel of falling crystal snow. He was headed toward the bars. She hoped nobody got shot.

She was sitting up in bed, wondering where to turn, when he arrived home. To her surprise, he didn't look or act drunk. She wondered what he'd been up to. His usual pattern after one of his explosions was to drink till he couldn't stand and then flop into bed.

"Honey," he said softly, "I made up my mind once and for all. I'm gonna quit the hard stuff. I'll wean myself with beer."

She listened without comment, trying to remember an expression she'd heard about reliving the same experiences.

"Honey," he continued, "just cut me a little slack." He took her hand. "Thank God for you. If it wasn't for you, I wouldn't be here today."

Déjà vu, that was it. . . .

"Honey," he said, squeezing her hand, "I'm learning. Gimme time. Remember how I used to hate addicts when I was a deputy? I understand them now. I'm an addict myself. I abuse my body the same way they did. What a goddamn hypocrite I am."

She wondered, Is this the beginning of the self-awareness that the therapist talked about? Did that gunshot knock a little sense into his head? It was probably too good to be true. Life-and-death problems didn't solve themselves so neatly.

"I'll beat this with your help, honey," he was saying. "You can take that to the bank."

Fifteen minutes later he was dead asleep. What a strange man you are, she thought as she looked at his relaxed face. Tonight you held a gun on your wife and fired a shot in the house where your sons were sleeping—*with all your knowledge of firearms!* And I still haven't heard an apology.

4

Joe didn't go completely dry, but as spring approached a measure of peace fell over the rental house in Bonners Ferry. He would come home from the woods with a six-pack of beer and guzzle it in front of the TV before going to bed, exactly as his father did in Fontana. Elaine vowed that she wouldn't tolerate one more serious slip. What would he do in his next outburst? Shoot the cat? *The boys?*

At night he called for Brenda in his sleep, and sometimes he would spring from bed, throw on his clothes and disappear around the block. In the morning, he always denied his dreams. Elaine knew what was going on. They couldn't discuss his bad nightmares because they were about an unbroachable subject: Brenda.

The boys, the real justification for the return to Idaho, were still haunted by the "the boogeyman" but showing signs of recovery. Money was shorter than ever. Joey and Mikey were growing fast and needed new clothes. The rent was always overdue. They were eating too much pasta and not enough meat. Joe seemed content to ride along on his disability check, drink beer and chop trees and rattle around town in his old Ford truck. Elaine didn't want to add to his pressures.

One morning after she packed the boys off to school, she drove to the post office to see if any civil service jobs were available. There was nothing in her classification, but the U.S. Forest Service needed a woodsman with carpenter skills. Soon she was rebuilding stockroom shelves, bucking up firewood, cleaning cabins, painting, shoveling snow, and clearing trails with a chain saw.

It felt good to be working in the icy mountain air, but sometimes it was hard to get up in the underheated little house. Every morning she padded into the shower on automatic pilot, a trick she'd learned as Big Ed's dairymaid in Fontana. You didn't wake up and decide to skip the milking. The cows wouldn't stand for it.

Michael Green's trial on two charges of first-degree rape was due to begin in Everett, and Elaine could see that the prospect of an innocent verdict weighed heavily on Joe. She was more optimistic herself. Since everyone in Snohomish County was convinced that the monster had killed Brenda, it wouldn't be hard to convince the judge to stack his sentences on the two rape charges, add ten or fifteen years for the assault on the Klawa woman, and another ten or twelve years for the knifepoint robbery of the florist in Issaquah. The Idaho and Utah robberies would add to the mix, and Michael Green would be stuck behind bars till his beard reached his shoes. Or until he decided to open up about Brenda.

Joe had lost faith in the justice system. He went hunting with Jim Nash and bored him with a backup plan of his own.

"I'm gonna kill the son of a bitch one way or the other," he told his friend as they sat in a tamarack grove waiting for a legal deer to graze into range. For a change, Joe didn't sound half-drunk. "Killing Michael Green," he said, his eyes narrowing. "That's my mission."

Nash was a gentle man, despite a love of hunting and 169 amateur fights in the Army and Marine Corps. "Joe," he said, "why don't you put this behind you? God takes care of people like that. Sooner or later Green'll pay the price."

Joe said, "Sooner or later's not soon enough."

A month before the trial was scheduled to begin, Joe took his wife aside and warned, "I'm gonna be going to jail for a while, honey. You'll have to take care of the boys." He said he was prepared to do hard time. "They don't like ex-cops in prison."

She studied his dark Magyar eyes. He looked serious. She almost wished he were high or drunk, but several weeks had passed since his last falling-down binge and he seemed in better control. It made his threats about Green more ominous.

"What're you gonna do, honey?" she asked.

He said he intended to walk into the courtroom, shoot Green in the head and throw down his gun. "Justifiable homicide," he explained. "Five years max, out in two."

"Joe," she said softly, "how's that gonna get Brenda back?"

"We're not gonna get Brenda back," he answered.

Elaine and the Nashes gnawed over the problem. "I used to think it was the alcohol," she said. "Him and his brothers and my brother Jimmy, they'd drink and talk about how they were gonna get Green. They'd forget about it in the morning. But this—this seems serious."

Nash said, "All that boy talks about is murder. He feels like less of a man 'cause he didn't protect his family. Let's hope he's not serious, Elaine."

5
___

The rape trial of Michael Kay Green opened in the old mill town of Everett, Washington, on July 14, 1986, with no Geres in attendance. Three hundred miles east in Bonners Ferry, Joe was vexed at being denied a chance to see the boogeyman at bay and up close. He'd made the mistake of confiding his attack plan to a friend in law enforcement, and the friend had tipped detectives. A tense phone call followed:

"Joe, we hear you're gonna hit Green. Don't come near the courthouse. If we see you in Everett, we're gonna have to lock you up."

Elaine was relieved when he recounted the conversation.

Green's lawyer put on a standard rape defense, heavy on mistaken identity and alibi evidence ("I was miles away at the time"). As in most rape trials, the defense attempted to exploit the tendency of jurors to regard rape purely as a sex crime committed by oversexed males.

Diana Green, a former Miss Mukilteo who used cosmetics to good advantage, was in constant attendance on her husband's behalf. As the football hero scribbled notes on yellow legal-size paper, projecting the image of a misunderstood young businessman, she sat in the first row and shot him adoring glances. The message was driven home to the jury daily: why would this Adonis have to rape when he had such a beautiful wife?

On the witness stand, Diana backed up his alibis and made sure the jurors knew that she believed in his innocence. At one point in direct examination, she called sweetly to the defendant's table, "Isn't that right, honey?"

Reporters learned that she'd sold the white Toyota to pay Mark Mestel's $5,000 retainer and was obligated to pay $37,000 more in installments. By legal standards, it was a reasonable fee. Mestel was a diminutive scrapper who won most of his cases.

* * *

Within the Pittman family, the tensions continued. Mother and daughter still weren't speaking. Donne Pittman had been quoted in the *Seattle Times*, "I can't believe he would hurt somebody. He's a likable person. If he did hurt somebody, he wasn't responsible for his actions."

Sharon promised her husband that she wouldn't volunteer any more information, "but I've got to answer the questions in court to the best of my knowledge."

He asked if she was trying to send their son-in-law in prison.

She said, "If he's guilty? I sure as hell am."

When she was called as a prosecution witness, Sharon tried not to look at Green as she described life in the Mukilteo house. "There were times it was good and times it was bad," she said carefully. "It fluctuated, depending on his treatment of Diana. We got along fine as long as they were getting along fine. But the times he abused Diana and the boys, I did not hesitate to tell him I did not like it and would not tolerate it in my home."

Diana glared from the front row as Sharon was asked how she felt about her son-in-law. "I don't hate Mike," she testified. "I feel he needs help." She was asked about his behavior around the house. "He spent most of his time working out and eating and doing household chores."

Donne Pittman took the stand and told the truth about Green's behavior as he saw it. He described a time when the son-in-law grabbed one of the boys by the hair and pulled him back into the house, throwing another son to the floor, and kneeing a third in the stomach. To the easygoing baker, it was "more like roughhousing."

Lesley Caveness, who with five or six others was monitoring the testimony for the Geres, found Sharon Pittman sobbing in the women's bathroom room after she and her husband testified. The compassionate Lesley said, "This must be the most god-awful thing for you."

"It's just, oh—awful," Sharon stammered. "Di's been abused by him. He's an animal. I don't know why she doesn't just leave him."

Observers noticed that the defendant's courtroom demeanor began to seem less and less appropriate. "He has a cocky, abrasive way," Debbie Simmons reported to the Geres. "He makes me so *damn* mad.

He has this 'I'm in charge' attitude, 'I'm the big shot here.' He fools around with the bailiffs and jokes with his lawyer. I guess the idea is to show he's a regular guy. I know it's part of Mark Mestel's job to make his client comfortable, but it just seems a little much.''

Elaine asked if Green seemed to recognize any of the Gere support- ers in the audience. ''Oh, God, yes,'' Brenda's former teacher replied. ''He's always giving us the eye. The other day he stared straight at me for the longest time. Eyes like a crocodile's. You know me, Elaine. I'm not brave, but I just hate him so much—I don't want him breathing our air another second. So I stared back till he looked away.''

''Watch your backside, Debbie,'' Joe put in from the extension phone. ''He might walk. You don't want him coming at you later.''

Debbie said, ''He asked his lawyer who I was and who Lesley was, and Mestel asked Patti Toth, the prosecutor. She can hardly bear to look at Green. He called her 'Patti' once, very condescending. And Patti said, 'You will *never* call me by my first name, Mr. Green!' He said, 'Okay, *okay*! Calm down, Patti. Don't get emotional.' When Mestel asked her who we were, Patti said, 'They're nobody that Mr. Green needs to know about.' I was so mad, I went home and asked Nate, 'Isn't there someplace we can buy poison darts?' ''

Debbie was unnerved when two brutish-looking men took seats directly in front of her in the first row of the spectators' section. ''The one guy looked strong and the other looked stronger—a chiseled look, T-shirt bursting,'' she told her husband, Nate. ''They kept turning around and staring at me, and the muscle guy finally asked, 'Why're *you* here?' I thought they were friends of Green, so I said, 'Well, I'm just interested.'

''After a while I realized they were making Green squirm. I couldn't hear, but they whispered at him whenever there was a break. The bailiffs kept edging closer. I thought, Oh, my God, there's gonna be trouble. Then one of the guards said, 'Cool it, Dennis. You too, IBar.' And they all just kinda laughed like they knew each other.''

''The bailiffs ran a metal detector down us,'' Dennis Mackey said later. ''Only us. IBar knew some of 'em because he's an auxiliary cop. We'd wait till they weren't paying attention and we'd whisper to Green, 'Where's Brenda? What'd you do with Brenda?' You could tell he heard us.''

On the fourth day of the trial, the cronies were busy with their war of nerves when a corpulent man stepped forward during a recess and exchanged a few words with the defendant. The palaver went on for three or four minutes, and Green was smiling.

Dennis said, "Look, IBar. He's got a male friend. Son of a gun!"

The man turned around and Dennis said, "Hey, that's Jamie the fat guy. Sells dope, snitches on his friends, hustles, fixes. I think he killed somebody once."

They caught up with the roly-poly man in the corridor. Jamie said, "I come to get a look at the monster."

"You don't know Green?" IBar asked.

"Naw. I just come to the courthouse to see about some drunk-driving warrants I got."

"How many?" Dennis asked.

"Two, three, six, I dunno. Fuckin' cops're bustin' my chops. Might have to do some time."

Dennis observed that he seemed to have a rapport with Green, and added, "That's pretty good, buddy. IBar and I've been looking for a guy that can get next to this asshole, 'cause he took a kid that belongs to one of our friends. Brenda Gere? Remember?"

Jamie the fat guy said he'd read about the case but didn't know that Green was involved. "Up to his ass," IBar said. "Probably killed her. But he won't talk."

"What d'you give a shit?"

"We want to give her a Christian burial," IBar responded.

"Him, too," Dennis said, "preferably alive. Listen, Jamie, what if we got the sheriff and the prosecutor to cut you a fat hog? You know, you get Green to point us in the right direction, and they drop the DUIs."

"I got no problem with that," Jamie said quickly. "I can reach Green in jail. You know me. Put me in that cellblock, I'll find out things."

Dennis said, "Lemme get back."

The sheriff's office didn't think much of the idea. "We don't make deals with pond scum," a high-ranking officer said.

Dennis said, "C'mon, man. This guy's a low-level dope dealer. You can make the deal and bust him later."

The official said, "Go on, Dennis. Get outta here."

Driving away, the old friends commiserated. "That was it," IBar said.

"Our hot chance," Dennis said.

"Never come again."

When they told the Geres the story on the phone that night, Joe said he felt sick.

6

As the trial entered its sixth day, the defendant's behavior turned more unlikely, leading some observers to suspect that he was setting up an insanity plea and others to wonder if he was psychotic. He babbled with his attorney and sometimes with himself, flirted with females, and glared at the Gere claque as though his eyes could draw blood. At best he seemed disoriented. He showed up for testimony in a camel-hair jacket, white shirt and red tie, and seemed to flop all over the witness box, grinning and laughing when he wasn't making apocalyptic statements in a voice that sounded as though it came from a closet.

At times he turned to the jury and almost seemed to plead. When Mestel asked him if he'd raped a woman on July 22, 1985, he said, "Absolutely not, absolutely." Did he rape a woman on August 13? He leaned toward the jury box and said in a plaintive voice, "Absolutely not. *Please* believe me."

Later on the same day, he testified, "I'm an avid weight lifter. I love weight lifting," and began a lengthy disquisition on European weight training and how Russians developed their muscles. While insiders like Sharon Pittman listened in astonishment, he said he was "very confident" that eventually he would beat the world's record of 891 pounds in the dead lift and that he had a good chance of making a team in the new United States Football League. He modestly described finishing "one point behind the winner" in the Mr. Arizona bodybuilding contest and failing to win the 1985 spring bodybuilding competition in Portland, Oregon. He made himself sound like a dedicated young idealist and health fanatic on the verge of a meteoric career. Could anyone possibly believe that such a paragon could commit rape?

Twelve jurors could. After four hours of deliberation, they found him guilty of one charge and innocent of the other. A TV reporter asked, "Now are you gonna tell where you put Brenda?"

He said, "It's a little late for that, isn't it?"

As he was being led from the courtroom, Dennis Mackey called out in an exaggerated faux-gay voice, "Bye *bye*, Mikey."

"Fuck you," the rapist replied.

7

Pre-sentence investigators and journalists dug into Michael Green's past and produced a picture of a shy, withdrawn child whose personality had changed abruptly and mysteriously in college.

The family was well-to-do. Diana Green told a reporter, "His father had a six-figure income and had real estate investments. Michael had a car as soon as he was old enough to drive. He had everything a child could want."

Old records showed that Green was born in Seattle in 1953 and adopted by Delbert and Kathleen Green as an infant. The father was listed as a "contract manager" in the defense industry and the mother as a former registered nurse but now a "homemaker." After moves to central Washington and San Diego, the family settled in Palo Alto, California, where young Michael attended Garland Elementary School and Jordan Junior High. In 1968 the Greens moved to Portland, and the boy entered Jackson High.

Encouraged by his father, he made the school's football team. His coach, Lynn Hewitt, told an investigator, "Mike wasn't a great natural player, but he worked harder than anybody. I remember him as a nice young man, shy, polite, friendly. A great kid to have around. A *perfect* kid." Another coach remembered him as "almost a wimp."

Green won two varsity letters as a tight end and tackle, and also played on the school's baseball team. Over the summer he jogged and worked out while his classmates vacationed. When school resumed, he spent most of his time in the weight room and seemed unconcerned about his studies. His graduation GPA was a lackluster 2.67.

In the fall of 1971, when Green enrolled at the University of Washington, the Husky football team was composed of virtuoso high school stars and beefy semipros who'd been groomed for years to take the team to the Rose Bowl and roll up gate receipts. At an early turnout, Green appeared as a walk-on and was unimpressive. At six-three, he weighed 170 pounds, barely enough to survive as a split end or punt returner, but he kept insisting he wanted to play in the line, where players who weighed less than 220 were considered petite. One of the Washington coaches noticed his dedication and put in a call to Green's old coach in Portland. Lynn Hewitt recalled his own response: "I don't know if Mike's gonna help you, but he's certainly not gonna hurt. He has a good attitude and he'll hit the weights and he'll work hard."

In three and a half months, Green put on twenty pounds and became No. 73 on the Husky team as a defensive tackle and middle guard, a member of the famed "Body Benders." In his sophomore year he was granted a football scholarship. By that time he exceeded two hundred pounds and was expanding rapidly. In a four-month period, he added thirty pounds of muscle and was dubbed Mean Mike Green, a reference to the star Pittsburgh Steeler pass-rusher known as Mean Joe Green.

A teammate and close friend told a pre-sentence investigator, "The change in his weight and physique was noticeable but reasonable to me considering the amount of time he spent working out."

Green had smoked marijuana since high school, but until much later no one seemed aware that he was shooting steroids. "Maybe somebody should've noticed," coach Lynn Hewitt said later. The star lineman seemed to prefer working out alone, running the stadium steps or flailing away at the big bag in the gym till his hands were bloody.

* * *

In college, Green was a B-C student with aspirations of becoming a professional writer. "I've tried some experimental writing—to see how far out I could get—and some structured stuff," he told a campus interviewer. "I like to deal with the lost American dream."

He acted as though his home life were unsatisfying. Friends described his father as "a strong man," "opinionated" and "domineering." Father and adopted son clashed frequently, often over Michael's heavy use of marijuana. An older sister, Cheryl, had left home in her late teens, and younger brother Jeff played in the line for the Huskies at six-five and 245 pounds, two inches taller and ten pounds heavier than his brother.

Michael complained to friends that he felt like a stranger in his family's home. In a questionnaire, he listed John Wayne and "Ted" as the people he admired most; most of the other players listed their fathers. On rare visits to the Greens' big house in North Seattle, friends noticed a coolness between Michael and Delbert, even though the son seemed to be trying to impress the father. They also noticed that Michael seemed to resent his predental student brother Jeff. But against Michael's claims of favoritism the friends also saw a trophy room set aside to glorify the Green boys' exploits, and most of the exhibits were Michael's. On the rare occasions when Delbert discussed the family's business, he emphasized that his three children had been treated exactly the same.

In his junior year, Green began to show symptoms of " 'roid rage," clashing with teammates and coaches. He became known as a difficult player and temporarily quit the team. He told friends that he was no longer welcome at his parents' home in North Seattle, complaining that his father had kicked him out for good over marijuana.

A surprise ex-wife turned up in the pre-sentence investigation. They'd met in the summer of 1975, before his senior year, and lived together off-campus. Michelle Lyons was a bright young woman with a good job at the Nordstrom department store. She told investigators that Michael's parents had warned her that he had "an explosive temper," but she'd found him charming and lovable. They were married in Spokane in 1976. After he graduated with a B.A. in English, he took a trainee job at Household Finance Corporation while nursing secret plans to become a pro football player. When he was passed over in the pro draft, he tried to repeat his college success as a walk-on by showing up at the Seattle Seahawks camp, where he survived two or three days as a tackling dummy and then was rejected. Michelle said he became even more depressed and decided to try prize-fighting—"from one marijuana dream to the next." He told her she could have the privilege of supporting him while he worked his way up to the world championship belt, cruiserweight division.

He spent days and nights in the University of Washington gym, working on the speed bag and the heavy bag, trying to find sparring partners, but the only fights he could arrange were at home, usually over his roving eye or his spendthrift ways. He smashed Michelle's collection of figurines and ripped out the phone when she tried to call police. He insisted that he had to quit his job at HFC to concentrate on the ring, and she said that she was tired of supporting his silly dreams. He told her that his new girlfriend would be happy to take over the role, then backed Michelle against a wall. "If you hurt me," she howled, "my father will kill you."

He'd always seemed cowed by the mere mention of men, and he quickly released his hold on her neck. Michelle left for good.

The new girlfriend, Julie Cutler, was a coworker at HFC. She told investigators that they moved in together in 1977. He'd slimmed down, and as far as she could tell, he used no steroids or other drugs except marijuana. He began jogging, doing aerobics, and frequenting natural food stores in Everett and Seattle. He went through a wheatgrass phase, acerola, safflower oil, tryptophan, vitamin E, spirulina, ginseng, ma huang and nasturtium root. He ate oranges by the dozen and sprinkled them with ascorbic acid, the pure form of vitamin C. If friends served wine or beer, he sipped politely.

Julie saw him as a paragon, bright, healthy of mind and body, an amusing and instructive companion who could talk on any subject. But after a while, she began to notice that he demanded total attention and control. If she came home ten minutes late, she faced a grilling. If she showed signs of rebellion, he became enraged, once dumping the contents of a hot frying pan on her arm in a disagreement over cooking time.

Just before Christmas 1977, he showed up with scratches on his face and said a sparring partner had caught him with his laces. At a New Year's Eve party, he chastised her for talking to an old boy-friend and stalked out. When she got home, she found her personal glassware shattered on the street in front of the apartment.

One night he held forth on the joys of urinating outdoors, told her that he frequently availed himself of nearby lawns—"All joggers do it."

How odd, Julie thought. Then he described the sexual goings-on of a neighbor couple. Similar accounts made her wonder if he was the peeper who'd been drawing complaints in the neighborhood.

She had a final flash of insight during a weekend at her parents' cabin at Lake Cavanaugh. As they walked down the main street of a nearby village, she noticed that he kept staring into store windows. My God, she said to herself, he's not shopping. He's admiring himself. *In every single window.*

She'd read some psychology, and it had been no great leap to diagnose him as an egotist, but now it was coming clear that he was something more—a full-blown narcissist, with all the grandiose, selfish, destructive characteristics of the breed. Narcissists made poor mates, and if crossed they could become downright dangerous.

She wasn't surprised when he drew up a revised set of plans for becoming rich and famous. He would be the next Mr. America.

Then Julie discovered that he was sneaking out at night to meet a woman named Diana Pittman, who worked at her father's bakery in Everett. The final breakup was mutual.

8

Two weeks after his conviction for rape, Michael Green was led into the Snohomish County courtroom in chains, escorted by four deputies. In a weak voice that barely carried to the first row, he accused the prosecution of "going mad" to win a conviction and said the trial had been "a nightmare." It was as though he were the only person who'd suffered.

After his lament, he was sentenced to ten years for rape and twelve years and eight months for felonies committed on the run. Stacked up, the sentences would have kept the women and children of Snohomish County safe from his sexual marauding till well into the twenty-first century.

But the sentences weren't made consecutive. Under an agreement worked out by the attorneys, they were concurrent.

Joe Gere was furious. "Ten fucking years?" he raved. "Back on the street in five or six? What kinda fucking justice is that?"

Elaine almost wished she could share the Gallo red he opened. She wasn't worried about his new style of controlled drinking. He was selling cars at Evergreen Motors, a thirty-minute commute from Bonners Ferry, and he'd been lead salesmen for three straight months.

Joe slept late the next morning and then opened another bottle. He said it didn't matter if he missed a few shifts at work—"I got a lot of things on my mind."

Elaine didn't argue. Nothing she'd said in the past had ever made him cork a bottle.

In the next weeks, both Geres made frequent calls to the Snohomish County authorities, demanding that they charge Green with Brenda's murder.

Lead investigator Joe Ward urged patience. "It's still a weak case," the sheriff's detective said, "and the prosecutor says it's not gonna get any stronger without a body. If he was acquitted, we'd never be able to try him again."

Elaine phoned first assistant deputy prosecuting attorney Michael Magee and asked why Green couldn't be charged "so he'll have something hanging over him. It might make him talk."

Magee was a precise, intense ex-lecturer on law, loser of only two minor felony cases in ten years as a prosecutor. His stiff mustache and brisk manner of speech gave him the appearance of a British subaltern. He explained that under state law, Green would have to be brought to trial within sixty days of being charged, much too soon to have any chance at conviction.

"Green's going away for a long time," he said. "Maybe he'll get careless, sloppy, start bragging to a jailhouse informer. A lot can happen in six or seven years.''

Elaine said that her husband would be gone by then. "He's talking about breaking into the prison—"

"Joe would never do anything that stupid."

"The old Joe just talked about it," she replied. "There's a new one now."

On a snowy night a few months after the trial, Joe Gere ushered his fourteen-year-old son into the living room for a serious talk. Joey thought it would be about his latest report card. If he brought home C's, his father demanded B's. If he brought home B's, his dad wanted A's. No grade was high enough. Joey wondered if his dad would be drunk and abusive again.

"I'm gonna be taking out Michael Green," Joe began. He sounded calm enough, and for a change he didn't have a glass in his hand. "I won't do it alone. Somebody's gonna help me get inside."

"The prison?" the boy asked.

"The prison, yeah. We already know who Green's talking to, what he's saying, how he acts. We even know what candy bars he buys at the commissary."

Joey asked how you could get inside a penitentiary without committing a crime.

"Never mind," his father said. He lowered his voice. "I need to know how you guys are gonna do without me. Would you take care of Mom and Mikey? I mean, if I had to serve a couple years?"

"I . . . guess," Joey said. He had no idea how he would take care of himself, let alone his brother and mom, but he didn't know what else to say. It was often that way between him and his dad.

"I got good backup," Joe went on. "A guy I met hunting. We've got a plan."

For an instant, Joey felt the manly warmth of being taken into his father's trust, the same feeling that came over him when they went out for a driving lesson or stalked deer. But mostly he felt like a boy on the verge of another terrible loss. He was just beginning to get over Brenda and he couldn't imagine a life without his father, alcoholic or not. He was a strict man, aloof, sometimes unreasonable, but Elaine had explained, "If your dad didn't love you, he wouldn't care *what* you did. That's how you can tell a good father. A bad dad wouldn't give a damn, let you run wild. And you'd end up pumping gas.''

Now his father was repeating, "I want to be sure you'll take care of things." He repeated himself a lot lately, as though he were growing old at thirty-nine. "You think you can handle it?"

"No, Dad, I'm not sure," the boy said honestly.

"Tell me somethin'. How d'you feel about Michael Green?"

This was an answer Joey could give without hesitation. He wasn't quite as afraid of the boogeyman as he'd once been, but Michael Green was never far from his thoughts. "I *hate* him," he said. "I never knew I could hate anybody the way I hate that guy. I dream about killing him with my bare hands."

"So I'm doing what's right, huh? Can I count on you?"

"I'll do my best, Dad," the boy said. "But . . . I wish there was some other way."

"Well, there isn't."

9

Elaine was afraid that something dark and final would happen soon if she didn't head it off. But what? Alcohol had been part of the warp of Joe's life even when Brenda was alive, even when he wasn't eaten up by grief and rage. Once when he came home drunk, he confessed, "All my life I was raised around drinking and partying, hon. That's what the Geres *do.*" Elaine told him she understood why he drank but not why he tried to get drunk.

"I don't try," he said. "It just happens."

One evening she came home to their Bonners Ferry house so tired that her legs trembled. She'd spent the day clearing icy slash from a Forest Service trail and hadn't been able to feel her fingertips since morning. It was already dark at this northern latitude.

Joe and one of his boozy companions were installing a rebuilt engine. A litter of crushed beer cans surrounded the old truck. As soon as Elaine stepped from her Chevette, he said, "Hey, hon, how about goin' downtown and getting some beer? It's, uh—for Shawn."

"It's not for Shawn," she said impatiently. "It's for you."

"Well, go anyway."

It was seldom that she denied his requests—her biggest joy was still what her mother called "doing" for her family—but she had to cook dinner and put the boys to bed.

"Joe," she said, "gimme a break. I'm cold and dirty. I don't want to go anywhere."

He raised his head from under the hood and said, "You goin' or not?"

She walked toward the door and said, *"Not!"*

He chased her into the house and slammed her against the kitchen wall. He insisted that she was going and she insisted that she wasn't. When he grabbed her by the shoulder, she spun away and said, "That's it. I'm outta here."

"You're . . . leaving?" He laughed. "Go ahead!" He smelled like her father's old bar rag. "Don't try to take my boys."

He knew she would endure anything before she would leave her children. Big Ed had played the same kind of game on her mother till Evelyn slapped him with divorce papers. Then he'd turned pussycat.

Joe turned his back and stalked outside. Elaine found Joey and Mikey playing video games in the basement. She quietly packed an overnight bag and detoured around Joe to her car.

"Where the hell're you going?" he snapped. His friend stared wide-eyed.

Joe tried to pull her out of her little blue car. She slammed the door, narrowly missing his hand. He reached through the window and clutched her blond hair, but it was too short for a good grip. She rammed the shifter into reverse and backed halfway down the block as Joe pinwheeled after her in a crazy-legged sprint.

At the Nashes' house on the edge of town, she yelled, "You gotta hide me! I'm leavin' Joe."

Edna steered her inside while Jim drove the Chevette into an enclosed shed and covered it with a tarp. Ten minutes later, Joe phoned and demanded Elaine.

"Haven't seen her," Jim lied.

Joe said he was on his way over, that Elaine had deserted him and

he didn't know what to do. Maybe Jim could help him find her and
bring her back.

Elaine hid in a bedroom while Joe raved and sobbed and insisted
that she was his life; there was nothing he wouldn't do to get her
back, even quit drinking. After a while he left.

She knew what he would do next: drink himself onto another
planet, his regular approach to crisis.

At one in the morning she drove home and slipped through her
back door like a burglar. Joe's pickup truck was in the driveway and
she could hear him breathing deeply in their bed. She tiptoed into
the boys' room and whispered that they were leaving on a trip.

When Mikey started to protest, she pressed a finger against his
mouth. Joey acted as though he'd known what was coming.

They drove till they found a vacancy.

Early the next morning she phoned and said, "Me and the boys are
at the Shiloh Inn in Coeur d'Alene, Joe. We won't be coming back."

"No, *no!*" he said. "Listen, Elaine, Jim's here. We've been talking.
I'll do anything you want."

Elaine, Joe and Jim stayed on the phone for an hour. Joe promised
to reform. When he insisted on speaking to the boys, Elaine said,
"They don't want to talk to you." If he was trying to wangle his way
out, she would drive a tough bargain. Anything less was a waste of
time, especially his.

At last the deal was struck. Joe would immediately join Alcoholics
Anonymous, an organization for which he'd always expressed dis-
dain. He swore a holy oath that he would never touch another drop
of liquor, not beer, "not even hard cider." The alcohol problem,
he said, was behind them at last. If he'd only known how much she
cared. . . .

Jim Nash agreed to help his friend by giving up alcohol himself.
Elaine drove her sons home.

After several months on the new regimen, Joe told his sister Linda
that his bond with Nash was making each of them stronger. "Jim
and me," he said in one of their infrequent telephone conversations, "we'll put a six-pack of beer in the middle of the coffee table
and drink Pepsi."

Linda's diabetes had blinded her right eye by now and she'd

undergone laser surgery to save the other. She told Joe she could distinguish objects and colors and was doing eye exercises every day.

"My God," he told her on the phone, "how can you be so calm? I've got sixty percent in my left eye and it's getting worse. Every night I dream I'm blind."

She tried to cheer him up and told him she intended to resume her teaching career.

"I wish I had your guts," he said.

Linda thought, What an odd comment! Has he completely lost touch with himself? Joe used to have enough guts for the whole town of Fontana and half of Bloomington. She still ran into fellow citizens who remembered his feats as a deputy.

"My life is a joke," he confessed to his little sister. "I'm nothing."

"Joe," Linda said, "that's just plain silly. What about Elaine and the kids?"

"What about Brenda?" he countered.

"What about your work?"

"My work?" A hollow laugh came over the line. "I sell fuckin' cars, Linda."

She was concerned enough about his tone to call Elaine the next day and ask what they could do to shake him out of his black mood.

"You tell me, Linda," Elaine said.

VIII

LIFE WITH MICHAEL

1

McNeil Island counselors drew up a profile of Michael Green and reported that he was intimidated by males half his size. He seemed to be mellowing and wrote his wife, "It is amazing how much clearer I see things since being off steroids for so long. I feel like that dreamy kid again."

His letters were an odd mix of lyricism, requests, demands and bombast, and were marked by frequent misspellings and grammatical errors, unusual for a college graduate in English (although not for a scholarship athlete). He lined the walls of his cell with *The Norton Anthology of English Literature*, Roget's *Thesaurus*, Strunk and White's *The Elements of Style* and other reference works. In the book on style, he underlined criticism of the misuse of *hopefully*. His love poems were free-form:

> *I watch her hunch her shoulders' line against the spring wind*
> *Wind carrying high slack tide heavy against the bulkhead.*
> *She doesn't notice. . . .*

When he wasn't referring to Diana as "the angel of my life" and drawing hearts with their names entwined, he was complaining about her attitudes and applying pressure: "You know you have me over a barrel, rolling for the downhill side."

He said he was writing a book, *The Harbinger*, under the pseudonym "Michelle K." The main idea seemed to be to expose the

Machiavellian oppressors who'd faked two rape charges to send him to prison for the abduction of a child he'd never even seen. He spelled out his credo: "Over the next few months, every time I take my pen in hand, I will be hurting them. They will respond by in turn, hurting themselves. When other convicts are playing cards or watching movies on Showtime, I will be in the law library. The very system they use to destroy me will in turn be their undoing. The laws they swear to uphold will be my final relief. Is that not final victory, to use ones' enemies own gun upon him. This I shall watch unfold from wherever they lock me away. In the words of Napolean—never interfere with the enemy when he is in the process of destroying himself."

He often indulged in abstruse philosophizing. "Most would say, the child becomes the adult when he no longer fears the dark," he wrote. "I say, the child becomes the adult when he knows his journey is his toil and he can stand on the threshold of darkness unafraid to flip the switch."

Despite his heavy tones, he was capable of an occasional stab at humor. "I am currently practicing my typing," he wrote Diana. "O boy! See Scott run! Wow! Look at the two convicts giving each other hand jobs. Yes, that is called 'on the knob training.'"

Di still loved him, but she wondered about his mental processes.

Word came back via the grapevine that he'd been raped by two smaller prisoners. "Let's hope so," said the angry Sergeant Tom Pszonka, speaking for his brother officers. "If it was only legal, we'd tie him to a tree and shoot off his toes one by one till he tells where he put Brenda."

Green's faithful wife made regular Sunday pilgrimages with gifts and clothing. She had to get up at 4:00 A.M. to catch an early ferry so she would be the first passenger to disembark at the island prison in Puget Sound, enabling her and her husband to find front seats at the TV football games. As always, he was as strident as an infant about what he wanted. If she missed the first boat and they had to sit farther back, he was surly all day.

Diana put money in his account, working one full-time job and two part-time jobs to provide for his special needs. The pressure was constant: "Please send any money you can afford *without hurting yourself.*" When her contributions came up short of his expectations, he played on her sympathy—"I think their plan is to starve me to death"—and finally on her fears—"I need money to pay a debt. It's a kill or be killed situation."

"Even in prison," Diana's mother Sharon commented, "he was controlling her."

She couldn't remember when it had been otherwise.

2

The relationship had been volatile from the start. They'd met in July 1978, when Diana was working Saturdays in her father's bakery and Green was barely hanging on at a small bank as a commercial loan officer and bad-debt collector whose alarm clock seemed to fail two or three times a week. He told her he lived alone in North Seattle and was training to be Mr. America and then Mr. Universe. Di could believe it. He looked like a demigod in a Brooks Brothers suit, and he had the rolling walk she'd seen in muscular members of the aerobics classes she taught at the Everett YMCA. He was clean-cut, had dark hazel eyes, a mustache, curly brown hair, and a manner so sincere and intense that sometimes he gave her the feeling that he was about to jump over the table to make his points closer to her face.

Their engagement was announced in the summer of 1979, but they couldn't marry, he told her, until he'd shaken off a previous girlfriend. When that was accomplished, Diana moved in with him, just in time to be thrown out of his car during one of their many disputes.

A week before the September marriage she arrived home to find an empty wine bottle on the coffee table.

"Who was here?" she asked.

Mike admitted he'd been entertaining his old girlfriend.

"Why was *she* here?"

"I had to break off our relationship."

"You told me you did that months ago."

"Well, I just didn't have the heart to tell her."

She explained to her mother, "I couldn't push him. If you push him, he gets mad. So I just dropped the subject."

It would be the style of their marriage.

The wedding was nearly called off over the selection of music. He said it would be his choice or nothing. It was his choice.

They moved into a little frame house at McKees Beach and soon found that their main community of interest was the shape of the human body, particularly his. Diana lacked less than a year of college to earn her teaching credential, and she'd been promised a cherished position at Mariner High School, her alma mater. The ambition was quickly forgotten in a whirl of athletic activity. The newlyweds pumped iron together, and sometimes he showed off by lifting her and her weights with one hand.

He pushed her to a fast pace in their daily jogs along Marine Drive. She had a trick knee, and it collapsed. "I can't go another inch," she moaned.

In an angry voice he told her that no woman was going to wimp out on Michael Green. The problem wasn't her knee, he insisted; it was that she was fat and out of shape. She couldn't understand. Since their marriage, she'd lost weight. Her stomach was flat and her muscles long and firm. She stood five-seven, weighed 115 and attracted stares. Her mother joked that if she got any slimmer she could celebrate Halloween night as a skeleton.

"You go ahead, Mike," she gasped, clutching her knee. "I'll walk back."

He lifted her by the arms and pushed, pulled, and dragged her the remaining three miles. The doctor said the injury to her knee would be permanent.

She soon learned that her husband was a neurotic perfectionist, and his obsessiveness seemed to include everyone involved in his life. He set rigorous physical standards for both of them, and when she didn't meet them, he withheld sex. Sometimes he shunned the marital bed "because I don't look good enough tonight." If the body in his mirror didn't impress him, he couldn't perform in bed.

She didn't get it. "What the hell do *his* looks have to do with it?"

she asked her mother. He seemed to regard her body as an extension of his, and refused to enter the holy temple unless both achieved perfection.

They'd been married a month when he slammed her to the floor and told her he couldn't stand women with protruding stomachs. She looked down. She couldn't think of anything that would make her stomach flatter, short of anorexia or bulimia.

After a few months he began ordering her to bring home pornographic movies from the video store. He peeped through a hole in the Y's locker room at naked women; he seemed to think this was his right as a man.

He came home from a dip in Puget Sound and dashed off a few lines about observing "the belch of Weyerhauser's plant 2 so easily visible to the south, covering Everett in a brown haze. Seeing Everett from where I lay in the water it resembled some artist's idea of an industrial soup." He dedicated the imagery to her. She thought it was beautiful.

They'd been married for three months when he maxed out their last credit card to pay for an ex-girlfriend's trip home from Alaska. Diana found unpaid bills in a drawer, some dating from before they'd met. It appeared that he'd consolidated some of his debts in a big loan at Household Finance and hadn't made a payment in months.

He insisted on handling the finances even though she was bringing in the only paycheck and he could barely manage long division. He seemed to prefer snarling up the books to relinquishing control. He took the same approach to their exercise programs, social lives, insurance and other family matters.

His inability to handle money was a steady source of friction with his meticulous father, who allowed them to move into one of his rental units rent-free but reserved the right to provide financial advice, which only seemed to annoy his son.

There was something odd about the relationship, but Mike wouldn't discuss his father, and Delbert was less than forthcoming. Now and then the successful defense contractor and real estate owner would visit Donne Pittman at the little bakery in Everett and ruminate about his son.

Diane's brother Dan noticed a slight narrowing of Mike's eyes whenever Delbert Green's name came up. Once he showed Dan a long letter from his father, full of paternal advice about minutiae. Mike said, "Can you believe he writes these things?"

Mike's reaction to the attempts at fatherly micromanagement was to accept a job as credit sales manager for Snap-On Tools Corporation in Phoenix, Arizona, at a starting salary of $450 a week. He told Di to start packing.

A few months after the move, Diana phoned her mother at eleven at night. "How come you're still up?" Sharon asked.

Di explained that she was waiting for Mike to get home. He'd been working hard lately, sometimes till dawn.

"Working?" Sharon said.

Diana said she didn't dare check on him. She'd tried it once, and he told her that if she ever did it again, he would divorce her after beating her so hard that no man would ever look at her again. She told her mother she was expected to serve a hot dinner when he came home, whatever the time.

Di was describing their new apartment when she interrupted herself. "Mom, I gotta go now. I hear him on the stairs. Oh, Mom, he's here—"

The phone was dead for days. Later Sharon learned that Mike had ripped it from the wall because his meal wasn't on the table when he arrived.

A year after the move to Arizona, Sharon and Donne flew south for a visit and found their smiling son-in-law eager to show them the wonders of the desert. Sharon was astonished at how massive he'd become, how cat-quick on his feet, how intimidating. He explained that he'd been loading calories and working out at a gym in preparation for bodybuilding contests.

He rented a luxury motor home to take them to the Grand Canyon in style, and when the engine failed midway in the trip, he kicked the tires and bumpers and slapped the side panels with his big hands, making a thunk like an ax against a tree. Sharon had the feeling they were dealing with 250 pounds of two-year-old boy, punishing the naughty RV because it had inconvenienced him.

3

In the Greens' third year in Arizona, Sharon took an emergency call from Diana's boss at a Phoenix escrow company. "If you want to see your daughter alive," the man said, "you better get her out of here. She's been coming to work with bruises all over, and she's down to nothin' but skin and bones. She claims she was in a car accident, but we know better."

Sharon alerted Donne at the bakery. Her distress was observed by her boss at Lynnwood Mortgage, a family man who'd long admired the female Pittmans, mother and daughter. He asked what was wrong.

She hated to ask for time off. It was the busy season and she was the top processor and underwriter. Her departure would throw a crimp in the operation.

"Come on, Sharon," he insisted. "You're no crybaby. What the hell's going on?"

After she told him, he said, "Take the next plane. Get that child outta there. And don't go alone. Take Donne for protection."

"Donne wants to stay out of it," she said.

"Then take one of your sons. You may save Di's life."

An hour passed, and Sharon was still trying to decide what to do. Her boss stuck his head in her door and said, "Pick up your tickets at the airport. I put 'em on my Visa card. Now get outta here!"

Sharon phoned Diana from a booth at Seatac Airport and told her that she and brother Dan had heard about the accident and were on their way. Diana acted surprised but not displeased.

A few minutes after Sharon hung up, she was paged to an airport phone. "Mom," her daughter said, "you don't need to come down. Really, I'm okay. It was a just a little accident, but I'm fine now."

Sharon said they would discuss the matter in a few hours.

* * *

At the Phoenix airport, mother and son were met by Di and her old friend Susie from San Diego. Sharon almost fainted at the sight of her daughter. It looked as though her fine, thin nose had been smashed. The skin around her eyes was a sickly blue-gray and one socket looked depressed. She clutched her side as she walked.

Susie drove them to a nearby motel. "I'm all better now, Mom," Di said.

Sharon shuddered. If she was all better, how come she looked like a broken stick? She couldn't weigh a hundred pounds.

"Come on, Di," Susie put in. "Tell your mom the truth."

Sharon held her hand over her mouth as the story emerged level by level. At first Di claimed that Mike had hit her only once. Finally she admitted that during an argument over his latest girlfriend he'd slapped her three or four times, butted her and pushed his palms against her cheeks and lifted her three feet off the floor, twisting her head and neck.

Sharon, Susie and Dan insisted that they drive straight to Susie's apartment in San Diego, six hours away. En route, the rest of the story came out. Mike had bitten her wedding ring out of shape. He'd threatened her with a knife and then with a gun. He was seeing several women on the side and trumpeting his infidelity to the world.

A few weeks before the final assault, he'd thrown a lamp at her, and neighbors summoned police. At the station he'd claimed that Diana had started it, and the desk sergeant told them that someone would have to spend the night in jail. Diana offered, but when a jail matron saw her bruises, Mike ended up in the cell.

Back in Mukilteo a few months after the unpleasant visit, Sharon wasn't surprised to hear via phone that Diana had returned to her job and husband. Di said that Mike had apologized sweetly and promised never to hurt her again. He was withdrawing from steroids and gaining self-control. "And Mom," Di said in a cheerful voice, "I'm—pregnant!"

Sharon tried to conceal her misgivings as she asked, "Does Mike know?"

"I just found out. I'm telling him tonight."

The next day Sharon learned what had happened in a call from a Phoenix hospital. Di said that Mike had "whacked out" at the news of her pregnancy, gulped a mouthful of tranquilizers, and stomped around the apartment while yelling about free will and determinism. After rattling the walls with his heavy fists, he'd punched her in the stomach. The miscarriage came within hours.

Snap-On Tools finally unloaded its problem employee in October 1984. In three years, Green's weekly salary had gone from $450 to $575, minimal raises for a college graduate in an executive position. His work evaluations ranged from "excellent" to "unsatisfactory," and he'd gained a reputation for toadying up to males and lashing out at females. The dismissal report cited "poor treatment of employees and sexual harassment."

In his off-hours he'd been bulking up for a bodybuilding contest, and two rent-a-cops were summoned to stand by as he was handed his pink slip.

"How stupid!" Diana told her mother over the phone. "What did they think he was gonna do? Wreck the place?"

His body glistening in oil and his muscles twitching like bagged frogs, Michael Green placed second in the Mr. Arizona contest, but the prize money didn't come close to matching what he'd spent on vitamins, steroids and other assists while ballooning up to 260 pounds. Diana's paycheck at the escrow company barely covered household expenses, and soon they were living below the poverty level. It was time to go back home.

Green drew on his knowledge of English composition to produce an all-purpose job application for banks and credit companies in the Seattle area. In classic résumé style, he rhapsodized about his work record and neglected to mention that he'd just been fired from the only job he'd ever held for more than a year. He claimed that he'd excelled at Snap-On Tools as credit sales manager, with "direct management and control of 54 dealers, seven field managers and four staff members." Under "hobbies," he wrote: "Weightlifting, 1984 Arizona State Superheavyweight powerlifting champion. 1984 Arizona State Bodybuilding Championship 2d Place. Second hobby: nutrition. Third: reading and writing."

The advertisements for himself concluded: "As you will see by my résumé, I am used to being the best at whatever I do and can be a major asset to any corporation which hires me."

His reputation and record were well known in Northwest financial circles, and no one wrote back to offer him a job.

4

Late in 1984, the Pittmans had offered to make their master bedroom available to the struggling young couple, bringing to nine the number of bodies in the large waterfront house. Sharon's sympathetic boss hired Diana to work alongside her mother at $1,400 a month, and Mike made a formal decision to earn his living as a bodybuilder and male model. "We'll make a ton off endorsements alone," he told his wife. "And that doesn't count the movies."

He'd barely slipped into his new routine when he met a weightlifting blonde at the gym and began staying out late. At a party in the Pittman home, Di caught him using the bedroom phone to wish the girlfriend a happy New Year. In the resulting battle, he body-slammed her to the floor. Police restored order and the marathon battle continued verbally.

Sharon intervened at two in the morning. "Just leave!" she told him. "Get the hell out of here!"

He continued sniping at his wife as though no one had spoken. Di sat on the floor and sobbed.

At last he stalked out the door and was gone until breakfast. Sharon turned him away, but Diana insisted everyone deserved a home and this was his.

"Okay," Sharon said, "you can come in, but only if you both agree to counseling. You guys can't go on like this."

For a few weeks there was peace, but on Mike's terms. Everyone in the house was expected to serve his interests. The understanding was that they would be recompensed in grand style after he'd supplanted his archrival, Arnold Schwarzenegger, in public adulation.

"His needs, his drugs, his food, his time always had to come first," Sharon said later. "Di had to tell him how great he was, how handsome. It was nauseating."

As his rigid regimen continued, he turned into a walking collection of personality distortions and tics. Impromptu decisions or the least suggestion of spontaneity or abandon seemed to disconcert him. If Diana said, "Let's go to the movies," he acted shocked. Such trips had to be planned in advance, the films evaluated and discussed, options weighed and rejected. Such trips had to be made under *control.*

He spent most of his time working out, eating, visiting tanning salons, applying bronzing lotions and oils, working out poses. He flinched at zits as though the devil stared from the mirror. For a while he used a carotene tanning lotion that turned his fingernails a sickly orange. Sharon didn't know how often he bathed at the gym, but at least three times a day he ran the Pittman shower till it was cold.

He was obsessed by cleanliness but expected others to do the work. Dirty dishes made him cluck with annoyance, as though he'd caught the women of the house in a serious malefaction. He never wiped out a shower or cleared a mirror or mopped the spot in front of the toilet where his sprinklings sometimes fell short because of his inability to see below his fifty-four-inch chest.

He seemed to enjoy lying for its own sake, telling stories that couldn't possibly help or hurt his cause. He sent the boys on fools' errands and laughed when they fell for his deceptions. Sharon developed a theory: by fooling others, he made himself feel less foolish. It was another way to show that he wasn't as weak as he felt.

Once he punched Di's face and claimed that she had run into a door. Sharon said, "You are the biggest lying jerk in the world. How can you do this? What the hell is wrong with you, Mike?"

He gave his usual bland reply: "I'm sorry. I'll never do it again."

He would treat his personal punching bag gently for a few weeks and then beat her up. He also bullied her brothers. Every now and then he would grab one by the hair and roughhouse him so hard he'd cry. He berated twelve-year-old Donovan for dipping into his ice cream. "Don't you ever touch my food!" he raged, and punched the boy in the side.

Trouble developed over Vincent, one of the Pittmans' newest charges, a veteran of nine foster homes. His first act after being led into the house was to put a BB-gun hole through the family TV. The word was that his next stop would be juvenile detention.

Sharon saw the dire possibilities and immediately warned Green, "You can't touch this boy. Don't do *anything* to him. They'll have the juvenile authorities on us in no time flat."

The big man seemed to take her admonition as a challenge, and soon his selective bullying reached such proportions that one of the younger brothers recorded an example of the abuse on tape. Vincent's first audible words were "I can't breathe!"

The 280-pound bodybuilder was sitting atop the eleven-year-old boy. "Oh, it hurts, huh, punk?" he taunted. He shifted his weight higher on the boy's chest and laughed uproariously.

Dale and Donovan were watching, and one of them said, "Come on, Mike!"

Vincent began screaming, gasped for air, then was silent, then gasped again. The torture continued for five minutes. When the boys played the tape for Sharon, she felt sick.

A few days later, Di called fourteen-year-old Dale into the kitchen, and when he didn't respond quickly enough, Mike threw him on the bed and punched him in the stomach.

Sharon came home from work and said, "Mike, I need to talk to you. I know there's a lot of people living here and I know the kids get on your nerves once in a while. You have the right to send them to their rooms, but I will *not* tolerate your hitting them anymore."

As usual, he apologized. Diana strode into the room and said, "What's going on here?"

"I'm having a talk with Mike," Sharon said. "You stay out of this, Di."

She turned back to her son-in-law. "So help me, Mike, if you ever lay a hand on any of my kids again, I'll take a baseball bat to your head."

Diana flew at her. "How dare you talk to my husband that way!"

Donne heard the commotion and asked what was going on. Father and daughter ended up defending Mike, and Diana accused her mother of being "off your rocker."

Sharon collected her sons and drove to the nearby Alderwood Mall, then took them to her sister Sandra's house for the night. Dale's stomach still hurt. Sharon considered rushing him to a hospital emergency room but was afraid to involve the police.

In the morning, Donne called and asked, "Is this gonna keep up?"

Sharon said, "Donne, do you realize that Dale's hurting?" She and the four boys returned later in the day.

The son-in-law's hold on Diana tightened. Before she left for work in the morning, she had to cook him a half-gallon pot of oatmeal and serve it in a six-inch baking bowl with four sliced bananas. If the bananas were unripe or overripe, he would throw them at the wall. His second course consisted of the whites of a dozen hard-boiled eggs. A dozen more were set aside for his midmorning snack.

For lunch he loaded carbs with a huge bowl of pasta and downed a pair of roasted chickens. Afternoon snacks consisted of a half-dozen beef tomatoes, three heads of lettuce, and a pound or two of cold white breast of chicken.

When Diana arrived home from work, she was expected to whip up his vitamin drinks, shoot steroids and B-12 into his butt, and prepare his main meal: more organic chickens, pails of salad, mounds of mashed potatoes, and brimming bowls of carbohydrates like popcorn and noodles. He finished off each sitting with seventy vitamin pills.

At one time he'd taken his meals in the dining room with the rest of the family, but his gorging turned Sharon's stomach and she made a face. After that affront to his dignity, he dined on a sagging card table in his bedroom while staring at the wrestling matches on TV.

Diana also served as his personal maid, dietetian and makeup artist. He slapped her across the room when she nicked his abdomen while shaving his genital area for a bodybuilding exhibition. He threw her new 35mm camera out the car window after she spilled Coke on the seats of the Toyota.

He seemed as concerned about her weight and figure as his own, as though she were an appendage to his splendor, and he sometimes ordered drastic measures. Sharon noticed how thin she'd become and served the two of them a big Sunday breakfast. Diana was halfway through her omelette when Mike frowned and said, "Diana?"

She jumped up and headed for the bathroom, and when she

returned her eyes glistened. Sharon thought, What's going on here? Am I missing something? Then she realized her daughter had vomited.

Later Diana admitted that she was expected to stick her finger down her throat whenever her weight exceeded 110 pounds. She became anorexic, and Mike blamed her boniness for his lack of interest in sex. When she tried to reason with him, he beat her in the privacy of their bedroom and instructed her to "scream silently." If she threatened to walk out, he threatened suicide. He told her how easy it would be to take a nap on the railroad right-of-way below the house. When he pulled one of his frequent disappearances, Diana always rushed to the tracks and searched for his head.

Every day Sharon fantasized about shoving her son-in-law off the end of the slip and into the screws of the little green-and-white ferryboat, but she didn't dare make an overt move. The ultrapatient Donne insisted that all Mike needed was a little encouragement and support, just as they'd supported so many foster children, and Diana insisted that her husband was a decent, fascinating man, despite his outbursts, and she loved him, which seemed to render other arguments moot.

Sharon thought she understood Mike Green better than either of them. To her, he was a yowling, demanding, uncontrollable, egoistical infant, wearing a bodybuilder's stringy jockstrap in place of diapers. He forced every confrontation to the limit, then sweet-talked his way out. "He was good at damage control, admitting what he knew you could prove but denying everything else," Sharon observed later. "He was the master of the half-truth and the untruth. He had three different affairs in the ten months he lived with us and talked his way out of every one."

A week before Christmas 1984, Mike stayed overnight with his blond weightlifter, and Di filed a missing persons report with the police. The woman had been spotting for him at a gym called Howard's Bodybuilding in nearby Marysville, and he'd once brought her home for dinner. The Pittmans didn't know that she usually wore his ring on a string around her neck.

A few weeks later, Diana and the woman found themselves riding stationary bikes side by side, and Diana recognized the ring. After a yelling match, she stomped out the door.

Mike came home and swore the affair was over. Diana took him at his word, but Sharon was dubious. (Later he wrote a girlfriend, "It wasn't enough to have two on the side. I had three on the side. Women always came after me.")

"He would hold court in our living room, being charming, funny, bright," his mother-in-law recalled. "When he was nice, he was very nice. He said he considered us his real family, called me Mom or Sharon. He'd give Di a bear hug and say, 'You're just dynamite.' He was a strange English major. He never read a newspaper or a book. I picked up one of his letters and it was full of third-grade mistakes. All he seemed to care about was how he filled his underwear. He had us believing he would be the next Mr. America. It was all he talked about."

At Howard's, the big man was an attraction. Everyone knew he was into "enhancing drugs," the euphemism for steroids, as were most of the gym's semipro bodybuilders. Eventually their skin thinned and grew puffy, their necks and faces bloated, and bluish lines appeared below the epidermis like the veins on a medical mannequin.

It became a game to see how much bigger "Mr. Hulk" grew each week. He took time out to answer questions and smiled at the women. Few gym rats could keep up with his focused intensity or pace, and he changed partners regularly. Members interrupted their own reps to watch him.

"He'd lift so much weight we'd have to get a guy on each side of the bar to spot, which was maybe six hundred pounds," said a gym habitué. "He was an easygoing guy, real likable. Everybody admired him. The only thing we noticed—whenever he talked to women, he looked down. But so do a lot of guys."

The Hercules of the barbells and fitness machines seemed exquisitely aware of each of his billions of cells. "My hair is very sensitive," he would testify later, "and it needs proper shampoos and stuff to use. . . . Because of genetics or whatever, I have a very difficult time holding a tan."

He spent hours rechiseling individual pecs or lats or delts. With Diana's diligent assistance, his skin stayed as cool and smooth as a slug's. He devoted an hour or two a day to Howard's sauna and ultraviolet bed, stripping to avoid tan lines. Before competitions, he applied body oil and other beautifiers. He used more eye makeup than his wife.

5
―――

In March 1985, after four months back in Mukilteo, Mike was invited to represent Howard's at a bodybuilders' event in Portland. A week before the contest, he began to bleed internally, a common side effect of steroids. His diet trainer, Elaine Craig, herself a nationally ranked bodybuilder, explained, "He was on a sodium load when the ulcer leaked. He'd reached his peak and his whole timing went off. When you reach your peak, your muscles are sharply defined, your striations show, there's no fat, water retention is down, your vascularity comes out. We had to change his diet to compensate for the bleeding, and he flattened out. He was the biggest and the best-looking contestant in Portland, but he never had a chance."

Diana and her parents went along as a cheering section but ended up sitting on their hands as the biggest and best-looking contestant finished last in the heavyweight division. Elaine Craig and her husband Brad, half owners of Howard's Bodybuilding, were embarrassed when Diana began cursing the judges. "I can't believe this. What were you blind bastards *looking* at?"

Elaine said, "Sit down! Everyone's staring." She felt sorry for Mike. He was such a big fish up in Marysville.

Mike tried to put the best face on his failure, but the Pittmans could see he was crushed. He made a halfhearted explanation that he'd taken a diuretic an hour before his appearance and "I lost all my fluids, lost the puff in my muscles, lost the sharp definition." He also thought that his tan had "washed out" prematurely, a continuing problem. And, of course, the judges were biased against him because he wasn't from Oregon.

Sharon was dismayed by the showing. Was this the end result of months of lifting weights and shooting steroids and eating whole chickens and *acres* of lettuce and broccoli and swallowing magnums of fish oil and pills? She knew nothing about the protocol of body-building contests, but she could tell that he was bombing from the time he minced onstage in his teeny-tiny briefs. "There were four in his weight class," she told a friend later. "If there'd been ten, he'd've finished tenth."

On the way home, she delivered a rare lecture to Di and the muscleman. "Well, now," she began, "it's time to go back to work, isn't it? Time to start looking toward different things? Donne and I have seen you through these first months. Now it's time to get on with your life."

Mike's answer was to take a double hit of steroids in his room. Then he left for Howard's Gym. He returned at three in the morning.

He claimed to be checking into the unemployment office daily. One day Diana asked him if he'd gone, and he snapped, "I told you, Diana. I went yesterday."

"Yesterday was Monday. The unemployment office was closed."

"Oh, yeah," he said. "I'm sorry, I forgot," as though that covered the subject. If she questioned him too sharply about his daytime wanderings, he would turn morose, blow up or threaten suicide.

He caught a one-day modeling gig for Kodak, then picked up a few small fees for posters and commercials. He claimed later that he'd earned $1,500 a day modeling, but was unable to name the agency that handled his bookings. A local bodybuilding magazine ran an article entitled "The Monster from Mukilteo." The story cited the healthier details of his training regimen but failed to mention the testosterone, Dianabol, Winstrol V, Deca-Durabolin, Anadrol and other fluids he injected, some imported from East Germany. Black-market steroids were expensive, and Sharon wondered where the money was coming from—surely not just from Di's $1,400 a month salary. He pawned his stereo and turntable and other valuables that seemed to pop up in his hands like a magician's rabbit and disappear just as inexplicably. It flashed through Sharon's mind that he might be stealing, but she didn't want to be unfair. He seemed to have an unusually close relationship with a pawnbroker.

* * *

After a while his drugs of preference escalated to Equipoise and several other racetrack steroids that were known to cause rectal bleeding and colitis in humans. They were easily available to gym rats. Sharon found rubber-capped bottles with images of cattle on the labels. Diana told her that Mike sometimes lost track of the proper dosage and overfilled the syringe.

His body became so stretched and inflated that he couldn't bend without strain. As his capillary walls thinned and weakened, he would develop a nosebleed if he tried to tie his shoe. A vein on the side of his head throbbed continuously. He resembled a museum statue but could barely carry out the trash. Di washed the Toyota once a week while he supervised. He tried to help, but it made him too tired.

In a routine checkup, the family doctor warned that his liver was being damaged. He went off his potions for a month, bickering with everyone he encountered and beating a tattoo on his wife, then quietly returned to his previous high dosages.

On the night of Diana's twenty-sixth birthday, April 11, 1985, Mike took her to dinner and a baseball game. On the way home he complained of neck pain. He stopped the car and got out.

"Look, Diana," he said. "Did you ever see so many frogs?"

Diana looked. There wasn't a frog in sight.

As summer arrived, Sharon grew more concerned. Her dislike for her son-in-law was becoming hard to conceal, and she was afraid the day was coming when he would start abusing her as he did Diana.

"I couldn't talk about my fears," she said, "because my husband and my daughter backed him a hundred percent. I walked around my own house scared to death. He had this look in his eyes. I stopped pushing him about moving out. I thought, What's gonna happen to Diana if they go? I can keep an eye on 'em here. If he hits her too hard, at least I can drive her to the hospital."

Then one day in September, a child disappeared from a home on Thirty-fifth Avenue S.E., and deputies came to call.

6

By November 1986, Michael Kay Green, convicted rapist, had been a ward of the Washington State Department of Corrections for three months, and his wife was beginning a process of reeducation about their relationship. Her mother no longer argued with her about Mike's guilt; the two females now lived apart, their feelings running so high that Sharon had resigned from Lane Mortgage and accepted a similar job so they wouldn't rub elbows at work.

One evening Diana showed her wedding pictures to a family friend who'd been a witness to an attempted assault by a very large man on two young girls at Scriber Lake Park in July 1985, the season of the jogging-trail rapes and the Gere abduction. "I can't believe it," the friend said, pointing to a full-face picture of Mike. "That's the guy!"

Diana didn't know what to think. In a small portion of her mind, she accepted the remote possibility that her husband had killed Brenda Gere, not as part of a rape but in a steroid-induced frenzy. But she couldn't imagine him as a rapist, especially since he sometimes went weeks without showing the slightest interest in any human form except his own. She was as convinced as ever that the conviction had been fabricated by Snohomish County to put him away for what they suspected he'd done to Brenda.

She decided on a deep reality check, exiled herself to the rarefied air of Arizona, and brooded about her marriage. Around Howard's Bodybuilding, she'd been happy to play the role of the dumb blonde and devoted wife—"Planet Diana," as some of the gym rats referred to her. Now she began seeing Mike in her nightmares, raping and strangling. She was afraid to sleep, hated being alone, and drank more than she intended, but she'd never been able to tolerate alcohol and eventually quit it altogether. When she returned to Washington, she began to consider divorce.

IX

DEATH IN THE RYE

1

After three or four sessions, Joe Gere began grousing about his Alcoholics Anonymous meetings. The lesson the counselors tried to pound home was that his early life, his beating in San Bernardino and other vicissitudes were extenuating but not exculpatory. He told Elaine that the AA people would sit in a ring and pepper him with variations on the same theme: *That's no excuse. . . . You make your own life. . . . You can't undo the past. . . .*

"They keep wanting me to open up. Open *up?* To guys I see in town every day? People I sell cars to? My God, hon, I garroted guys in the DMZ. I accidentally killed a man when I was a deputy. I broke arms, heads, balls. How can they expect me to open up?"

Elaine realized that he'd reverted to his oldest thought patterns. Hungarians didn't reveal themselves, at least not this Hungarian. He would risk losing his livelihood, his family and maybe his life rather than offer a few snippets of personal information to strangers. She had a sick feeling that he might be constitutionally incapable of change, that it wasn't a matter of his sincerity but of his makeup, his genetic programming, his social background, and she and the boys were doomed to engage in a delicate holding operation with an incurable drunk for the rest of their lives. Divorce was out of the question. She had married for life.

*   *   *

After a few more weeks he quit AA. He said that a female counselor had advised him that 2 percent of alcoholics were unreachable, "and she's pretty damn sure it includes me."

He turned to another tried-and-failed solution: a change of scene. On a whim, he rented a house on Lake Pend Oreille and moved their sparse collection of furniture. The view from the picture window looked torn from *Field & Stream*. Ripples of blue-green water lapped at their floating dock and the fringes of their lawn. Canada geese wheeled overhead. Slate-colored Cooper's hawks chased dickey birds into the treeline. The lake itself was forty-three miles long and home to record-sized Kamloops trout; fishermen came from all over the world.

In bed that night, Elaine thought of their earlier houses, conventional, boring, suburban, most of them constructed of particle board and Sheetrock, plastic imitation shakes, prefab windows and other ticky-tack. They weren't so much built as glued and stapled. The log house and the beach place in Dana Point were exceptions, but they were distant memories.

This lake house was a major tonic for Joe. He might have alcoholism in his genes, as he admitted himself, but he also had an ingrained love of the outdoors that dated to his earliest years in the mountains of West Virginia. Now he could cast for big trout from his lawn. It would be like another childhood.

In the morning Elaine was awakened by a sound like the squeeze-bulb horns and squeaky axles of the Fontana Days parade. A carpet of honkers was breakfasting on their grass and depositing the residues in gloppy gray puddles. She slid into her flip-flops and ran out to chase them into the lake.

The lake was gone.

She rushed inside. "Joe!" she said. *"The lake!"*

He looked out the window. "It's okay, honey," he said. "They just drew it down."

"Drew it down?"

He explained that the lake was actually an impoundment in the Pend Oreille River, so big that it had its own tides like the Great Salt Lake, and the damkeeper must have released water to allow for heavy rains.

"It's no big deal, honey," Joe promised. "The water'll come back. They don't draw it down very often."

Their wooden dock rested at an angle in a few inches of slime. She tried to reach it but sank to her ankles in guano and mud. Before she could pull free, mosquitoes dive-bombed her face and hands.

That night she dreamed that Brenda's body was locked in the mud.

Elaine remained unhappy in the strange new setting until they moved a few months later, this time to a remote bungalow on five acres just outside a logging village named Laclede, on the Pend Oreille outflow southwest of the lake. To reach home, they had to turn off the blacktop at the Riley Creek Mill and follow a washboard dirt road. The house abutted a quarry that had been hacked from the side of the mountain.

"There's elk and bear out my back door," Joe told Jim Nash on the phone. "*Conventions* of deer. We got grouse like you got robins! Come down and help me thin 'em out."

Their new address was a twenty-minute drive from Evergreen Motors in Sandpoint, where Joe continued to rack up sales, and the Sandpoint schools were an upgrade for the boys. Elaine found a clerical job, indoors at last. It was still winter, and she had to drive Highway 2 every morning in the dark. Log truck drivers ruled. If the lordly loggers thought she was too close, they would swerve a foot or two onto the shoulder and spray her car with pebbles and rocks, a practice known as "dusting." Not long after the Geres moved in, a citizen was crusned by a speeding log truck, by no means an unknown occurrence. Elaine whispered a little prayer every time she left for work. Ground haze snaked up from the river bottoms and grayed out her windshield. Black ice caused skids. Wild animals frolicked on the road. After Elaine wiped out her third deer, she told Joe, "This is depressing, honey. Are you sure we didn't go a little *too* far out?"

He insisted that the place was perfect.

2

By New Year's Day 1987, with the short days lengthening by fifteen minutes a week, Joe had evolved into the advanced sort of boozer who seldom appeared drunk. As long as he maintained a high level of alcohol in his bloodstream, he was able to go to work on time, help with his sons' homework, even hunt and fish with friends. At Evergreen Motors, he wore a path to the nearest bar, working out deals, consummating deals, and celebrating deals over drinks. Elaine remembered the style from their real estate days in Southern California, back when they'd owned twin Corvettes and a forty-two-foot boat. He'd also drunk heavily as a deputy, soldier, and teenage boy. He'd been drinking the night they met. She'd thought it was kind of cute. Now she wondered, When *wasn't* he pickled in alcohol? In the womb? Nope. Joe Sr. said that Reva had enjoyed her pint a day even when she was pregnant.

After a day of doing business over ice cubes, Joe would come home and drink till he slumped into bed. He took less and less interest in the house and his family. Elaine changed lightbulbs, burned leaves, shoveled snow. When the clothes dryer quit, she didn't even bother to tell him. She unscrewed the repair port, bought new parts, and replaced the burned-out wiring.

The family doctor ordered some tests and warned that Joe's liver couldn't survive much more abuse. Elaine bit her lip and kept quiet. The problem was plainly beyond her and maybe beyond the doctor. If Joe was truly oppositional, as a psychiatrist had said a year ago, they could only make him drink more by objecting.

Every few weeks Joe Ward or another detective would faithfully report that there was nothing to report, and every few months someone from the sheriff's or prosecutor's office would visit the Idaho panhandle for a chat. There was no more disagreement on strategy. The decision about charging Green was being left up to Joe and Elaine, or so they were told, and Joe agreed that they should wait till they found Brenda, and if she wasn't found, bring the charges a few days before Green's release from prison. It was the best they could do.

In Clearview, the last of the dogged searchers had rolled up their sleeping bags and gone home. On a tip, Debbie Simmons and a small party searched weed by weed around the perimeter of Paine Field in Mukilteo, where Boeing rolled out its 747s. It was a two-day job on hands and knees, and there'd been no tips or sightings since. Julio DeSantis laid down his machete and Dick Cress his compass. IBar Arrington and Dennis Mackey were forced to the cold conclusion that the key to the mystery lay neither in rural bars nor gyms nor midnight phone calls to the Pittmans, but in the jumbled brain cells of a psychopath who was being shielded from outsiders by the system he'd defied.

To most Idaho friends and neighbors, Joe Gere continued to give a stable impression. Behind closed shades he would drink himself horizontal, and Elaine and the boys would tiptoe around his inert form. Her mask of equanimity slipped only once. Joe turned up his nose at the eggs Benedict and waffles she prepared for a Sunday breakfast and marched straight for his Kool-Aid stash. "Damn it, Joe!" she yelled. "You're killing yourself. Why can't you just *stop?*"

"Because I'm in pain!" he cried. *"I hurt!"* She remembered his mother Reva using the same words. His tone put her in mind of a trapped animal. He'd been having nightmares about Brenda again.

Elaine began to fear that he would be killed in a head-on crash. He confessed that sometimes he had blackouts and pulled his new black Camaro IROC-Z off the highway.

Jim Nash told Elaine, "We gotta do something, honey. His fuse is already lit. This boy's a walking time bomb."

"Why don't you talk to him, Jim?" she suggested. "He respects you."

"Do you think it would do any good?"

"No," she said.

On the two friends' next hunting trip, Joe missed a step while crossing a frozen stream and slid through the ice. As Nash helped him to his feet, he realized that Joe was dead weight. He'd been nipping again, but he didn't seem drunk so much as petrified, preserved, his body shut down and his reflexes on hold.

"Joe," he barked in his glass-shattering voice, "you're a damn fool. You're gonna lose your family. You're gonna die."

Joe sat on the bank and blinked, his head wobbling. Nash wasn't even sure he realized he was being addressed.

On the way home in the pickup, Joe revived and ordered Nash to stay out of his business. The two men almost came to blows.

When Elaine heard what had happened, she realized with a chill that half of the fortune-teller's prediction had come true. *He'll get in a big fight with his best friend and he won't be around much longer.* She didn't take as much stock in psychics and mystics as she'd taken before a dozen of them had failed to find Brenda, but this prediction was too close to ignore.

3

By March 1987, the Geres had been gone from Snohomish County for thirteen months, and there wasn't a single new lead in the abduction case. Michael Green refused to talk to detectives and carefully avoided inmates suspected of being informers. He was written up for smoking marijuana but engaged in no more altercations. He spent most of his time writing stories and poetry. Fellow prisoners gave him a wide berth, partially because of his size—he'd bulked up on the starchy prison food and Diana's weekend baskets—and partially because of his moony attitude and erratic ways.

Prison psychologists found no obvious psychopathology, yet acknowledged that there was something wrong with his head. His reputation remained that of a rapacious wimp who abused women and children. Such inmates were low on the pecking order, barely a step above snitches and cops.

4

In the spring of 1987 the Geres' family doctor took Elaine aside and warned that Joe's life could be measured in months. No human organism, not even one so sturdy and powerful, could stand up to such poisoning.

"His heart'll quit, or he'll have a stroke, or he'll just collapse from trauma," the doctor told her. "Elaine, prepare yourself and the boys."

Joe began to have attacks of delirium tremens, explosive fits that made her shoo her sons outside while he struggled with his visions and delusions. He screamed at God and the devil, "No, no! I can't go yet! *Not yet!*" He ordered Brenda to do her homework and slow down on the three-wheeler and look out for the manatees swimming through the walls. In lucid moments he would ask Elaine to summon a priest, even though he was neither Catholic nor religious. Every time the symptoms subsided, he opened a bottle.

Late one afternoon an attack of hiccups became so intense that he couldn't hold anything down, including liquor. By midnight he was writhing in bed yelling, "They're coming to get Edna. Save her, Jim! We gotta get her out. . . ."

Elaine held him all night. He refused to let her summon an ambulance or a doctor. "Okay," he said around four in the morning. "You can call the priest now." Then he turned to the bedside lamp and said, "Whattaya mean I *can't*? Okay, okay. . . ." She figured he was negotiating with God again.

A few minutes later he was talking to Brenda, reaching out with his long arms as though he were stroking her light brown hair.

"Joe," Elaine said. "Joe! Wake up!"

He turned dumbly and asked her who she was and what she was doing in his bedroom.

At seven-thirty, still hiccupping, he told Elaine, "I just saw God. It's okay to take me to the hospital now."

She deposited her sons in the emergency waiting room as nurses started IV drips. Joe ripped out the tubes. "I don't wanna be at this party!" he yelled. "Take me home!"

A doctor told Elaine that he was still in delirium tremens. When he revived briefly, he demanded to be released. Elaine argued with him for an hour. When a nurse approached with a hypodermic syringe, he ordered her to back off. "You're not knocking *me* out. Goddamn it, *I'm going home!*" His dark eyes were wide and unblinking. The hiccups resumed, louder than ever.

"Joe," Elaine said, "if we go home we'll just have to come back."

The doctor beckoned her into the hall. "I can't make him stay," he advised, "but if he leaves now, Elaine, he won't survive. Microscopic pieces of tissue are toxifying his bloodstream."

Elaine ran back to the room. "Joe!" she said. "You are staying *here!*"

She sent the boys home and stood guard.

In a week Joe was stabilized and transferred by ambulance to the Northwest Treatment Center in Seattle. Evergreen Motors granted leave with pay, and his family and friends provided support. On visits the boys would laugh and joke with their father, share junk food and videos, shoot a game of eight-ball when he was well enough to sight a cue.

Joey was ecstatic. "For the first time, I felt safe with my dad," he said later. "Up till then, the littlest thing could set him off."

In three weeks a program psychiatrist told Elaine, "Your husband's not treatable by the usual means. He's so bright, he tends to take over groups. And he's pretty cynical about therapy. Whenever anyone mentions religion, his eyes cloud over."

"Is it hopeless?" Elaine asked, convinced that the answer was yes.

"No," the doctor said. "There's one more route we can take."

A month later, Joe was back home and selling cars. He was hardly recognizable to his friends. There was energy in his step and color in his face. He'd lost flab and gained muscle tone, and his spirits seemed elevated. Elaine said he was "the happiest I'd seen him since high school. It was like he stopped being a Hungarian. It was a miracle."

The miracle was Librium.

5

Joe swallowed his capsules twice a day and seemed repulsed by alcohol. He attended an AA picnic and burbled to Elaine, "You wouldn't believe how much fun they have without drinking." He was always happy to discuss alcoholism in general or as it pertained to members of his AA group, but, as before, the subject of Joe Gere seemed to unnerve him, and he switched to other topics.

Every night he drove his black Camaro home and joined the family for dinner, sometimes helping to cook. He scraped the dishes and slotted them in the dishwasher. After dinner he helped his sons with their homework, but not in the snippy sarcastic style of old. He talked up his favorite authors, and soon had Joey rushing to bookstores.

He was patient about Mikey's ailments, and didn't complain about the cost of medicines and treatments. "Mom and me, we'll get you through all his," he told the chubby boy. In the past, he'd acted as though Mikey's frailties were self-induced.

The hunting season arrived in Joe's fourth straight month of sobriety, and he taught his sons how to track bear, how to walk like a ninja on the ball of the foot, how to take little crisscrossing steps to keep from spooking deer, how to analyze tracks and scats ("If it feels firm, like clay, it's fresh, and the deer's not far"), how to read a stream for Dolly Vardens and cutthroats, how to tie nymphs and dry flies and mix up foul-smelling bait for sturgeon and catfish. He bought a .22 for Joey, a .410 shotgun for Mikey, and a reloader and Redfield telescopic sight for himself, augmenting his armory. Sometimes he took Elaine to rifle ranges, where she tried her best not to outshoot him.

On weekends, he and Joey went on overnight hunting trips into the high mountains, first stopping at a deli for a stock of gourmet food: pepperoni, Coke, and French bread. After one trip, Joey told Elaine he felt as though he were getting to know his father for the first time.

"The boys are finally seeing their real dad," she told Edna Nash excitedly. "They're seeing the man I married."

Joe began collecting bigger bonuses at the car lot. "He used to think you couldn't sell cars without getting sloshed with your customers," Elaine said, "but he found out he sold even more when he was dry. He would come home with his pockets stuffed with cash, and he'd say, 'Let's go to the drive-in and dinner. Let's go bowling.' He threw money at the boys and surprised me with gifts. The doctor warned that he might have mood swings on his medication, but he seemed to stay level. He showed a playful side that I hadn't seen since Brenda left. He thought it was funny to grow a beard, but it itched him so much he shaved it off."

On a whim she bought him a red rose and ordered the florist to deliver it to his desk at Evergreen Ford. Her message was pilfered from one of their favorite Lee Greenwood songs: "I don't mind the thorns when you're the rose."

Joe came home and told her he'd had to step outside to compose himself. She'd always known that the Geres hid deep sentimentality under their cold exteriors. How rare this was! It was like seeing him at the Cinnamon Cinder for the first time and realizing that he was different.

"He bought me a new IROC," she recalled, "and we argued about which was faster, mine or his black 'eighty-six. One morning we pulled up side by side at a red light in downtown Sandpoint, and he gunned his engine. I held up my thumb. He had a shift kit, so he jumped right out when the light changed, but I nailed him at the corner. Our tires were squealing and smoking. It was a twenty-five zone and we were probably doing fifty.

"I ran into a cop the next day and he said, 'Who won the race?'

"I said, 'Well, Joe got me out of the hole, but I won.'

"He said, 'We heard ya. Blew off his doors, huh?' He acted like it was kinda funny."

6

In November 1987, a fire gutted the house in the country, and the Geres rented a condominium in Sandpoint during repairs. Fires had been traumatic in Joe's life, and he often relived the scenes in his dreams: his mother's charred nightgown flaking off her body, the car fire that ended his police career, the heater fire in Bonners Ferry when Brenda saved the family.

After the Laclede blaze, Elaine thought she detected subtle changes in his behavior. He seemed a little uneasy, less joyous, jittery. He begged off homework sessions with the boys—unlike the new Joe—and began avoiding household chores. On the night of an AA meeting, a member called to ask why he hadn't arrived. When he came home at midnight, Elaine didn't have the heart to question him.

Thanksgiving approached, and Joe always seemed to miss Brenda more on holidays. He'd made it through the second anniversary of her disappearance, September 19, by working a double shift at the car lot and taking the family out. The longer Brenda was gone, the more Elaine and the boys felt the necessity of talking about her, but Joe persisted in his solitary grief. Whenever he discussed the case on the phone or met with visiting detectives, everyone in the house gave him space. Apparently the subject would remain taboo in the family circle for the rest of their lives.

His physician had warned that no one could take Librium indefinitely, and the process of withdrawal was begun in November. On Thanksgiving Day, Joe ran out of the little capsules and the doctor refused to renew the prescription.

Elaine found a half pint of vodka under a mattress in the guest room. Two days later she was visiting the Laclede house and noticed empty liquor bottles on the rubbish pile. Joe said they belonged to the workers.

He began to smell of mints and alcohol, insisting that someone must have spilled a few drops on him while he was closing a sale at the bar. She decided it was unfair to everyone to pretend there was no problem. Christmas wasn't far off, a trying season for the disturbed and depressed. "Honey," she said, "the boys and I were talking. We want the new Joe back."

She was pleased that he didn't insult her intelligence by acting as though he didn't understand.

"Hon, don't you realize you'd be better off without me?" he asked. "You've got my disability pay and your own job, and you'd save all the money I piss away." He paused. "And you've got my insurance money."

"The insurance wouldn't pay off," she observed, "if you, uh . . . did away with yourself." She wished she remembered the fine print in the policy she'd bought from Julio DeSantis.

"No," Joe agreed. "Not for two more months." It bothered her that he was counting.

"Honey, we don't *want* insurance money," she said. "We want *you.*"

His head slumped. "I'm a drag on you," he said. It didn't sound maudlin, more like a simple statement of fact. She couldn't let it stand.

"Joe," she said, "you *cannot* leave us. Those boys need a father. They need *you.* We love you, Joe. We couldn't go on without you."

"Sure you could." It sounded as though he'd made up his mind.

Two days later, while driving his sons to school in Sandpoint, Joe told them, "If it wasn't for your mom, I wouldn't be here today. I'd be—" He broke off the sentence as though he'd already said too much.

"You'd be where, Dad?" little Mikey piped up.

"Just, uh . . . not here."

Joey tearfully reported to his mother that Dad was hinting about suicide again. With Jim Nash's assistance, Elaine hustled Joe to the clinic to reactivate the weaning process; obviously it had gone off track. The doctor reluctantly wrote a new Librium prescription and ordered Joe to take one each morning till further notice.

The medication wasn't enough to ease Joe's pain, and he began nipping from the bottle earlier in the evenings and walking around groggy from the mix of drug and alcohol. His moods were unpredictable: he was as likely to fling a glass against the kitchen wall as arrive home with flowers for Elaine and toys for the boys. But most of the time he was simply a lump.

The doctor prescribed an antidepressant, which had the effect of making him irritable, high, and lusting for alcohol. Soon he was mixing drugs and losing track of the amounts.

In February 1988, while the Laclede property was still under repair, he phoned Elaine at the county office where she clerked and asked her in a slow deliberate voice what she would do if he went back on liquor for good—"just a few drinks now and then, like other people, so I don't feel so bad all the time."

In desperation, she said she would take the boys and leave.

"You *would?*"

"Yes, I would, Joe. Because you're two different people. Look how you were when you weren't drinking. Now you're so depressed you want to kill yourself. We've got two boys to think about."

Two days later he called her again from the condo. "I'm sitting on the floor in the kitchen, next to the garbage," he said. "I got my forty-four pointed at my head. I'm gonna blow my brains out."

Elaine begged him to wait. "You're just feeling bad right now, honey."

He explained that Brenda was alone, without a single member of her family, and he couldn't bear the thought. "I'll be with her and you'll have the boys."

"Honey, just lay down." She tried to keep her voice calm and soothing. "Take a nap and we'll talk when I get home."

He was snoring on a daybed when she arrived. He told her the TV had been showing Mel Gibson pointing a gun at his head in the movie *Lethal Weapon.*

"I don't know, hon," he said, his head heavy on her shoulder. "It just seemed like the right thing."

A few days later he interrupted her work again. "Good-bye, honey. I'm going to the mountains and kill myself."

She rushed home and found the front door standing open and the condo empty. He returned in his pickup just as she was picking up the phone to call for help. She could smell the alcohol three feet away.

7

By the end of the winter of 1988, suicide feints had become a regular part of their family life. Elaine never became accustomed to them or took Joe's threats lightly. He could do away with himself in a second in this apartment full of guns. The latest was a Colt .38 that he'd bought her "for protection." They kept it atop the mantel, loaded.

Friends and relatives provided solace but no real answers. The doctor restored a full regimen of tranquilizers; they calmed him but barely slowed his drinking. Joe's brother Bob, still fighting the liquor habit himself, warned on one of his long-distance calls, "Joe hasn't been right since the injury, Elaine. Don't let him out of your sight."

Another alcoholic, Dennis Mackey, usually a source of comfort over the phone lines, spoke with his typical Halls of Montezuma bluntness. "Maybe it's cruel to say, Elaine, but if he won't lay off the sauce, you could wake up next to a dead man. I love Joe, love all of you, Elaine. You better be ready."

"He's been talking about moving again. Maybe that'll help."

"How many times have you moved?"

"I was just counting up the other night. Thirteen times."

"In—?"

"Twenty years."

"What did it solve?"

Jim Nash told Elaine that Joe had taken to discussing his own death daily. "He'll sit right here in this front room and tell me how he's gonna do it, the same damn story, drunk or sober. He says he can't live without Brenda. He says, 'It's time now, Jim. My insurance is incontestable. They'll be better off.' "

Elaine reread the policy. They'd been making payments for just over two years. The company would have to cough up $50,000 on Joe's death, no matter what the cause. She didn't like the timing.

In late March, he turned over in bed and asked, "Would you remarry if I died?"

She said, "Never," and meant it.

The next morning he instructed his sons not to permit their mom to date after he was gone. "People are supposed to mate like wolves, for life." Mikey waited till he left for work, then cried.

For the first time in her life, Elaine was apprehensive about the approach of Easter. She tried to talk Joe into attending services on Ash Wednesday and again on Good Friday, but he brushed her off. He looked like someone who'd just stepped out of his coffin. His handsome face had turned blimpy and soft, his skin a pale yellow. He walked like a sixty-year-old and squinted in sunlight.

As he was leaving the house to visit the Nashes on the morning before Easter, Joe made a macabre little joke. "I'm already half dead," he said. "I might as well do the other half."

Elaine started to tell him she was getting tired of sick remarks like that and they weren't funny, but he was already gone.

Jim Nash was pleased to see Joe's new 4x4 demonstrator pull into the driveway around 11:00 A.M. The Geres had been feeding up some piglets on the Laclede property, and Joe used Jim's tools and shop to build pens.

Jim and Edna were surprised when their friend didn't step right into the house. Instead, he leaned against the trunk of a small tree about fifty feet away and slid into a sitting position. Jim thought, What's the poor guy up to now? It was a bright day in the north woods, unusually warm for early April. Joe raised his face toward the sun and leaned against the trunk.

Hours passed, and Joe hardly moved. Jim thought, Why doesn't he go home to Elaine and the boys? He's a grown man with a family, not Huckleberry Finn.

A ray of sunlight glinted off Joe's hands. "Come here, Edna," Jim called out. "Is that a bottle?"

Edna took a look and said she was afraid so.

Jim sighed. "Tomorrow's Easter," he said. "He's got that little girl on his mind."

Just before dark, Joe stumbled through the back door. "Jim?" he croaked, his voice off-key. "Edna? I'm, uh—*here*."

Jim steered him to the couch. His hands were empty. An afternoon in the sun had provided time to knock off the whole bottle.

Edna brewed coffee as Jim tried to decipher his friend's mumbles. After a while the weak voice strengthened. "I'm gonna kill you, you son of a bitch," Joe said, gesturing in the busy style of his father. "Say your prayers, asshole."

Jim asked if he was okay, and Joe blinked hard. "I'm gonna hire somebody," he said. "Or else I'm gonna get inside and do it myself. I dunno which."

After a few cups of scalding black coffee, he demanded a beer and began to talk. "Either me or the guy I hire, we'll break some law in Washington and have ourselves sent to McNeil Island."

"Simple as that?" Jim asked.

"Simple as that."

Jim started to point out flaws, but the plan was too ridiculous to merit discussion. What kind of selective crime would Joe commit? Robbery? Assault? Who would be the victim? A little old lady who might die of a heart attack and convert the offense into a homicide? A bruiser who might break Joe's skull? A cop who might shoot him? And how would he manage to get himself shipped to McNeil Island instead of Walla Walla or Monroe or some other Washington prison? Unless he committed a felony, he would end up serving his time in a county jail. Then how would he get to Green? And who would take care of Elaine and the boys?

Nash realized that the alcohol had corroded Joe's brain and the damage was probably permanent. What else could explain such a lunatic plan or such deadpan seriousness in presenting it?

"Joe," he said, putting his big ex-boxer's hand on his friend's forearm, "you're not making a damn bit of sense. People like us don't kill. You can get revenge other ways. Murder's out of the question."

Joe's eyes glistened as Edna entered the room. He turned away and murmured, "Brenda, Brenda. She was my life."

He stayed late, chugging beers, mumbling to the Nashes, shadows on the walls, sometimes to visions of Elaine and the boys. "I'm so sorry," he said toward the end. "I'm *so* sorry."

"About what, Joe?" Jim asked. He felt as though he were talking to someone in a trance.

"Didn't give enough . . . enough attention," Joe mumbled. "Teach, teach her . . . how to protect . . ." His voice faded.

It was 10:00 P.M. when he staggered toward the Ford pickup. Jim offered to drive him home, but Joe didn't seem to hear. He was so drunk, Jim said later, "that I don't think he even knew when he left or who he was leaving. Edna and I knew something was about to happen. I called the condo a while later and I couldn't believe it—Joe answered the phone. I guess that truck had autopilot."

8

At five in the morning, Joe shook Elaine and said he was going out to the Laclede property to check on the fire repairs, feed the two pigs and plant some rye. He'd plowed the front field a week earlier.

As she turned off her alarm in the dark, she thought, Better you than me, hon. She'd had problems with hogs in Fontana, and the relationship hadn't improved through the years. The boys felt the same. But even at his lowest ebb, Joe dreamed about running live-stock. He'd fenced four of the five acres at Laclede with cedar rails and posts that he'd cut himself, and lately he'd been talking about buying feeder calves. Elaine knew who would end up doing the heavy lifting, but she didn't object to anything that brought him closer to reality.

She intended to take the boys to Easter mass and then join Joe in Laclede. Just before he left, he said, "Bring lunch. We'll make a day of it. The boys can use some target practice." Seven or eight hours earlier, he'd collapsed into bed dead drunk, and now he sounded like a businessman planning his day. She'd always marveled at the Geres' resilience.

At ten o'clock she awoke for the second time and realized she'd overslept Easter mass. She roused the boys, prepared picnic lunches, and headed for Laclede.

When they arrived at eleven-thirty, Mikey threw up and flopped on the couch, his regular reaction to the tortuous dirt road. Joe sat at the kitchen table sending out whiskey fumes so strong that Elaine half expected them to be visible.

"Did you guys go to church?" he asked. He seemed in a good mood, but Elaine knew it could change with his next swig.

"No," she said. "We slept in."

"I had my own Easter sunrise service. I watched the sun come up while I was feeding the pigs."

Elaine broke out some sandwiches, but he didn't seem interested. He seldom ate when he was drunk. After a while she began laying down shelf paper, and Joe and Joey went outside to broadcast rye. Joe drove around the four-acre patch while his son flung handfuls of seed from the bed of the pickup.

Around three in the afternoon, Mikey was asleep on the couch when Elaine heard a honk. The truck was parked out front. Joe called out, "We could sure use some help."

She figured he was lonesome and wanted company, but then she noticed his soused and silly look, the one that signaled trouble.

She climbed into the back of the truck with Joey.

"Dad's drinking hard," the boy whispered. "He threw a bottle of vodka over the fence."

Elaine thought, Our Easter celebration is over. Of all his hallucinogenics, vodka made him the craziest.

He started up the truck and resumed the circles in the field. After about twenty minutes, he yelled, "Hey, don't throw so much! We gotta make it last."

It was just turning dark, and Elaine noticed fresh seed on the ground below the tailgate.

"Joe," she called out, "we already planted this spot."

The truck lurched to a stop. "Get up here!" he bellowed.

Elaine slid off the back and walked to the driver's side. Joe's head bobbed against his chest. He asked in a soft voice, "Are you telling me how to plant grass?"

Her heart told her to reach out to the suffering man, but her mind told her it really didn't matter. At this stage of inebriation, he might take offense at a hug, a compliment, any little gesture. The safest course was to walk away, which could also set him off. It was so discouraging.

She lowered her eyes and said, "Oh, Joe, what's the use?"

"You're right," he said without raising his head. "There's . . . no use."

He reached to his right and picked up the .357 Colt revolver he kept in the truck to finish off deer. He raised the muzzle toward her face.

She reeled backward toward a small tree, then turned to run. She heard a shot and yelled, *"No!"*

Joey vaulted off the back of the truck to her side. She was holding her head with both hands, and at first the boy thought she'd been shot. Together, they wrenched open the door.

Joe was slumped over the wheel, the pistol clenched in his hand. She pulled it away and set it on the dash. As she did, his cigarette lighter fell from the same hand that had held the pistol. Apparently he'd been too drunk to feel the extra metal in his palm.

Blood welled from his nose and ears and dripped down his chin. The front of his head was a crimson mass of tissue and bone. His face was lopsided. It looked as though he'd thrown up, but then she realized that the white stuff on his lap was brain matter. She'd seen it when she dressed out animals.

She grabbed his wrist and felt no pulse. She leaned into the car, kissed his lips, and said good-bye. She didn't cry, nor did Joey. Instead she stood in front of the sapling, saying, "Why why *why?*"

Then she let out a scream that echoed off the craggy bluffs behind the house. She kept repeating, "Why why . . ." Joey figured she must have said it a hundred times before he stopped her by squeezing her tightly. For five or ten minutes they rocked in each other's arms, sobbing.

"I can't accept this, Joey," she said. "I just can't accept this."

At last she calmed. "Go get the neighbors," she said. The nearest family lived a hundred yards across the field.

Joey banged on the door and banged again when it wasn't immediately opened. A woman answered. "I need help," he said.

"What's wrong?" she asked.

He couldn't bring himself to say the words. "Please," he said, "just come."

He stumbled back across the furrows. His mother sobbed softly, and he pulled her close again. It seemed to both of them that they stayed in the field forever.

The neighbor took in the scene and led Elaine away while Joey went to the Gere house to get Mikey. "Don't tell him," Elaine said. "Let me."

The sheriff was called, and the three Geres huddled in the neighbor's living room. "Mikey," Elaine said, "Dad shot himself."

The eight-year-old boy looked stricken. Joey had stopped crying. Elaine tried to compose herself. It would help to calm the boys. They were all that mattered now.

A businesslike deputy sheriff wanted to know why so many firearms were racked in the rear of the cab. Elaine explained, "We were gonna take the boys target shooting."

He surveyed the scene, circled the truck, then conducted a field interrogation. He asked, What hand held the gun? How could the victim have held a gun and a cigarette lighter in the same hand? He asked Joey where his mom had been when the gun went off.

"Standing outside the door," the boy said. "She put her hands to her head and screamed."

Through her confusion, Elaine finally comprehended that she was a murder suspect. The deputy asked if she'd washed her hands since the shooting. "No," she said. "Do you want me to take a paraffin test? A lie detector test?"

She willed herself not to be upset. The deputy was doing the same job that her husband and her beloved Uncle Hank had done for years. Joe was dead and she had two boys to raise. Nothing else mattered. *I have to be strong for my boys.* She couldn't afford the luxury of going to pieces.

After the coroner arrived to transport the body, Elaine drove the boys to the condo in Bonners Ferry and started making calls. Jim and Edna Nash said they would be right over. Her mother Evelyn promised to drive straight to the airport in Reno. When Elaine told Joe Sr. what had happened, he said, "My Joe? Dead?" Then there was a hollow silence, followed by a dial tone. She learned later that he'd been unable to catch his breath and collapsed. The old miner had fought emphysema for years.

When Joe Sr.'s wife Pat passed the message to Rick Gere, Joe's little brother and idolater, Rick yelled to his wife in the kitchen, "Joe died. We gotta get to Dad's house right away."

On the way in his car, he said, "My God, if I have a serious problem now, who do I call?"

Elaine's last message went to Dennis Mackey. From the instant the ex-Marine had arrived at the log house with his friend IBar, Dennis had been the Geres' main source of information and encouragement. Whenever there was the slightest development in the case, he was on the phone to report. If Elaine or Joe needed an errand performed back in Snohomish County, Dennis did the job.

"Dennis," she said, "we lost Joe. He killed himself."

She had to repeat twice before he understood. He sounded as though he'd been drinking. He told her he was sorry, discussed how Elaine and the boys were bearing up, then said, "If you ask me, Elaine, it was a merciful bullet. You'll never have to move again."

Elaine comforted her sons on the big bed. Early in the morning, she started to doze off and reached out to touch her husband before she remembered that he wasn't there. She fought an urge to cry. The boys were asleep, and she couldn't get up without waking one or both. She remembered the time she'd shaken her mother by the shoulders and warned her that she had to go on after Beverly left home and everything looked bleak. *Mom, you still got two kids to raise!*

That's what'll see me through, Elaine said to herself. My boys . . .

9

In the morning, she heard from the sheriff's office. Joe's blood alcohol level at the time of death had been .25 percent, two and a half to three times the amount that signified statutory intoxication in most states. The deputy told her where to claim the body and apologized for his sharp questioning the day before.

She drove her sons to school in Sandpoint and continued to

Spokane International Airport to pick up her mother. Evelyn seemed much calmer than she'd been after Brenda's disappearance. For years, mother and daughter had been anticipating Joe's death over the long-distance phone lines. The final act was no surprise.

The two women made arrangements to fly the body to Fontana so Joe could be buried next to his mother, as he'd requested. Big Ed rested in the same cemetery, along with other Mayzsaks and Geres. Elaine reserved an adjacent plot for herself and another for Brenda.

She arranged a joint memorial service. For the last year she'd been studying up on grief and loss—anthologies of poetry, pamphlets and books and mailings from Families and Friends of Missing Persons and Victims of Violent Crime, articles in the *Reader's Digest* and inspirational magazines—and she'd learned that her family needed something called "closure." She hoped the double service would help.

"Joe was sure heavy in that cargo hold," she told his sister Linda when they arrived at the Ontario airport. "Right after we took off, I heard a thud, like the coffin slipped back. Me and the boys looked at each other. We knew who it was."

Linda commented that her big brother had always made his presence known. "He went out in a dramatic way, didn't he? That was Joe's style. Read too much Hemingway, I guess."

Southern California newspapers ran the human interest story—EX-COP KILLS SELF OVER MISSING DAUGHTER—and TV crews crashed the funeral. Elaine insisted on simplicity. At the mortuary, she pressed the rosary from Brenda's first Holy Communion into Joe's fingers. His hands felt like plastic. He wore his best blue suit, and his face was still crooked. "Why does he look like that?" she asked the director.

"There wasn't a whole lot to work with, ma'am," the man said politely. "We had to rebuild his forehead." She ordered the casket closed.

Her irreligious husband had called for a priest every time he thought he was dying, so the ceremony was Catholic. The chapel was decorated with a crucifix, wreaths, flowers and a large photograph of Joe, eyes hidden by dark glasses, cop-style. A bouquet at the head of the coffin bore a ribbon marked BRENDA. Some twenty friends and relatives attended.

Just before the ceremony began, Elaine stepped up to touch the coffin for the last time. To her amazement, it was open.

Her mother said over her shoulder, "That doesn't even look like Joe."

Evelyn raised her camera. For years the matriarch had memorialized her loved ones with photographic portraits in their coffins.

"Mom!" Elaine said. "Don't take that picture."

It was too late. Elaine swore never to look at the print, and never did. "To me it was no longer Joe," she explained later. "From the second he died in that rye field, he was gone."

She reminded an attendant that she'd ordered the casket closed, and the lid was lowered. A priest from the Mayzsak family's home church offered a blessing and sprinkled holy water. He ended the ceremony by looking upward and saying, "Brenda, rest in peace with your father." Elaine squeezed the boys' hands and thought, I'll bet that's the part Joe liked best.

Her mother arranged Elaine, Joey and Mikey in front of the closed coffin and took a final family portrait for her album. Joey looked tearful, Mikey bewildered, Elaine numb.

Joe's childhood friend Deputy Sheriff Paul Curry joined five pallbearers including Joe's brothers and stricken father, who looked as if he hadn't stopped crying since the night Elaine phoned the news. An honor guard emerged from two patrol cars, and a six-man rifle team fired a volley over the sloping hillside facing the Jurupa Hills. After a deputy folded the American flag and handed it to Elaine, the man she'd married for life disappeared beneath the gritty, sandy earth of their childhoods.

10

The three surviving Geres returned to the Northwest with its remind-ers of Joe and Brenda, and Elaine resumed her weekly practice of phoning Snohomish County and asking when Michael Green would be brought to trial. Joey auditioned for the role of man of the family, bossing Mikey and echoing Elaine's commands, until she took him aside and said, "Joey, let me be the parent. Mikey's only in fifth grade. You just enjoy life."

Both boys remained fearful, clinging to her on trips away from the house. It took her awhile to realize that they were overly con-cerned about her well-being. "Don't leave, Mom," Mikey would say as she started to leave. "Stay here. Me and Joey'll take care of you."

The boys paid a price for their notoriety. "People didn't know how to react," Elaine explained later. "Joey's best friend stopped coming over, and I asked why. Joey said he didn't know.

"So I called Jeff and said, 'Did you know Joey's dad killed himself?'

"He said, 'Yeah, I heard.'

" 'Well, he's really feeling pretty bad. He sure could use a friend.'

"He says, 'Oh, okay. I didn't know whether I should come over or not.' He was at our door in ten minutes and they were friends again."

It took only a few months for her to realize that her sons weren't recovering from their trauma. "In their minds, every street, every tree, every trail connected up to their father. It was like they were walking around in permanent shock."

She decided to move to Carson City, Nevada, to be near her mother and sister. When the boys asked why they were leaving, she said it was time to start a new life.

X

THE WAY BACK

1

They gave up the Laclede property, losing the $3,000 equity, and used Joe's insurance payout to make an $18,000 down payment on a white elephant in Carson City. When they moved in, Mikey cracked, "Hey, Mom, where's Grampa Munster?"

Elaine went to work as a legal secretary and enrolled in a general studies program at Western Nevada Community College. "I've got to get an education to be the breadwinner for these boys," she explained to her mother. "I've got to improve myself."

The sagging house needed attention, and she soon found herself hanging wallpaper and sanding floors at three in the morning. The work came naturally; what she hadn't learned from her father about home improvement, she'd learned by using Joe's trick of studying workmen.

As soon as she met one challenge in the creaky house, another developed. The dining-room chandelier hung by a twisted thin chain, and one of the baguettes fell into her soup. She repaired the unit and redid the wiring. She laid down a wall-to-wall rug in the living room, patched the kitchen linoleum, and papered the shelves.

"Mom, we gotta get more sleep," Joey said one morning, digging at his dark hazel eyes. "What was that racket last night?"

Elaine explained that she'd been replacing some warped paneling and using a rental staple gun. "That wasn't all I heard," the boy said.

"Well, no. I was using the circular saw for a while. And . . . the jigsaw."

"Well, gosh, what's next?"

"The bathroom."

She'd intended just to install new linoleum but found that the flooring around the toilet was rotting. She ripped out the spongy boards, installed plastic plumbing, replaced the floor with water-resistant plywood, then discovered that the bathtub was leaking around the edges. She chipped out the tile till she reached more rot, and ended up having to replace the tiles and set a new tub in waterproof gypsum board.

She felt a twinge of anxiety when she stepped back from puttying a window one night and realized that her home-improvement job was essentially done. The place gleamed like a realtor's show house. The makeover had cost about $2,000 in materials and months of elbow grease, but she'd turned the white elephant into an attractive residence. Gee, she thought, it must be time to move.

Her losses seemed to weigh on her mind when she was inactive, and she gained another month of stability by helping to hang new wallpaper at her sister Beverly's house. The finished product looked so stylish that she did the same for her mother.

The boys weren't adjusting as well. Mikey was enduring his usual succession of arcane ailments, most of them rooted in an unstable immune system, and missing weeks of school. His asthma attacks worsened, and there were nights when Elaine wondered if he would draw another breath.

Ninth-grader Joey maintained a good attendance record but found the multiethnic school with its youth gangs and racial conflicts a big adjustment after the bucolic students of northern Idaho. Panhandle towns like Bonners Ferry and Sandpoint were known for survivalist originals who collected weapons, got drunk, and detested lawmen, but their children didn't carry knives and zip guns to school.

Both Gere boys were slow to make friends in the urban setting. So was Elaine. "I spent my time with my boys, and I wanted it that way. Men asked me out and I'd say, 'No, no. It's too soon after Joe.' To me, it would always be too soon."

* * *

One night she went into her sons' bedroom to kiss them good night. Mikey was asleep, but Joey seemed pensive. "What's the matter, kid?" Elaine asked.

Joey turned his face toward the wall and said, "I was thinking about Dad." He seemed reluctant to go on. "The way he always gave us candy and stuff."

"Well, honey," Elaine said, "we talk about Brenda all the time. Why not Dad?"

"I don't know, Mom. It's just . . . I don't want to make you sad."

Dear God, Elaine said to herself, how stupid I've been. Everybody's been protecting everybody. She held her son tight and they talked about Joe.

The discussions continued over the next few days and began to include Mikey. She learned that her supersensitive sons had been so reluctant to cause her any pain that they'd been holding back a secret: they considered Idaho their home and wanted to return. The Gem State might remind them of their dad and his death, but it also had mountains, streams and woods, horses, old friends, playmates, maybe even gems. They'd hated Carson City from the first.

"Okay, boys," Elaine said, "let's go home."

2

She sold the Carson City house at a $10,000 profit. Back in Sandpoint, she enrolled the boys in their old school and herself in a community college in Coeur d'Alene, an hour's drive. She bought a house on Hickory Street for $61,500 and began hacking away at the interior. They'd hardly moved in before Joey dropped a tin-can lid down the toilet and stopped it up. A rented snake failed to dislodge the metal. Elaine got out her tool kit and began chipping at the tile at the base of the toilet.

For a few minutes she wondered if she was fated to spend the rest of her life fixing bathrooms. She lifted off the toilet, cleared the obstruction, then decided to replace the flooring. When the two-day job was finished, she had to reseat the toilet, an occult technique known only to plumbing contractors, her father and her late husband. A friendly hardware clerk sold her the required waxy ring and showed her how to attach it to the base of a toilet and bolt it down.

"Real easy," he said. "A woman could do it."

She laughed. As Big Ed's daughter and Joe's wife, she'd heard such remarks all her life. After three false starts, she reseated the toilet. The clerk was right. A woman could do it.

Her first job after the return to Sandpoint was with the U.S. Census Bureau, driving the back roads and helping citizens to fill out forms. At first she was uneasy. Historically the Idaho panhandle had sheltered fugitives and runaways—her husband and Jim Nash had once encountered Christopher Boyce, the spy of the book *The Falcon and the Snowman*, while Boyce was on the run from the FBI—and she was always afraid she would enter a mountain cabin and never come out. She wore baggy clothes, heavy engineer's boots, and hid her flashy blond hair under a wool cap.

One day an owl-eyed logger invited her into his shack and couldn't seem to stop staring at her face. "Say," he said after several uncomfortable minutes, "aren't you . . . the widow?" He paused.

"Gere," she said. "Mrs. Joe Gere."

"That Green fella," the man said. "You want him dynamited? Or should I just chop off his head?"

A carpenter in town asked a similar question. Her brother Jimmy bought an AK-47 and told Elaine on the phone, "That son of a bitch Green won't be in jail forever. I'm gonna take care of business."

There'd been a lot of bourbon-based bluff and machismo from Joe, Dennis, IBar and even Joe Sr., down in Fontana, but she didn't have the slightest doubt about Jimmy's intentions. A few Hell's Angels still limped around San Bernardino County in his memory.

After the census job was phased out, Elaine clerked for the Bonner County Planning and Zoning Office. At lunchtime and after hours, she Xeroxed building and repair codes to help with her renovations.

One of her bosses had a home-repair encyclopedia on his desk, and she copied it page by page and smuggled it home in sheafs.

When she sold the Hickory Street place for $79,500, an $18,000 profit in only a year and a half, she realized she could make almost as much money improving houses as she could at a regular job.

3

For the next four years, Elaine and the boys bought and sold run-down properties, living rent-free and always turning a profit. At sales time, she would use her California real estate experience and save the 7 to 10 percent commission. Soon she had enough money to invest in some land and other properties. She and the boys continued to collect Joe's $650 monthly disability pension, plus $1,350 a month from his Social Security, giving them a sound financial core. She was scoring A's and B's at North Idaho College, and she'd opened college funds for her sons. Maybe, she thought, we can save a few bucks on graduation gowns by using each other's.

She would always love Joe and revere his memory, but she realized that she was becoming reconciled to his loss, although she maintained her relentless pressure on the Snohomish County police and prosecutors. She still refused to date. "When you've had the best," she explained to her mother in one of their long-distance gabfests, "why bother?"

Brenda remained a permanent lump in her throat. One night in early 1991, five and a half years after the disappearance, Elaine saw her daughter in an unusually vivid dream. An angelic-looking Brenda floated into sight, smiling sweetly, her head moving gently from side to side and her hair flowing behind her as though she were bobbing in a river. Her body was covered with a gray-black shroud. A slender arm reached out as though to beckon Elaine closer. Then she faded away.

By dawn, Elaine thought she'd figured out the dream. It meant that Brenda had been found. She couldn't wait to call Joe Ward.

When she reached him at 9:00 A.M., he said there was nothing to report.

Once again the diligent Ward put down the phone feeling that he'd let Elaine down. By late September 1991, the lead investigator had kept a picture of Michael Green on his wall for six years, and the case stayed on his mind like a malignant, untreatable tumor. He'd always been convinced that the child lay dead in the woods, but that hadn't relieved him from the obligation of checking out the leads that still arrived at the rate of one a week: *I saw this girl at the 7-Eleven in Madison, Wisconsin, and she looked so sad. . . . Your Brenda Gere's dancing in a strip joint in Tacoma. . . . We got the missing Gere kid in our lockup. She's a runaway. . . .* The number of investigative hours had reached the thousands. Then there was the rat-a-tat-tat of calls from Elaine, never diminishing as the years passed: "Joe, what's new? Any signs of Brenda? What about Green? Are you ready to charge him? Would it help if I came over?" He never begrudged her the calls, and he never rushed her off the phone. But each time he hung up, he felt a little less worthy of his badge.

Ward and his colleagues calculated that Michael Green had had no more than an hour to dispose of the body, which meant that Brenda could lie anywhere within a forty- or fifty-mile radius of Thirty-fifth Avenue and Grannis Road. The whole U.S. Forest Service and a division of infantry couldn't have searched every square foot of the second- and third-growth forests that ran to the Cascades on the east, Puget Sound on the west, Seattle to the south, and the Skagit Valley to the north. Ward figured that all the volunteers and helicopters and dogs and police officers might have managed to cover 2 percent of the area at most.

Not that they hadn't turned up plenty of bodies and parts: Michelle Koski, Robin Maria Kenworthy, Hazel Gelnett, Jay Roland Cook, all stabbed or strangled to death; the skull of a Korean national named Sun Nyo Lee; unidentified bits of scalp, hair and ear in a trash dump; a severed human leg along the Skykomish River; the dismembered body of a male near the village of Gold Bar.

But . . . no Brenda.

The intense Ward had never known such a frustrating case. The killer was already behind bars, serving time for rape, not murder. His earliest release date was July 1992. The prosecutor's office planned to charge Green a few days before his release even if Brenda wasn't found, but the prospects of conviction were poor unless some unexpected physical evidence turned up. And what could that be, after six years?

Every day Ward stared at the picture of Michael Green and wondered what he would do if the monster returned to Snohomish County a free man. Maybe justice would take another form. The last anyone had heard from IBar Arrington, he was busy learning Green's hangouts so he could be on hand when the killer was released.

"We'll get into a fight," the former heavyweight boxer explained to a deputy, "and I gotta fight back, don't I? Green's gonna make my day."

Ward was a by-the-books cop, but he sympathized with IBar's attitude. So did colleagues like Tom Pszonka, Bryce Siegel, Rick Bart and Clyde Foot. "If IBar doesn't do the job," Pszonka offered, "maybe I could help out." He sounded half serious.

As lead detective, Ward was responsible for tracking Green's whereabouts, and every three or four months he checked in with the McNeil Island facility to make sure the big man was there. The Department of Corrections had a habit of quietly transplanting its charges, sometimes for their own safety, sometimes for the tranquillity of the prison, sometimes for reasons known only to itself. Because of his bulk, Green was monitored more closely than most.

In May of 1991, fourteen months before Green's earliest release date, Ward checked with McNeil Island and was told that inmate 917391 remained in residence. As always, the detective reminded prison officials to advise him of any change. He presumed that a flyer had been attached to Green's jacket to this effect.

Less than a month later, Ward returned one of Elaine Gere's periodic calls and assured her that if it was up to the Snohomish County Sheriff's Department, Michael Green's feet would never touch free soil again.

"My boys still worry about him," she said. "I've got a loaded thirty-eight in my purse."

"Relax. Unless he's a helluva swimmer, he's still at McNeil Island."

On a hunch, the scrupulous detective double-checked the prison. "How's Mike Green doing?" he asked an official.

"Which Michael Green? We got two."

This was news to Ward. "Michael Kay Green," he said, and read off his prison number.

The voice on the phone said, "Oh, he's been moved to pre-release."

"He's been *what?*"

"He's at Pine Lodge."

Ward put in a call to the correctional facility, three hundred miles across the state in the town of Medical Lake, just west of Spokane. A clerk informed him that Michael Kay Green was being held under minimum security but was allowed to perform supervised work by day. At the moment he was cutting brush. Sometimes he helped to fight forest fires.

Ward thought, My God, the guy's not far from the Geres!

The prosecutor's office was three flights downstairs in the county courthouse building, and the lanky Ward didn't wait for the elevator. He burst into the office and told a deputy prosecutor, "I want murder charges filed against Michael Green right now! He's working in the woods fifty miles from Elaine Gere. He could run the same as he ran before, and hurt more people."

The prosecutor promised to look into the matter. An hour later, Ward was told that murder charges would be filed against Green on September 19, the sixth anniversary of Brenda's abduction. It was three months away. A hot conversation ensued. The deputy prosecutor explained that witnesses had to be tracked down and re-interviewed.

Ward said, "Frankly, I'm not burdened by your problems with trying the case. I've got different problems. I don't want the public at risk. I don't want more children killed."

"Joe, the decision has been made. Why don't you start putting the case together?"

Ward called Pine Lodge again. "Look," he said, "Michael Green is a suspect in the homicide of a twelve-year-old girl. I have an agreement with the prosecutor that he's gonna be charged with murder in three months. Can you limit his freedom till then? Keep him inside?"

He was told that an arrest warrant or court order would be required. "We got four hundred inmates here," the prison official said. "Green's earned his good time. Don't worry yourself. We know our job."

Ward backed off. He didn't want Green singled out for observation; it might make him suspicious. All the guy had to do was slip away from a work crew.

After the conversation, he pulled out his files and ran his finger down the list of earlier interviewees in the disappearance of Brenda Gere. There were just under a hundred names. With Green headed for trial, each would have to be located. Ward knew from experience that some would be thousands of miles away, maybe even out of the country. He had a dozen hot cases on his clipboard and a stack of old cases to track on behalf of the taxpayers who paid his salary. It would be a busy few months.

He called Elaine and said, "It's full-bore now on Green. He'll be charged in September."

Elaine said she didn't want to wait another minute. She'd drafted an open letter to the U.S. Congress asking for federal intervention. If that didn't produce results, she intended to fly to Washington and trudge from office to office till someone took an interest.

"I don't know if it'll work," she said, "but I'm not gonna let this thing drag. Let 'em try him in the Supreme Court."

Ward begged her to hold off for a while.

4

Counselors at the Pine Lodge Corrections Center found Michael Green to be moody and withdrawn, but a model prisoner. He used weights and workout machines and helped other inmates with their lifts and spots. In nearly six years of incarceration, his jacket showed a single infraction, for a marijuana violation, and he'd earned every possible day of good time. Unless he was charged with another crime, he would return to society in July 1992.

His wife Diana had spent several years in exile in Florida, Arizona and Alaska in an attempt to recover from the painful marriage. An MMPI (Minnesota Multiphasic Personality Inventory) test revealed that she tended to conceal her feelings, had many "resentments to uncover" and was easily influenced by others.

She'd written Green that her therapist didn't seem "to understand our love and thinks I don't know what love is." And: "I guess I have to dig deeper & see why I stayed in a relationship which was some-times violent and why I just really do not want to let go." In every letter, she professed her love.

Late in 1988, she'd met another man and finally let go of her personal monster. The no-fault divorce, in January 1989, confirmed that the marriage was "irretrievably broken" and there were "no children."

The loss of the woman he claimed to love more than life hadn't seemed to affect inmate 917391. Ever since his time in the Snohomish County Jail, he'd had pen pals and handmaidens to whom he ladled out lavish admiration in poetry and prose. They seemed to come and go.

Like most psychopaths, he made a seamless adjustment to prison life and almost seemed to be enjoying himself. "It is beautiful over here," he wrote his current girlfriend about Pine Lodge. "I cannot get over how much freedom their is after staring at razor wire and gun towers for almost six years. I will be fighting forest fires for the Department of Natural Resources this summer. Then I hope to transfer to one of the Security Crews working in the Parks or the local hospitals."

He seemed disturbed by another life event: the abrupt and unex-pected discovery that he and his older sister Cheryl had been adopted as infants. He exchanged information about the revelation with his forty-year-old sister, who'd also been kept in the dark. In a poignant letter, she wrote her brother that she now understood why there'd been no baby pictures of either of them, or pictures of their mother during pregnancy. She said that she'd phoned Delbert as soon as she found out that their brother Jeff was a natural child but she and Michael were adopted. "He cried," she wrote. "He really was very touching, said Jeff was a surprise—but you and I were from *heaven*—

they wanted babies so bad & hadn't had any after 7 years of marriage. . . ."

Cheryl wondered about their real parents. "Where did I come from?" she wrote. "Where was I for 3 mos? (you were 3 mos old too when they got you. . . .) What nationality am I? . . . Maybe none of this is important to you—but in the future you may feel differently."

She referred to Green as "my baby brother" and said she still had an old snapshot of the two of them, "you sitting on your tricycle with me standing on the back. I'm five and you're three and it was taken at 112 Churchill Ave., Palo Alto, in that little white rental house by the railroad tracks that we rented before moving to Mountain View."

She reminded him of the time she'd beaten up a sixth-grade bully "who was trying to choke you" and noted that "I love my baby brother so much & I still do."

Green wrote an impassioned reply with his usual disregard for the niceties of punctuation.

"I am excited by the prospects of finding out something about myself," he wrote. "Little things like, 'Who am I?' 'Where am I from?' 'Why was I put up for adoption?' I mean, aren't these things every human being wonders?"

He apologized for not writing earlier and telling Cheryl how much he loved her. "For only you can understand the pain we felt as kids growing up, knowing in your heart something was wrong just not knowing what. How, maybe it was all your fault and maybe thinking you were a little crazy. . . ."

He mentioned their youngest sibling's battle with cancer and claimed that "Dell acted like he wished it was me not Jeff who was sick." And he reminded his sister of "the most painful memory of my childhood," how their father had punished her after she'd wandered away from a campground in California. "I remember staring up at the stars," Green wrote, "and thinking, I would kill him if I could."

5

Lead Detective Joe Ward and his colleagues accelerated their efforts to send the bodybuilder to the gallows. Michael Kay Green had become an obsession with him and his colleagues. The usually restrained Bryce Siegel said, "I try to find something good about everybody, but that Green is bad to the core. If he was an animal, you'd shoot him."

Sergeant Tom Pszonka said, "There were two faces I could never forget: his and Brenda's. Every dead body that I heard about, in the newspapers, in police reports, on TV, every time there was bones, that was Brenda to me."

Prospecting for informers, the detectives interviewed Green's past cellmates and blockmates and found a man named James Pittman in the Monroe Reformatory, a short drive from the sheriff's office. Pittman (unrelated to the Pittmans of Mukilteo) had been Green's "cellie" in King County Jail, and he told Joe Ward that the muscleman had bragged that he'd raped and killed a child and buried her body in the woods near Black Diamond, an old coal-mining village in the Cascade foothills.

Ward asked, "Will you help us prosecute?"

Pittman shook his head. "No way," he said. "I got daughters. This guy gets out, they could be next on his list."

Ward pressed, but the inmate was adamant. "No, sir, Mr. Ward," he insisted. "I'm sorry, but . . . no."

Another former Green cellmate was also too frightened to help. He claimed that Green had often talked about the case, admitted that he'd studied the Clearview neighborhood and had known when Brenda would be home alone. He said he'd walked in, found the child upstairs, overpowered, raped and sodomized her, then "beat the shit outta her" and "choked her out." Green told his cellmate that Brenda wasn't his first victim and wouldn't be his last.

Then Ward heard about a "mad-dog" killer named Tim Caffrey, who was given to outbursts of rage and was led around by his guards like a chained bear. Despite his volatile temperament, there was an inner integrity to Caffrey's story that convinced Ward he might make a credible witness. The man had nothing to gain; he was serving life without parole plus 185 years. His motive, Caffrey insisted, was that he'd hated pedophiles ever since he was abused as a child.

The informer had shared a cellblock with Green at McNeil Island. He noted that the big man seemed to lack any trace of remorse or feeling, except about himself and his plight. He made sexual advances to Caffrey, who brushed them off as if they were jokes. "He'd say crazy things out of the blue and then watch for your reaction. One day he says, 'Hey, Tim, what would you do if I told you I've killed and some day the pigs would catch me?'

"I said, 'So?'

"He said, 'Hey, Caffrey, who knows? You might be next.' "

On another occasion, Green said, "If I told you I killed and buried three women, would you tell on me?"

Caffrey told Green he wasn't a snitch.

Later Green said, "I know I shouldn't have killed, but it's too late now."

Caffrey described Green's unexpected reaction to the Florida execution of serial killer Ted Bundy. In a freewheeling conversation among several inmates, Caffrey had said, "Fuck that rapo. I'd like to beat the shit out of him."

Most of the other convicts echoed his feeling, but Green turned red and said, "How about if I beat the shit out of you, Caffrey, you asshole? I might be confronted with the same thing as Bundy someday. So shut your ass!"

Caffrey himself was too unstable to be lie-tested, but the chief prosecutor on the case, Michael Magee, said his testimony might be of use.

Other informers passed polygraph tests and were listed as prosecution witnesses. Dana Rice, a meek little man who looked more like a bookkeeper than a hardened criminal, said he'd been sharing a courthouse holding cell with the notorious bodybuilder when Green asked, "What are you in for, man?"

Rice said, "Fencing and forgery. How about you? Did you do what they say?"

Green clenched his fists and said, "I choked her out and raped her." He stared intently at Rice and then asked, "Have you ever eaten human flesh?"

After a few more remarks, the big man said, "You should try it sometime." When Rice asked why he was incriminating himself to a stranger, Green explained that no one would believe the story if it was repeated. "And then he said some more repulsive stuff," the inmate told Joe Ward. "He acted like he was getting off on it or something." Rice said he'd returned to his cell and vomited.

A career convict named Eugene Hillius told Ward about a scene in the Snohomish County Jail. Green was kibitzing a cell block poker game when he began a strange stream of chatter in which he bragged about raping Brenda Gere and beating her to death with his fists.

"Everyone knows I did it," Hillius quoted him, "but I'll beat it on a technicality." Hillius said he was willing to testify because he had a twelve-year-old daughter of his own.

A deputy sheriff's daughter came forward and said that Michael Green had tried to lure her into his car during the Monroe County Fair in 1985, a few months before he'd shown up on Thirty-fifth Avenue. A deputy prosecutor told Joe Ward that the information was irrelevant to the Gere murder charges, but both men found it revealing. Apparently Green had spent the entire summer of 1985 indulging his libido. Ward had no doubt he'd committed other outrages. Victims of sex crimes often failed to report. They would be especially fearful in a community where two women and a child had had their throats slashed by a vengeful rapist whom one of the women had sent to prison.

Ward didn't enjoy canvassing the three or four miles of Thirty-fifth Avenue where Green had been seen walking and driving his Toyota, but it was part of the scut work known as "trial prep." He recontacted the Munsons, Bonadores, DeSantises and other dramatis personae, including a few whose contributions to the case had been so insignificant that he'd forgotten some of the details of their statements.

One was Barbara Chambers Adams, seventy-three at the time of the abduction, seventy-nine now. She invited Ward inside and before she'd finished pouring her first cup of tea she was telling him, "Isn't it weird how of all the times in the world I could pick to leave my house and drive past the Gere house, I had to pick the time that Michael Green was driving out of her driveway with the body in his car?"

Ward said, "Yes, ma'am. Imagine that." He was thinking, What the hell's this lady talking about? I've never heard any of this before. He'd perused the field interview report on her earlier observations before leaving his office, and unless his memory had slipped a cog, it said only that she'd seen a big man in a small car turn around in her driveway.

The elderly woman spun a long story, how the last school buses had passed by at three o'clock, and she knew about their schedules because she'd put five children through the local schools, and she'd seen the big man and his "bone white car" in her driveway a little bit earlier, and then she'd driven toward town to run an errand, "and as I'm driving by the log house, there's the same big guy in his car. And I looked at it because I didn't know which way he was gonna come out. I didn't think a thing of it and drove by."

"That's truly amazing," Ward repeated, truly amazed. "Did you mention this to anybody else at the time?"

"Well, I thought I told somebody over at Elaine Gere's. They had a potluck one day and I took some food over."

Ward thanked her and drove back to share his serendipity with prosecutor Michael Magee. Both men were excited. Citizen Adams would make an impressive witness. She could put Michael Green at the scene of the crime at a crucial time, not innocently walking up to the door in the mistaken belief that there was an open house, as he'd admitted, but driving off the Gere property in his car.

The case looked a little stronger.

6

By August 1991, with Green's release date less than a year away, Ward was feeling increasingly anxious about the murderous predator who was already mingling with civilians on forest trails. Word came that he would soon be assigned to a work detail in a state hospital. Ward cringed at the prospect. Law officers and the Department of Corrections often worked at cross-purposes.

Once again he communicated his anxiety to the prosecuting attorney's office. Legal experts told him that the law seemed clear enough: there was no way Green could be set free until July 1992.

"That's reassuring," Ward argued, "but what if he kills somebody while he's out with a work crew? How're we gonna explain *that* to the public?"

On Friday, August 2, 1991, the year Brenda Gere would have graduated from high school, chief assistant deputy prosecuting attorney Michael Magee met with Ward and deputy prosecutor Ken Cowsert for another evaluation of the case. Magee had intended to charge Green with murder on September 19, the sixth anniversary of the abduction, but Ward argued that citizens' lives would be at risk in the interim.

Magee said, "Let's file right now."

Elaine Gere was elated at the news. "It's about time he paid for what he did," she told Ward on the phone. "What happens next?"

"We'll transport him back to the county jail. That'll get him out of your neighborhood."

"How does the case look? I mean . . . without a body."

"Still weak. We may never find her."

Elaine said, "Oh, yes we will."

When she came home from her classes in Coeur d'Alene that night, Elaine found a prayer to the Virgin Mary that had helped her through many long hours. Her losses hadn't altered her attitude about religion. She still attended mass, but she didn't propagandize her sons or take much part in church activities. She'd assigned the problem of Brenda's whereabouts to the highest authority long ago. He didn't seem to be doing much. Maybe the Blessed Virgin would intervene.

She repeated the prayer over and over, each time adding, "Please help us find Brenda," till she fell asleep.

The next night, Saturday, August 3, she tried a different tack, praying directly to Brenda. "Please, honey, help us find you. . . ."

She knew the approach was unorthodox, maybe even sacrilegious, but she doubted that God and the Virgin would take offense. Maybe they could all work together with Brenda, using her as their instrument. She recalled later that she prayed almost all night. "I never prayed so hard."

7

Three hundred miles to the west of the praying mother, on the moist side of the Cascade Range, the next day arrived warm, dry and sunny. It was Sunday, August 4, the time of year when the drip stopped dripping, the drizzle stopped drizzling, and Northwesterners looked forward to a month or two of Riviera weather, a closely held local secret.

It was such a nice day that two brothers-in-law and their wives took a walk in the hilly woods of the Tulalip Indian Reservation near the little town of Marysville. In the same general area, twelve bodies had turned up in recent years, some believed to be Green River Killer victims.

The foursome followed an overgrown road that hadn't been used to skid logs since the thirties. Jim Moore was walking apart from the others when he reached a gully and spotted a discoloration on the ground about eight feet ahead. Pale lime motes filtered through a canopy of vine maples, alder saplings, salmonberry bushes and other young growth and illuminated a human skull covered with moss.

His brother-in-law caught up, and the two men glanced around a grotto set off by two cedar stumps. Mixed in a mulch of dead leaves and sandy soil that had slid down the sides of the ravine, they found a pair of red pants, a fragment of discolored nylon stocking, a frazzled comforter with a faded rainbow design, and a patchwork coat with one sleeve. A large bone lay in plain sight, and a few splintered pieces poked from the ground. The men surmised that coyotes or bears had made off with others.

They studied the skull without touching it. The lower jaw was missing. The upper teeth were encased in tarnished silver braces. A few loose teeth were scattered around. Off to one side lay a military-type entrenching tool, still in a rotting canvas cover that had turned as soft as wet paper, plus an empty knife sheath, a weathered cigarette pack, and two worn tires that had been rolled over the lip of the ravine through the years.

The observers backed away from the sylvan sarcophagus and called police.

Joe Ward had just returned from an interview with a potential witness when he heard about the find and rushed to the scene. The medical examiner's chief investigator, an anthropologist by training, was digging up a thighbone that somehow had become buried upright in the sandy soil.

"Look at this," Ward interrupted, and pulled a photograph of Michael Green from his briefcase. "This is the guy that killed this child." The tough cop fought tears at the sight of Brenda's braces. All these years, he thought. *All these years.* . . .

The ME's investigator pointed out that many bones were missing and some were gnawed and splintered. "This is not from rodents," he said. "This is large-carnivore activity—coyote, dog, maybe bear."

The remains told a terrible story. The child's nose had been driven into her brain. Her skull was cracked above the eye. A thin groove in one vertebra and an indentation in another suggested that she'd been stabbed twice, the instrument stopping at a rib on the first thrust, piercing to the innards on the second.

The child's collarbones and some of her other vertebrae were intact, but the shoulder blades were missing. A brownish-colored rib bone resembled a twig. Several small bones were found an inch or two below the surface. The ME said it looked as though the killer might have tried to conceal the body with dirt but gave up after a brief attempt. The remains weighed twelve pounds.

Ward was glad to find the entrenching tool; it might help to prove premeditation. He remembered that the child had been wearing a bra when she disappeared, but no underclothing was in sight. Her cotton flannel shirt had dissolved into threads and patches, but the label was intact: GAP. He examined the red stretch pants that Elaine Gere had bought a few days before the abduction. They were separated from the remains by seven or eight feet of tangled brush. One stirrup had rotted away. The weathered pants had what appeared to be two knife holes but were otherwise undamaged. The ME said he didn't see any obvious semen, blood or tissue stains but would make more tests in the lab.

Ward realized that if the stretch pants had been on the child while animals scavenged the body, they would show signs of teeth and claws, as well as the stains of human decomposition. Since neither was evident, it was obvious that they'd been removed first. He also noticed that the extra-wide red patent-leather belt was unbuckled. That might help to prove rape, upgrading the crime to "aggravated murder" and qualifying the killer for the death penalty. As Ward said to himself, the only large carnivore that can undo belts is man.

His thoughts turned to the forest trails near the Pine Lodge Corrections Center. Hordes of hikers would be out this Sunday afternoon. Some would be twelve years old.

The slender detective slipped several times as he made his way toward the road. He pulled free from the clutch of a blackberry whip and realized how Green must have ripped his pants in the crotch. Carrying a body through this landscape would strain anyone's clothes.

Ward couldn't make any official notifications, not even to Elaine, till the body was positively identified, but he informed Pine Lodge that an arrest warrant for Michael Kay Green was being typed up "and I'll be there to serve it as quick as I can."

He asked that Green be secluded from other inmates. "I don't want him to find out what's going on. Please, don't let him out of the compound! I don't want him to run the way he did the last time."

The telephone voice said that it was raining in the eastern half of the state and the prisoners had been inside all day. "Good!" Ward said. "Keep him locked down. Don't let him read any newspapers. If he learns about the body, I'll lose the element of surprise. I want the first face he sees to be me. Maybe he'll tell me something."

The prison spokesman said he would pass the message.

8

The next morning, Elaine was getting ready to drive to her job at the Coldwell Banker real estate office in Sandpoint when she took the call from Joe Ward. "We found her," the familiar voice said.

She said, "Thank God." She promised to drive to Everett as soon as she could find someone to take care of the boys.

"Elaine," Ward said, "there's not much more than bones."

"But . . . you're sure?"

"It's her."

Elaine felt sorrow and relief. She said to herself, My baby's been dead all this time. She hasn't been living in misery. We can lay her to rest by her dad.

She cried a little, redid her face, and left for work. It was a new job and she couldn't risk losing it.

Diana Pittman had just returned from Alaska when she opened the *Seattle Post-Intelligencer* to look at job opportunities and discovered that "unidentified remains" had been found thirteen and a half miles out on the Tulalip Reservation Road. She clipped the small item and scribbled "Brenda Gere?" above the headline.

Her mother Sharon called from work to report that Mike was being charged with the child's murder and that the body had turned up a mile from the house that Diana and Mike had rented before they'd moved to Phoenix. As young marrieds, they'd jogged past the gully almost daily.

Diana screamed, "That son of a bitch! *He did it!*"

She thought about how she'd been used, abused, lied to, manipulated. She remembered the reprovisioning trips to McNeil Island, the information she'd withheld from police, the good-hearted deceptions on her husband's behalf. She cried, yelled, and slammed her fist into a pillow.

By noon the body had been positively identified from dental charts and an arrest warrant drawn up, vetted, and signed. Ward and a colleague, Sergeant Tom Greene, booked a flight to Spokane.

Just before leaving the sheriff's office for the drive to Seatac Airport, Ward phoned Pine Lodge and was told, "We moved Mr. Green to Spokane City-County Jail."

Ward felt sick. *"Why?"* he asked.

"Because it's what we decided to do."

He took a deep breath and hung up. "It wasn't my place to chew the guy's ass," he explained later. "I informed my sheriff right away and then called the Spokane jail and told them who I was and why I was calling. One of the jail officers says, 'It's my understanding that Mr. Green already knows why he was moved. He was told by the staff at Pine Lodge.' I thought, So much for the element of surprise."

Ward and Tom Greene canceled their airline tickets and took off in a police cruiser for the five-hour drive, arriving in Spokane around 10:00 P.M. A wary Michael Green was led from his cell. He looked tanned, fit, and healthy, back to an apparently normal weight in the mid-two hundreds, his body bulging through his gray sweats.

It took about ninety seconds for Ward to read the arrest warrant, and Green listened without comment. An occasional hard blink of his close-set eyes and the throbbing of a jaw muscle were the only indications that he was surprised about being charged with the murder of Brenda Gere. When Ward asked him to sign a Miranda card, he said, "I know my rights. You got a witness. That oughta be enough." Glowering, he finally scrawled his signature.

The interview lasted less than ten minutes. Green said he remembered the lead investigator well, called him Joe, and looked him in the eye instead of staring off into space as before.

"I don't have any hard feelings, Joe," he said, "and I hope you don't." He apologized for his public accusations that Ward had railroaded him on the rape charges.

What typical psychopathic bullshit, the detective said to himself. "That's okay," he told Green. "You'll probably be saying the same things before long."

The big man listened politely, didn't pace or try to control or dominate the detectives as in earlier interviews. But after five or six minutes passed, some tension began to show. He twiddled his thumbs, tapped his fingertips together, picked at his hand, rubbed his nose and lips. He gave the impression that it was an effort to remain calm. The lawmen weren't surprised that he was upset. He'd been six weeks away from work release when they'd barged back into his life. From now on the gallows would be on his mind.

After a good night's sleep, the detectives took custody of their prisoner at 8:00 A.M. Ward was thinking, This big freak's in great shape and he's capable of moving fast.

"Go to the can now," he ordered. "We're not stopping."

Before they drove out of the jail's sally port in the Snohomish County sheriff's car, Green was placed in handcuffs and leg irons. He sat in back, in a locked cage. They'd hardly crossed the frothy Spokane River and headed west on I-90 when he said, "Look, I don't want to talk to anybody except a lawyer."

Except for a few exchanges about his intelligence and his college degree in English, he kept to his word. In Everett, he was driven through a gauntlet of press photographers and TV cameras, and the county jail swallowed him up.

On Monday night, Elaine Gere answered dozens of calls, some from relatives and acquaintances, most from the media. A priest called to remind her that Catholics believed in forgiveness, but she advised him that Michael Green would have to seek absolution elsewhere.

Reporters had always treated her with deference, and she thought of them as friends. She was quoted in the Seattle Times: "I'm sorry I'll only be able to see her bones, and not her little face. I'll just leave it up to the judge and jury. Now my promise is to bring her killer to justice and see him dead, just like she is, and her father."

She told a TV crew that "Brenda finally found a way to help us find her, to set our minds at peace and to know that she's with her dad now." In a phone interview, she said, "I believe in the Bible, an eye for an eye and a tooth for a tooth, and I'll live the rest of my days seeing that her killer is destroyed."

She was pleased to hear from Joe's childhood neighbor, Paul Curry of the San Bernardino County Sheriff's Office. He'd known Elaine well and always referred to her as "the salt of the earth."

Curry told her that California newspapers had been inquiring about covering Brenda's funeral. "Oh, Paul, I'm sorry," she had to tell him. "We can't bury her till after the trial. Her remains are evidence."

He said that his sheriff and Joe's old friends sent condolences and were standing by to assist.

Up and down Thirty-fifth Avenue S.E., neighbors laughed and cried when they heard the news. Gretchen Bonadore leaped from bed and yelled to her daughter, "Melanie, turn on the radio! They found Brenda." Julio DeSantis, "the Rambo of Clearview," held back tears. Gordon Munson slammed one hand into the other and said, "We got the son of a bitch!"

Lesley Caveness, Judy DeSantis, Debbie Simmons and several of Brenda's teachers made plans for a memorial service at Canyon Creek Elementary School. A nearby nursery sent a Christmas tree— a card said it was "because Brenda loved Christmas"—and a cemetery provided a marble plaque with the inscription PLANTED IN MEMORY OF BRENDA S. GERE, 1973–1985, REMEMBERED WITH AFFECTION. At the ceremony, several alumni of Brenda's sixth-grade class, some now six-footers, shoveled dirt on the tree's roots. Others planted marigolds as Brenda's favorite song played in the background on a boom box:

> *We are the world.*
> *We are the children . . .*

Teacher Charlene Richardson opened her purse and pulled out photos of the students when they'd been sixth-graders. The children gathered around and commented. "Oh gross! Look at the haircuts! . . ." "I remember who *you* liked. . . ." "Here we are on the ferryboat to the San Juans. . . ." "There's Brenda, roasting a hot dog by the fire. . . ."

The teacher explained later, "We didn't feel like we were being morbid or reliving the past. It was more like we were bringing Brenda up-to-date, up to the present. She was the liveliest presence there.''

9

The second trial of Michael Kay Green turned out to be as bizarre in its own way as the crime itself, thanks to the star performer. From the earliest hearings, Green presented a new persona: a ditsy, befuddled, paranoid wreck who sincerely believed that everyone, including the judge and his own attorney, was engaged in a conspiracy to destroy him and the civilized world.

The incredible shrinking bodybuilder had made a poor adjustment to his latest stay in the Snohomish County Jail. He'd lost forty or fifty pounds, muscle tone and his deep tan. He was no longer fastidious about personal hygiene and seldom worked out. When he appeared in court for pretrial motions, his dark gray woolen suit looked five sizes too large and his straggly neck-length hair was an unnatural black that suggested the use of a coloring agent.

He seemed obsessed with the conspiracy against him and filed a half million words of complaint, the size of two fat novels, against his lawyers, police, judges and the prosecutor. He dispatched hundreds of pages of handwritten and single-spaced typewritten appeals to bar associations, potential witnesses, friends and victims of his earlier crimes, appealing to their logic and reasonableness. *Keep an open mind. I am not crazy. I am just fighting to get the truth out. . . .*

His claims further disturbed those he'd already traumatized with his knives and his erection. *Something is terribly wrong in this county. My efforts to get at the truth landed me in Western State. . . .*

He had no trouble enlisting fellow inmates in his support, persuading them to sign affidavits to the effect that ''Mr. Joe Gere was a White Supremicist . . . shared beliefs with Posse Comitatus. . . . Their ideas disseminated through a religious body called 'Reform Church' with a large membership in Snohomish County and many law enforcement personal.''

A semiliterate affidavit on his behalf proclaimed that ''Diana Green recieved a call from Joe Gere, he played Nazi Marching Music over the phone.''

The defendant refused to file a witness list, as ordered by Judge Gerald L. Knight, and explained that ''he doesn't want his witnesses assassinated or murdered by 'the network.' '' Court officers on both sides exhibited uncharacteristic patience as he orated for hours about ''the network,'' an evil organization drawn from the Lutheran Church, the ''Aryan Church,'' the Gere family, the Boy Scouts of America, lawyers and public officials. His letters showed connect-the-dot relationships among disparate organizations and events, including the death of an Everett woman in a SWAT raid, a recent string of arson fires, the Vietnam War, the Patty Hearst case, certain cabalistic happenings in the woods of Idaho and Rhode Island, the CIA and FBI, the publication of a ''Dear Santa'' letter by a destitute child in western Washington, the latest University of Washington football scandals, the Food and Drug Administration and other items. Threatened with contempt for his antics, he wrote the judge, ''The defendant will spend a thousand lifetimes in prison before he allows another person to be hurt.''

Twice the trial was postponed for mental tests at Western State Hospital. Green's behavior so puzzled the experts that a fifteen-day commitment was extended to thirty. At first he refused all cooperation with psychiatrists but talked for hours to fellow patients about ''The Family of Friends'' and other sinister forces. He also provided several versions of the murder of Brenda Gere.

A therapist observed, ''You had to wonder, is there another person in there? One a crazy paranoid and one a cold killer?''

Michael Magee didn't think so. The urbane prosecutor tried to avoid smearing his fellow humans with simplistic labels, but when he looked into Green's deep-set eyes, all he saw was ''deception or evil or both.''

Magee had had long experience with major criminals. ''In private practice, I defended murderers and kidnappers and rapists, father stabbers and mother rapers and everything in between. One of my clients murdered two fifteen-year-old girls after he'd walked away from Western State Hospital. I thought, My God, I might win this case!

"I couldn't do it. Another attorney stepped in and lost. Soon afterward I got a guy acquitted of rape, and a month later he was charged with aggravated murder. The final straw was a client who'd been acquitted of rape six months before and was arrested for raping a paraplegic. The jury acquitted him in thirty-six minutes and came down from the box to tell him how sorry they were that he'd been put to so much trouble. I felt major unclean. I drank about ten shots of Irish whiskey and swore a solemn oath I would never represent another criminal."

"Green knows our case by now," the prosecutor explained to a colleague, "and he knows he could lose. So he goes into court and insists he's sane while trying to act insane, which he thinks will work much better on the judge than frothing at the mouth and making strange noises. He figures he'll be declared incompetent and sent to Western State, a hell of an improvement over a penitentiary. After four or five years he'll say, 'Okay, gang, I'm cured now. Go ahead and try me. Where are your witnesses? Where's the evidence?' We've already lost six years on this case."

Psychologists couldn't make up their minds, and some said later that they'd never been confronted by such an enigma. Green's second observation period was extended by another fifteen days, making forty-five in all. He was subjected to longer and longer interview sessions, a total of seventeen hours, and given five or six medical and behavioral tests, including a repeat of the Minnesota Multiphasic Personality Inventory by the same examiner who'd tested him in 1986 and again a few months before trial, three MMPIs in all. Despite a test-taking style exhibiting "reticence to self-disclosure," the results showed that "Mr. Green is functioning with a stable and long-standing personality disorder."

And yet the psychologists found that "his affect was appropriate" and "his thought processes were grossly normal." He showed no signs of clinical depression or anxiety, or of major mental disease or defect. He described himself as "obsessive," but standard personality tests showed otherwise.

In an exhaustive report to the court, psychologist R. M. Hart noted that subjects with Green's profile "are typically described as angry, unhappy individuals who exhibit maladaptive behavioral patterns. They are known for their difficulty with authority and rules. They frequently are involved with substance abuse [Green's were steroids and marijuana] and can have serious difficulties with law enforcement agencies. Their life pattern is punctuated by unpredictable change and frequent interpersonal difficulty. They are considered shallow, superficial individuals who do not form long-standing interpersonal relationships."

Dr. Hart concluded:

> It is my clinical hypothesis that Michael Green is functioning with a long-standing personality disorder, that is, an enduring set of values, attitudes and behaviors having their origin in early childhood or late adolescence and enduring over time. At the core of Mr. Green's personality, there appears to be a state of insecurity and poor self-concept.
>
> We are told that Mr. Green was raised by an authoritarian father and that Mr. Green tried desperately to gain his approval. Mr. Green's sister [said] that "no matter how hard Mike tried, and he tried with all his heart and soul, it was never quite good enough." Jim Champagne apparently had discussions with Mr. Green about his parents and stated, "I feel that his relationship with his parents had an adverse affect on his self-confidence."
>
> It is my clinical hypothesis that early in Mr. Green's life, he developed a set of attitudes and behaviors in order to compensate for his insecurity and lack of self-esteem. Today, he appears as an individual with an exaggerated sense of self-importance. He exhibits very strong needs to be in control and to control the events in his life and a tremendous tenacity in pursuing his own personal goals. These goals, for the most part, are set by himself in isolation and directed at increasing his self-esteem. . . .
>
> It is understandable why Mr. Green's interpersonal relationships are fraught with conflict. Ms. Cutler described Mr. Green as egotistical, narcissistic and intelli-

gent. She stated that when he could not control a person or a situation, he would lose his temper. . . . When Mr. Green's motives or self-indulgence were challenged, he appeared to act out in a childlike or violent manner. It is quite understandable how an individual with Mr. Green's self-doubt and constant need for self-improvement could abuse anabolic steroids with the known sense of euphoria and bodybuilding capacity that these drugs possess.

Officers of the court were impressed by the seven-thousand-word report, one of the most voluminous ever issued in a Washington case, but had varying reactions to its conclusion that "in his present mental state, he does possess the basic and fundamental capacities to understand the nature of the proceedings against him and he does possess the capacity to assist defense counsel in formulating his defense, if he so chooses."

Those were the legal tests, and Michael Green would go to trial. Defense attorney Anthony Savage disagreed with the finding. He'd been appointed by Judge Knight after three other lawyers had fallen into Green's disfavor and been asked by the defendant to resign. The judge warned that no other lawyers would be appointed. If you can't work with Mr. Savage, he told Green in effect, you'll stand trial naked and alone.

Tony Savage was a large, rumpled man with a shape and voice that put older observers in mind of the folksinger Burl Ives. He was a longtime hero of Michael Magee and other students of the law as a ferocious opponent who fought fair, an unusual combination in the opportunistic defense bar. Magee confided to friends that Judge Knight appointed Savage so that "Green can never complain to an appeals court that he wasn't properly represented."

If this strange man is capable of assisting in his own defense, Tony Savage asked himself, why are he and I spending so many hours talking about the Lutheran Conspiracy etcetera and so few about the real issues?

"We met for the first time in Snohomish County Jail," he said later. "He was very serious, good-looking in an intense sort of way, with a look in his eyes that showed he was all tied up, angry. He would pace, clench his fists, raise his voice. The visiting rooms are very small, not more than six-by-eight, and there's only one small window for the guard. We were locked in.

"For the first hour I sat and listened. He was talking about the Mafia and Joe Gere and everything under the sun, and I just couldn't follow. It all came out in a rush."

The pattern continued over several months. "He wasn't hard to work with," Savage recalled, "if you accepted his premises. He wasn't rude, didn't swear, didn't swing at me. He called me incompetent, and I guess from his perspective I was. You were incompetent unless you were willing to jump into this bizarre theory of his—and it grew by multiples as I went back to interview him. He had all these things bound up in one package, and in the middle was Joe Gere, out to get him with the assistance of everybody except Barbara Bush.

"I'd go up to the jail and say, 'All right, Michael, today we're gonna talk about so-and-so's statement to the prosecution.' We'd start, and within five minutes we'd be back on his conspiracy ideas. I'd say, 'Will you *please* get down to discussing this statement with me? This statement's gonna hurt you!' He'd say, 'Oh, all right.' I'd get fifteen seconds of conversation and then off he'd go on the conspiracy again. And he was *not* acting. I've seen plenty of liars and actors in my work, but this man believed every word he said."

Both prosecution and defense attorneys had presumed from the beginning that Green's best defense would be temporary insanity due to abusive use of steroids. Such a plea could result in a lesser verdict and shorter sentence, perhaps even a hospital commitment.

Savage said, "I'd heard from everyone that he was a nice, nice guy as a young man. What changed him? The steroid defense was obvious."

It was not only obvious; it also represented the facts, to a greater or less degree. Anabolic steroids had long been known to cause aberrant behavior, including murder and mayhem. Dr. Harrison Pope Jr., associate professor of psychiatry at Harvard Medical School, had examined Green's records and concluded that his crimes "might well never have occurred if he had not been using steroids at the time." Pope cited numerous examples of steroid abusers who'd developed "a veritable Jekyll-Hyde personality."

Everyone agreed on a steroid defense except Green, who steadfastly refused to discuss the idea. Savage would wait for a lull in his client's conspiracy rhetoric, then insert some practical questions about steroid use, his dose schedules, where he obtained the drugs, how they were administered, their effects and side effects. The big man would shrug off the questions and continue with his theorizing.

"If I can't use the steroid defense," Savage confessed to a colleague, "I'm dead."

The lawyer began receiving irate letters from Green urging him to withdraw voluntarily.

"I told him I'm not gonna withdraw because I haven't done anything to withdraw for," Savage explained. "I said, 'Fire me.' But he didn't want to do that, because the judge had made it plain he wouldn't appoint another attorney. Michael might have been crazy, but he had enough sense to know the old cliché about a man who is his own attorney."

So the elephantine judicial ballet dragged on, from the original trial date in 1992 until the spring of 1993, five continuances in all, with everyone trying to juggle calendars and rearrange appointments to match the latest delays. Teachers who were scheduled to testify against Green booked substitutes and then had to unbook. Elaine and her sons made three six-hundred-mile round trips across the Cascades, jeopardizing her GPA at Lewis Clark State College and her job at the U.S. Bureau of the Census, and setting the boys back in their own studies.

Evelyn Mayzsak flew up from Carson City and returned in two days, then repeated the same futility a month later. Her son, Elaine's little brother Jim, offered his opinion by phone from Wyoming: "No more bullshit! Let's give the guy a fair trial and hang him." He dubbed his AK-47 "my Michael Green gun."

Teacher Debbie Simmons said, "We feel victimized. He's playing us for puppets, enjoying his power over so many people. All these lives depend on how Michael Green feels today."

Anthony Savage came to the conclusion that he was representing a madman, and the madman was trying to run the show.

10

By April 14, 1993, after nine months of delay, the last preliminary motions had been heard and trial began on the merits. There were tearful reunions in the corridors as witnesses saw one another for the first time in years. A morose Gordon Munson chatted with the Geres' former next-door neighbor Gretchen Bonadore. "I just totally blame myself," he said. "I should've warned Brenda, but I didn't know her that well. I know Elaine blames me."

"Oh, no, Gordon!" Gretchen said, and threw her arms around him.

Elaine had long since stopped blaming Munson. How was he to know that the man walking a hundred yards ahead of Brenda was a murderer? She blamed Michael Green exclusively, and she made up her mind he would pay. But it wouldn't be with his life. The gallows was no longer a possibility; the state had announced it would seek a life sentence without parole. It would be hard enough to sway a jury without trying to convince them that the former University of Washington football star deserved to be put to death.

Michael Magee warned Elaine, "This trial is not a guaranteed win by any means." He pointed out that Green was personable and presentable, well educated, and bright in an offbeat way. "He's not your typical defendant, poorly educated, from the lowest socioeconomic classes, lacking the presence or ability to present a false image successfully. We've got one shot, Elaine. It's like Stan Freberg's old routine: 'Live! One time on stage! In person! *The hydrogen bomb!*'"

Elaine asked to be the first state witness so she could remain in the courtroom to assist.

"You'll see me crying a lot," she warned her sons. "Don't get upset. I'm gonna let it out. It might do some good."

Joey said, "Mom, I saw them bring Green in. I didn't know what hate was till now."

Before she took the stand, Elaine exchanged hugs with Sergeant Tom Pszonka in the hall. The big cop said he was surprised that she remembered him after so long, and she assured him that she remembered every person, every scene, every minute of the summer and fall of 1985.

Pszonka told her, "We're gonna get the son of a bitch, Elaine. He's going down."

IBar Arrington squeezed his taut form into a front-row seat, as close to the defendant as the law would allow. He explained to Elaine that Dennis Mackey would be staying home. "He doesn't trust his feelings. He hates that guy so much, he'd try to strangle him in the hall."

Green's assault victim Krista Klawa said she shared Dennis's sentiments, as did several of Brenda's childhood friends.

Brenda's friend Crista Crownover sat in the second row clutching a letter she intended to deliver at the first break.

> Michael—
> A few words to you. . . . You took away a young girl's life. For that life her father claimed his own just to be with his daughter. When you took Brenda you changed the lives of a whole community. What you did was sick and I hate you for what you turned my life into. The nightmares will never go away. The hurt, the loss and the pain will always be here. I hope you rot in prison. When you do die I hope you die a slow and painful death. I don't believe you have any remorse for what you did, and that's sick. Maybe the time in prison will give you time to feel what Brenda felt. All I can say is "I HATE YOU!"

When she tried to hand Green the letter, a bailiff warned her away. "Green had that Mr. Cool smirk," she said later. "I just wanted to rip his face off. I scooted over to where I could catch his eye. The guards were talking to him, and I thought, How can you be so nice to this guy? He murdered the best kid I ever knew. I glared at him, and he finally turned and looked back, didn't smile, didn't change expression, no movement, just . . . nothing, boredom. It was irritating.''

Melanie Bonadore was surprised at how much weight the big man had lost. "He turned around and peeked at me, then looked forward, then said something to his lawyer and looked back at me again. It freaked me out.''

Her mother Gretchen noticed the interchange. "Those deep-set eyes, cold, evil. I got the feeling he recognized Melanie from our neighborhood, and I wondered if he'd been scoping her out when he found Brenda. He scared me so much I was shaking.''

11

Her mother's snoring had limited Elaine to two hours of motel sleep, and she expected to be nervous and intimidated when she was called to testify, but as she walked past Michael Green she felt such a wave of revulsion that it pushed the fear from her mind. She said to herself, Brenda! Joe! *Watch.* . . .

She hoped she looked conservative enough in her business suit. She'd intended to darken her little layered shag, but her sons had had a fit when they found out. "That's the way Dad liked it and that's the way *we* like it,'' Mikey chided her. As she arranged herself in the witness box, she was acutely aware of the jokes about bleached blondes.

She spelled her name for the reporter: "E-l-a-i-n-e G-e-r-e.'' She'd made up her mind that by the time she completed her testimony, the jury would know that a warm, radiant, frisky, lovable child was involved here, not someone long forgotten or a collection of moss-covered bones found in a gully.

"I was Brenda's mother and friend,'' she said, speaking slowly and looking from juror to juror. "She was the joy of our lives, my husband's, mine, both her brothers'. She was full of life and she lived every day to the fullest. She loved getting up in the morning and doing something—going out, riding a horse, swimming. She was like a little mother to her six-year-old brother. When I would be at work, she would take care of the boys. When she was only three years old—"

"Your Honor," Anthony Savage interrupted, "this is no longer responsive."

Elaine took a breath and plunged ahead. "She went to gymnastics, she swam. She just was starting seventh grade and she wanted to go out for the cheerleading squad. She had a lot of girlfriends. . . . They would talk about boys and giggle and say he's cute or something. And I would ask her a couple times, 'Do you have a boyfriend?' And she said, 'Oh, Mom.' And she was just too embarrassed to talk and say anything. Just typical little-girl ideas. She hadn't even been to a dance. She was expecting to go to her first school dance the following month."

As the prosecutor led her toward the events of September 19, 1985, Elaine's eyes caught Michael Green's for the first time. It occurred to her that sharks must have such eyes. She held her stare till he looked away.

Michael Magee asked her to identify a few pictures. "This is Brenda with Crista's cat over at Crista Crownover's house," she said. "And they also had a horse there, so she liked to go over there. And this is Brenda's soccer picture. She had just started playing soccer and she was really good at it. She was goalie. She loved rainbows and unicorns. . . ."

After she described her daughter's bright new clothes, Magee asked, "Where is your husband?"

"He's dead," she said, so softly that the judge leaned forward. "He committed suicide three years after. He said he didn't want to live without Brenda."

On cross-examination, Savage confined himself to a few innocuous questions about the damage to the side porch railing. No defense lawyer had ever become rich by bullying widows in front of a jury. There was nothing that Elaine could say that could bring anything but harm to Green's case.

*   *   *

Elaine joined her sons in the row behind the prosecution table and watched the familiar figures troop by, all seven or eight years older than when she'd first encountered them. Annie DeSantis had met Brenda in the sixth grade, and now she was a woman of twenty. Elaine felt as though she'd entered a time warp. To her eye, the lawmen seemed to have aged the most. Except for a few fitness fanatics like Bryce Siegel, they were paunchier, looser in the jowls, duller of eye. She knew what policemen went through and wondered how any survived. *You understand, don't you, that cops have the highest divorce rate? The highest suicide rate? The highest rate of alcoholism? And one of the highest mortality rates?* She still remembered the words of Joe's first commanding officer. In those faraway days when the immortal Geres drove their matching Corvettes in the desert sun, the warnings had seemed like a challenge.

Detective Joe Ward was the last witness of the first day, and then Elaine and her entourage reconvened at the motel to begin a nightly routine that was to last through the two-week trial. Her mother and sister weren't speaking—a long-standing feud between the two stubborn women that had begun over something so earth-shaking that Elaine couldn't remember the issue and doubted if *they* could— so she'd booked two large rooms, one for Beverly and her two daughters, and one for herself, Evelyn, and the boys. Support team members trouped in and out: Elaine's sister-in-law Georgeann Mayzsak, Debbie Simmons and other teachers, Lesley Caveness, Dick Cress and other members of Families and Friends of Missing Persons and Victims of Violent Crime, former neighbors on Thirty-fifth Avenue, reporters, well-wishers.

Elaine tracked down a regular bingo game for her mother. Evelyn insisted on taking Joey and Mikey the first night and kept them out till 2:30 A.M. so she wouldn't miss the bonus round. Mikey fell asleep over a winning board worth $200 but cleared $70 overall, and Joey picked up another $20. Grandma lost but insisted that winning wasn't the point of bingo, another of her lifelong rationalizations.

As the case against Michael Green unfurled, Michael Magee verbally rebuilt Thirty-fifth Avenue S.E. like a Broadway set designer and recounted the events of the warm September day through the mouths of a long string of witnesses: Deputies Stan Breda and Bryce Siegel, Joe Ward, Sergeant Tom Pszonka, the Munsons, Seattle PD detectives John Boren and Richard Steiner, the Pittmans, James Champagne, the informers Caffrey, Rice and Hillius, forensic experts, Gere neighbors like the Bonadores and others who'd seen the giant in the area.

Some of the circumstantial evidence sounded weak on its own, but the web was strengthening. The expectation was that the former star football player, dressed in his dark business suit and shrunken to a reasonable size, would take the stand and refute the testimony strand by strand, make eyes at the women on the jury, and eloquently depict himself as an upwardly mobile college grad who was being victimized simply because he'd stepped from his car to stretch his sore muscles on an Indian-summer day. As in all murder cases, Green needed to make only one convert to force another trial.

Elaine held her sons' hands through the farrago of testimony. She abandoned her plan to indulge her emotions and look weepy; she was too angry for playacting, even in such a just cause. But her eyes brimmed over when a forensic witness held a picture of Brenda's skull in his hands and turned it around, catching the courtroom light. She wondered how God could allow any mother to be subjected to such a sight.

She also served as backup researcher and prompter for the prosecution. When a prospective witness had difficulty remembering a crucial time, Elaine reminded him of his original written statement; he checked and found she was correct to the minute.

The defense began scoring points with a mistaken-identity argument based on Green's svelte new shape. One by one, witnesses had to admit that the serious-looking man at the witness table seemed much smaller than the loitering hulk of 1985. Where was the three-hundred-pound behemoth who tossed full-grown women over fences as others tossed Frisbees?

"He wasn't a whole lot bigger'n me in court," recalled Deputy Bryce Siegel, himself a hard 195 pounds. "They don't serve steroids or whole chickens in jail, and he'd been off his diet for years."

After one more witness appeared confused by Green's size, Elaine recalled a photograph that had run in a Denver newspaper at the time of his original arrest. He'd looked twice as big as his police escort, and his muscles strained at his dark V-necked T-shirt.

During a recess she mentioned the picture to Michael Magee, and the prosecutor's face lit up. "Find it," he instructed her. "We've got to show the jury what he really looked like."

Elaine extracted the news picture from her "Michael Green" file at the motel, and Magee succeeded in admitting it into evidence. One by one, jurors looked down at the picture and up at the former Adonis. A few of them nodded.

12

After several more days of trial, Elaine realized that the key to her sanity was to stay busy in the off-hours, one of her oldest rules. She started giving her relatives and friends hairdos, a long-standing family tradition. On vacation trips south from Idaho, the honors graduate of Ferguson's Beauty School would roll into Carson City and give her mother a perm on the first night and her sister a perm on the second. She would proceed to Fontana, rework sister-in-law Linda's coiffure, then administer to the beauty needs of other Geres and Mayzsaks and even a few old friends. She never traveled without her curlers and potions.

"The trick to making really permanent curls," Elaine lectured to her support group in the Everett Motel as she shoved her sister's blond head under the faucet. "is you gotta roll 'em just a certain tension and not crimp the ends of the hair, or you'll have frizzies. Wrap each curl *very* carefully. Then put the solution on and time it twenty minutes, rinse out for a full three minutes, blot it, set with neutralizer, wait five minutes, rinse out for a full three minutes, blot it, set with neutralizer, wait five minutes and rinse under the faucet. Then take out the curlers and blow your hair dry."

She laughed and raised Beverly's head by a hank of her dripping hair. "You're gonna be a new woman, Bev—and you saved fifty bucks."

On the fifth day, the elegantly coiffed Gere delegation watched eagerly as Diana Pittman Green took the stand, this time on behalf of the prosecution. She was dressed down, no longer the glamour queen of Michael Green's rape trial, when she'd shown her loyalty to her husband by casting loving glances and asking him impromptu questions from the witness box, as though he were a court officer instead of a rapist.

Diana and most of the other Pittmans were still intimidated by the big man, and she'd shown her trepidation in pretrial interviews with Michael Magee and his colleague Doug Fair. "She'd say one thing one time, one thing another," Magee said later. "She'd contradict the most obvious facts. I think I understood. She'd been Green's victim for years. Even after he started bad-mouthing her, even after she divorced him and claimed she hated the sight of him, she still vacillated between protecting him and sending him to prison. So we had to hold her testimony to a minimum."

Diana confirmed under oath that they'd often jogged near the place where Brenda's body was found. She told about finding one of the Pittmans' kitchen knives in the trunk of her Toyota and wondering why it was there. She also confirmed that Michael had once been "quite a bit larger . . . very broad-shouldered, broad-chested," and that his hair now appeared darker because he no longer lightened it for competition bodybuilding events.

After a reprise appearance by Joe Ward, the prosecution rested, and the long-simmering difficulties between the defendant and his court-appointed lawyer immediately surfaced. In their private strategy sessions, Green had continued to shun a steroid defense and insisted that Savage call FBI officials and various local lawmen for questioning about Joe Gere's involvement in the Lutheran Conspiracy. Savage addressed the court:

"Last night my client and I had a discussion about the tactics that I propose to employ in his defense. Those tactics are, as I understand it, my call. I advised Mr. Green that I thought that certain witnesses . . . should not be called and that I did not propose to call them.

Mr. Green takes strong disagreement with my position. I was advised this morning that Mr. Green does not intend to testify."

Hamstrung by his client and chief witness, Savage was reduced to questioning members of the Snohomish County Sheriff's Department in an attempt to impeach some of the prosecution testimony. While his case was being presented, Green seemed to sag, slumping in his chair, his chin on his big chest. His dark eyes looked flat and lusterless. He stopped taking notes and whispering suggestions. He seemed to be distancing himself from the proceedings.

Michael Magee observed the change and thought, The guy's failed all his life, but he could always create an illusion. He never made Mr. America, but he could strut around gyms and bars. Now he has nothing left to show, not even the physique.

After a half hour of light sparring with Bryce Siegel, Joe Ward and Stan Breda, Anthony Savage rested the only case he had.

Joey Gere waited in the hall. He was a six-footer now, as slender as his father had been at the same age and almost as muscular. As the trial proceeded, he'd grown restive. He still missed the big sister who'd been sidekick, mentor and instigator, and he still awoke at night to the sound of his father's .357 Colt. He'd complained to his mother, "It's so frustrating, sitting here watching. It's like letting somebody else take care of your problems. It doesn't give you the same satisfaction."

Green and his keepers emerged from the courtroom and passed within a few feet of the boy. "Bye-bye, Michael," Joey said, echoing Dennis Mackey's remark at the rape trial seven years earlier.

Green didn't react, but before he returned for the next session of court, word was passed that he'd thrown a small fit in the jail. He was led back in belly chains, and a bailiff warned witnesses and spectators to avoid irritating the defendant because it could lead to exile from the courtroom or even a mistrial.

Joey thought, Good. The son of a bitch heard me.

13

Prosecutor Magee had worked till dawn on his closing arguments. He'd recently won a death struggle with lung cancer and was still weak, but his voice reached the last row of spectators.

"When I was a little boy," he began, "my old grandmother used to tell me fairy tales. One of them I remembered real well, and it scared me, and I still remember how it ended: 'The boogeyman will get you if you don't watch out.'

"And I was scared. And my dad told me, 'Don't be scared. There's no boogeyman. That's just a story.' And I believed just about everything my dad ever told me.

"But he was wrong. There is a boogeyman. And on September the nineteenth of 1985, Brenda Gere met the boogeyman."

Anthony Savage jumped up to object, an uncommon move in the opening minutes of an opponent's closer. He asked the judge to strike Magee's remarks and instruct the jury to disregard them.

"Overruled," Judge Knight said. "It's argument only, counsel."

Magee held up a large photograph of the smiling child, light glinting off her braces, wispy bangs drifting over her forehead. "Before she met the boogeyman, this was Brenda Gere."

Then he held up an enlarged picture of the child's scattered bones. "After she met the boogeyman, *this* is Brenda Gere."

Savage interrupted again. "May I have a running exception to counsel referring to my client by the name of 'boogeyman' or any other appellation?"

"You do," the judge answered.

It took almost an hour for Magee to review the testimony and advise the jury what the state expected of it. He depicted Green as a liar and child-killer who'd spent days trolling for a young victim before selecting Brenda. He asked the jurors to "consider his flight, consider his statements, consider his size. Somebody picked up a one-hundred-and-ten-pound-dead-weight little girl and carried her, not only carried her out of her house, but carried her down that trail and left her to rot. Nobody else. Nobody else did it.''

He wheeled and pointed to the impassive Green. ''*He* did it! And it's your job to not let him get away with it.''

Experienced observers could only sympathize with Anthony Savage when he arose to respond. The only tool left to him was the dazzling elocution for which he was well known. He started by saying that he admired Magee, ''a decent man and a good prosecutor,'' but he had to take exception to his use of the word ''boogeyman'' and his admonition to the jury ''to not let him get away with it.''

''If you follow that argument to its logical conclusion,'' Savage said in his rumbly voice, ''it means every time a jury in this country acquits, they have let somebody get away with it. Now, if that's the feeling, we should do away with trials. When Mr. Magee indicts, the man should go directly to prison, because we can't let him get away with it, whatever it is. All verdicts of not guilty are improper because people are getting away with it.''

He raised his voice: ''Monkey business! . . . All of you swore under oath that if the evidence was insufficient, you would acquit, recognizing that would be the proper verdict even if you weren't convinced that Mr. Green was totally innocent.''

Savage spoke for almost twice as long as his opponent. He was careful to show his sympathy for the Geres: ''What happened to Brenda Gere was a tragedy. It brings up sadness, sorrow and anger. I'm sure all of you, as I did, thought of your own children or grandchildren. And it's a terrible thing. But I don't think we serve anybody—society, Brenda Gere, the Gere family—by rushing to judgment and convicting somebody on the theory that, well, we've got to do something. We've got to even up. We've got to show that we care.''

He analyzed the testimony and found gross contradictions between original statements to police and the testimony in court. Seven years seemed to have sharpened memories rather than blurred them. Certain evidence, once soft and nebulous, had hardened into absolutes.

Savage lingered lovingly over the credibility of the informers. ''Mr. Caffrey,'' he said, emphasizing the *Mr.*, ''Mr. Caffrey didn't like Mr.

Green. Mr. Green was always belittling Mr. Caffrey and Mr. Caffrey says Mr. Green made a lot of statements to him. And he only waited two and a half years before he got in touch with anybody about those statements.

"And Mr. Rice. He says that he was brought up on September the fifth with one other man. Never met Mr. Green before. But within the space of five or ten minutes' meeting, Mr. Green is telling him all of these terrible things. . . . And Mr. Rice is so upset he goes to his cell and throws up. . . .

"Mr. Hillius. He'd never met Mr. Green before. . . . And on December nineteenth Mr. Green comes up to where he's playing cards. . . . Mr. Green at this point is yelling so everybody in the cell block can hear him, shouting about I did it and everybody knows I did it, blah blah blah. And of course Mr. Hillius, he doesn't like that, but it only takes him five days to get hold of the sheriff and tell him. . . ."

Savage asked a rhetorical question: why would snitches lie? "Well, folks," he answered himself, "if you think that our prisons are repositories for truth and honesty and logic, I beg to differ with you. They would do it to spend Christmas with their families. They would do it because there's something wrong with their heads, like Mr. Caffrey says. They would do it to get even. They would do it for some perceived possible benefit for themselves, if not now, then the next time they get in trouble."

Having tarnished the informers, Savage began to tear apart the state's fragile web of evidence. He argued that detectives had picked and chosen which items to present and which to forget or lose. The FBI's latest laser equipment had turned up a fingerprint and palm print in the Gere house, he said, but "they were not Mr. Green's. Whose are they? Isn't that something that interests you?"

The veteran defense attorney closed with a reminder that had swayed dozens of other juries. "A verdict of not guilty does not mean a finding of innocence. . . . A verdict of not guilty does not mean you approve of Mr. Green. You probably dislike him right up to here. It doesn't mean you approve of me. I'd like you to like me, but a verdict of not guilty doesn't mean you're patting me on the back. . . . You don't have to smile at Mr. Green as you leave. You don't have to shake me by the hand. It just means [the state's case] isn't good enough."

By the time he'd finished, Savage had created a measure of doubt in the minds of many in the packed courtroom. Elaine Gere hated him for his persuasiveness, and when somebody told her he was just doing the job that the judge had assigned him, she said that he should have resigned.

Michael Magee took almost as long in rebuttal as he had in his original argument, reinforcing his witnesses' testimony, underlining pieces of evidence, and attempting to rehabilitate his three informers in the eyes of the jury.

"I said we were here about Brenda," he told the jurors. "I said we were here about murder. I said we were here about Michael Green, not the Michael Green who sits there in a suit and looks so nice, but the Michael Green who is so big that everybody who saw him was amazed.

". . . We're here about justice for Brenda . . . for Brenda's mother and brothers and for her father. . . . In this trial right now you are the conscience of this community. You are the law. You will decide exactly what justice is and what Michael Green deserves. . . . And it's not going out that door a free man."

14

The jury deliberated all afternoon and retired for the night. Back at the motel, the evening chatter was about the closing arguments and how convincing each lawyer had sounded. Elaine helped her sons with their schoolwork and touched up her mother's hair. She and the boys turned in at midnight, and for once Evelyn's snoring didn't bother her. She had too much to think about to waste time on sleep.

Just before noon the next day, Friday, April 23, Elaine and her group were sitting in the witnesses' waiting room when word came down that the jury had reached a verdict after a total of nine hours of deliberation.

Before the Gere and Mayzsak delegation was allowed in the packed courtroom, purses were checked and everyone was patted down for weapons, including the boys. No other spectators were searched.

The foreman began, "We the jury find the defendant Michael Kay Green—"

Elaine squeezed her sons' hands.

"—guilty of the crime of aggravated first degree murder as charged in Count One."

She didn't hear the rest. Someone let out a whimper of joy, and someone else cried, "Yes, *yes!*" Michael Magee raised his face and said, "Thank God." Tom Pszonka's heart pumped so fast that his badge jiggled. Gretchen Bonadore mumbled under her breath, "Now if he could only die the death he gave Brenda."

The attorneys agreed that there was no point in delaying sentencing. Under the law, the judge had no discretion.

The convicted killer was asked if he had anything to say. "No, sir," he answered without emotion.

"Mr. Green," the judge intoned, "I sentence you to life without possibility of parole."

Michael Magee stepped up. "Your honor," he said, "I've spoken with Brenda's mother. Under the statute, she has the right to address the court. She would like to."

A few reporters had rushed from the courtroom, but they scrambled back as Judge Knight beckoned Elaine to the bar. She'd known for weeks what she wanted to tell the judge before sentencing—that he *must* find a way to bend the law and send Michael Green to the gallows, the way good judges did in the movies. But she hadn't expected the occasion to arise so abruptly.

She was still too angry to be nervous, even though she'd always hated public speaking. As she gripped the smooth wooden rail and looked up at the judge's black robes and the Stars and Stripes and the forest-green flag of the Evergreen State, she thought, Hold on here! I don't have to talk to the judge. He's already passed sentence. *I can talk to Green!*

She turned and faced the man who'd punched her daughter to death. Their heads were a few feet apart, and she stared unblinking.

He folded his big hands and stared back, his face as impassive as the stone on Brenda's grave.

Behind her she heard a stage whisper: "Is she talking to *him?*"

"Mr. Green," she began in the most scornful tone she could squeeze from her limited voice box, "you have affected my life and my two sons' lives, my dead husband's life, my daughter's life. I will never be able to understand why a monster like you has no feeling for normal people."

Green broke off his stare and looked down. The walls of the courtroom seemed to close in as reporters elbowed toward the front.

"I'm so glad the jury saw through you," she went on, "and I hope you rot in hell. And I hope that Brenda and her dad can rest in peace now." She turned and looked at the judge. "And I want her remains as soon as possible. At least I have that."

She heard soft sobbing behind her as she turned back to Green. It came from Debbie Simmons, Brenda's former schoolteacher, seated with Lesley Caveness and the boys.

"And I wish I could throw you on the side of the road like you did her," she finished, "like the piece of garbage you are."

She resumed her seat and clutched her sons' hands. Applause filled the room till the judge gaveled it down, and Lesley and Debbie and several others patted the backs of her hands.

In the hall, young Joe Gere told a TV reporter, "I feel that half of me died with my sister and the other half just kinda died with my father. And up until now, my whole life, I've been waiting for this one moment."

Mikey Gere told a newspaper reporter, "Now he can't hurt anybody else. I feel better knowing he's gone."

The boys were standing outside the courtroom door when Green shuffled by in his irons, escorted by bailiffs and reporters. Joey thought, How many hours have I wasted, wondering if I was next on his list? Mikey, too. How many others suffered the same?

This time he made sure he was heard. "Bye-bye, boogeyman!" he called out. Green didn't seem to react.

Joe felt better than he had in months. Never again would any child have to cringe in fear of Michael Kay Green. There was something called justice, and they'd just seen it work.

* * *

As Elaine headed for the courthouse exit, her mother said, "Imagine. If the bastard was acquitted, he'd be walking down this same hall, free."

"Not for long," Elaine said.

"What's that supposed to mean?"

"We'd follow his car. He wouldn't get away. If Dennis or IBar didn't get him, Jimmy would. And if he got away from Jimmy, I'd kill him myself."

Michael Magee caught up and said, "I want you down in my office right now." His mustache seemed to stiffen, and she wondered what she'd done wrong.

The chief deputy prosecutor's office wasn't much bigger than a confessional, and she wondered how he was able to do such complex research. Law books, journals, briefs and other files rose in out-of-plumb stacks. She thought, Someday Michael Magee will sneeze too hard and it'll take Lesley's bloodhounds to find him.

He said, "I've been waiting for years to see you do this." He handed her a Magic Marker and pointed to a blown-up picture on his wall. "Put a big red X across that face," he ordered.

Elaine applied the X and added horns and goatee. Magee said, "Thanks. That's one less criminal I'll have to look at every day."

She said, "We'll never forget what you did today," and added expansively, "You outta run for governor."

Magee said he would give the matter some thought over an Irish and a beer at Kate's Bar.

Young Joe Gere's hallway farewell to the killer was picked up by a TV microphone and broadcast that night to an audience that extended to six or eight states and Canada. Elaine only wished his dad could hear.

The next morning she picked up a Seattle newspaper and saw a color picture of herself on page one. She wished she'd spent less time on other people's hairdos and more on her own. It made her feel good to learn that the community was acknowledging her cause. She told the boys they should be proud.

She didn't want Brenda's remains shipped to Sandpoint in a UPS van, and she didn't want them lying around in a dingy evidence locker, so she arranged for a Monday cremation and took the boys on a dizzying round of weekend activities to occupy their minds. In the lower level of Seattle's Pike Place Market, they found a store called Golden Age Comics where Mikey picked up a rare Captain Marvel and a Batman. They browsed the musty corridors of Zanadu's Bookstore, repository of thousands of titles, including the Edgar Rice Burroughs Mars Series beloved by both her Joes, and her sons' latest craze, the Star Wars sagas.

At noon on Monday, they drove to the funeral home and picked up a cardboard box wrapped in silver and gray like a Christmas present. At her request, the mortician had pried loose a tooth, still in its brace, and presented it to her as a memento.

Joey lifted Brenda's ashes from her hands and said, "Here, Mom, let me take her."

He gently lowered his sister and adviser into the trunk of the blue IROC-Z for the seven-hour drive to Sandpoint. When they reached home, Elaine put the box on the mantelpiece next to her loaded .38.

A few weeks after the trial, Diana Pittman Green was sipping coffee in the Sea Horse Restaurant in Mukilteo when a woman walked over and said, "You're Diana Pittman, aren't you?"

"Yes," she answered.

"Well, I was on your husband's jury."

"My *ex*-husband."

"I felt so sorry for you when you were testifying. He looked like such an attractive man. My heart went out to you."

Diana said, "Thank you."

"You know," the woman said, "I still wonder if we made the right decision. I'm having nightmares about it. There was no physical evidence, you know."

Diana put her hand on the woman's arm. "Go home and don't have any more nightmares," she said. "The man's an animal."

"Well, I just wish I had an opportunity to sit down and talk with him."

"No, you don't. He would charm you. You'd believe him. You'd be more confused than you are now. You made the right decision."

15

Brenda's ashes remained on the Gere mantelpiece for four months, except for a brief excursion on Mother's Day 1993, when a priest in Coeur d'Alene blessed the remains and read from the Bible about ashes and dust. Elaine liked his description of Brenda and Joe as "two little lambs, taken by God."

When friends asked about the handsome cardboard box on her mantel, she said, "I just want to be with my daughter a little while longer." She knew it didn't make sense to others, but Brenda wouldn't be there forever. Elaine planned to use her vacation time in August to lay the child to rest in Fontana. After the services, she intended to drive her sons to San Diego and the biggest comic book collectors' convention of the year. The two legs of the trip would be like the New Orleans funeral services she'd read about, the mourners shuffling to the cemetery and dancing on the way back. It seemed like a therapeutic way to handle death.

The IROC-Z sagged on its springs as they pulled out of Sandpoint for Carson City. Elaine had been under the hood of the 350-horse-power car late the night before, replacing the leaky radiator reservoir and some filters. Brenda's cardboard tomb rode on suitcases in back.

Elaine picked up her mother in Nevada and continued south to San Bernardino County, where she dropped Evelyn off to spend time with friends and relatives and play a little bingo. The old home-town never changed much, but glossy new suburbs were crowding the badlands between Fontana and Los Angeles.

"It's a goddamn shame," Joe's brother Bob complained when Elaine stopped to visit. "They're conglomerating everything."

The three Geres bunked with Joe's sister Linda and her husband. The ex-schoolteachers welcomed visitors. Diabetes was clouding their vision, Linda's faster than Bob's, and they no longer qualified for driver's licenses. Elaine shepherded them around and helped them catch up on errands.

Toward evening they all paid a nostalgic call on her childhood neighborhood. The house on Juniper Street was still standing, minus two or three outbuildings and some hog pens, but an upscale development of Spanish-style homes had replaced most of the vineyards.

"Where're the pigs?" Elaine joked. "Where're the turkeys? This place is going downhill."

Just north of the freeway, the ruins of the Kaiser Steel Corporation's great mill, once twenty stories high and as long as a football field, resembled a bombed-out city block, so awesome in its ugliness that part of Arnold Schwarzenegger's apocalyptic *Terminator 2* had been filmed among the skeletized remains of Basic Oxygen Process Shop 2, which once had turned out three million tons of carbon steel a year. The furnace itself had been dismantled and sold to the Chinese government, and a Brazilian-Japanese consortium was cannibalizing the rest of the mill, part by part. The landmark slag heap at the west end of town had melted to half its size as salvagers sold the inorganic residue for paving.

At six o'clock on her second morning with her in-laws, Elaine awoke early and stepped into the courtyard. Pepper trees, spidery ocotillo and ketchup-colored hibiscus blossoms scented the air. Mourning doves passed overhead, and a pair of mockingbirds mocked from a burro bush.

Elaine knew it wouldn't take long for the August sun to burn off the chill. She closed her eyes and willed herself back to the Jurupa Hills, doing chores in her flour-sack dress, splashing in the weir with Beverly and Jimmy and the Mexican boy who lived down the road.

All night long she'd been thinking about Joe and Brenda, and how much better they must feel on this day. Then it came to her that she'd never visited Joe's grave alone. She made the short drive to Green Acres Cemetery and walked up the grassy slope as the sun rose over the San Bernardino Mountains to the east. She was pleased to see that her instructions had been obeyed; Joe's bronze military marker was gone and in its place was a double headstone for him and Brenda.

In every direction radiating outward from the grave, plaques bore the names of deceased members of the San Bernardino chapter of the Hell's Angels. She could have thrown rocks and hit a dozen. She doubted that Joe was bothered by the company. He and the Angels had always understood each other.

She remembered the red rose that she'd sent to the car lot when he was doing so well on Librium, and how it had made her stoic Hungarian as emotional as an I-talian.

"Joe," she whispered over his grave, "Brenda's gonna be with you today. You can rest in peace."

She didn't feel morbid or sad. This was a happy day for the survivors. The strange human process called "closure" was doing its work.

The graveside ceremony was brief, with only the boys and a few close relatives attending. Formal services had been held for Brenda and Joe years before, and Elaine didn't want to burden anyone with another solemn mass.

She was glad that the church had assigned a black priest. She loved the Idaho panhandle, but she'd never been comfortable with its undercurrents of racism. Hardly any African-Americans lived in places like Hayden Lake and Sandpoint and Bonners Ferry. It was good for her sons to see a black man doing something besides shooting hoops and pumping gas, just as it had been good for her to grow up with Hispanics, African-Americans, Asians and a dozen other ethnic groups. She remembered how Brenda had copied out Martin Luther King's best-known quote the year before she died: "I have a dream. . . ."

Elaine was also pleased when the priest likened Brenda to the martyred Saint Maria Goretti. In the inspirational literature she'd been studying, Elaine had read about the saint who put up a fierce battle before being raped and murdered. It made Elaine proud to have her daughter bracketed with a heroine of the church.

Then the pyramid vault was opened, the Christmas-wrapped box laid gently inside, and the vault resealed. Two old friends were together for good.

The comic book convention boosted the boys' spirits, just as Elaine had anticipated. Joey specialized in collecting "The Punisher," books about a vigilante policeman whose wife and children had been killed by gangsters, and he found three ancient editions in a stall.

Mikey was always on the lookout for "The Death of Superman." He had two of the prize issues back home, sealed in clear plastic bags against a white acid-free cardboard backing, "bag and board" as the technique was known to serious collectors. In San Diego he bought another "The Death of Superman" for $50 and couldn't stop smiling. It was worth at least $75.

16

M other and sons were enjoying their first dinner back home in Sandpoint when a sudden realization snapped Elaine's hazel eyes wide open. They'd finished the mission that had given direction to their lives. Michael Green was gone and wasn't coming back. Their crusade was ended, and so, for the most part, was their mourning.

"What're we gonna *do?*" she asked her sons. "We did our job. Why, it's like we're starting all over again. Like—"

"Babies," said Joey.

Elaine said, "Like babies. That's *right,* Joey."

Her oldest child reminded her that he preferred to be called Joe.

Later Elaine sat at the dining-room table listening to the tape-recorded voices of Brenda and her friend Heather, doing a fake interview of the pop singer Michael Jackson.

"Do you like Boy George?" Heather asked.

"He's okay," Brenda said in a squeaky voice, "but he's really down there compared to where I am."

"Do you like his songs?"

"What songs?" asked Brenda as Michael Jackson. "I sing most of them for him."

"You must be a big star then. I got your picture and everything—"

Brenda broke in with a giggly commercial: "Bounty! The softener that always softens. How do you get your laundry so soft? One day my son Joey came home. He slid into first base, second, third and home. I said, 'Joey, why'd you do that?' Next day he was paralyzed so he couldn't go to baseball."

Mikey and Joey entered the room as a childish voice sang out, "Mah headache's jes' gonna split mah haid open. My husband tol' me about his turrible time at work, and what am Ah s'pose to do? Ah'm s'pose to take *Tylenol.* Thank yew."

The girls broke into an off-key song and the performance ended as their raucous voices sang, "In a flash you took aholt of mah heart. . . ."

Elaine glanced at her sons. They were smiling. The tape had been made when they lived in Cherokee Bay Park and Brenda was nine. This was the first time she'd dared to play it.

She ran it again at the boys' request. Then she dragged out the old photo albums. Tradition required a respectful pause at the formal picture of her great-grandfather, Franc Misjak, 1843–1925, squeezed into the Gilbert and Sullivan uniform of the Imperial Austro-Hungarian Army, bedecked with medals, stars and a hat bearing an eagle that looked heavier than his head. Across a century and a half, he bore a marked resemblance to Joey.

They turned to pictures of Brenda, wearing a Seattle Seahawks T-shirt with the number 10, headstanding on the rail of the log house, sleeping in the pickup with her head on her father's shoulder, feeding Canada geese on Lake Pend Oreille, trimming a ten-foot Christmas spruce, riding various horses and ponies.

There were pictures of Joe, too: the sun gleaming on his big hair as he held up a drink, instructing his sons in how to aim his dogleg .44, smiling out of the front windows of Corvettes, Camaros and 4x4s, standing with Mikey alongside a dead elk, trapshooting, helping Joey lift a string of trout.

Elaine suppressed a giggle as she came to a two-shot of her husband and Kanga, staring from their Magyar eyes like cousins off the boat. There were even a few photos of the family's slave photographer: Elaine picnicking alongside a mountain stream, smiling as she arranged Brenda's hair, bursting from a bikini that had fit the summer before, collecting dirty dishes from the back of the RV, gutting a bear. Everyone looked so happy, even Joe. He'd always been at his best around dead animals. Her father was the same. Men, she thought. What an experience . . .

Then she realized, How lucky I am, how blessed! I have such fine children. Joey—*Joe*—was almost nineteen now, an honors graduate in English and headed off to college. Mikey was fourteen, so bright it was scary, battling his ailments and never losing his gift of humor. Brenda was as vivid in Elaine's mind as though she were still whirling around the yard on her three-wheeler, flying through the air on her swing, or teaching her little brother how to ditch school and other high crimes and misdemeanors.

Elaine pondered the natural stages of grief, how friends had predicted that her pain would ease and someday she would be able to think of Brenda without having to freshen her makeup. A priest had told her, "God doesn't let us suffer forever." Her mother had sworn that when she reflected on Big Ed and Fontana, she remembered only the good times. "That's the way it'll work for you too, honey."

Elaine thought about the miscarriage before Brenda was born, and how she'd never seen her baby. She'd had twelve good years with Brenda and remembered every minute. She thought, Kids grow up and move away. Bonds slip. I'll soon be fifty. But Brenda will still be in our memories with her silly stories and jokes, her pranks. Brenda will still be *in this house.*

Instead of hiding her lost daughter's pictures, Elaine displayed them in the living room. Mikey set Brenda's stuffed dog Bernard on his headboard, and Joey positioned her koala bear on his dresser so it would be the last thing he saw when he turned out the light. Mother and sons read aloud from Brenda's baby book and journals, giggled and clucked and shook their heads—"Remember when you guys were little and she dressed you up as reindeer for Christmas?" "Remember when she put the cat in the fridge?"

It was almost as though the child had just stepped out for a few minutes but was expected back. Brenda Sue Gere was her captivating old self, a source of joy, a benediction. And she would always be twelve years old.

EPILOGUE

1

Many who had known the Geres moved away from Thirty-fifth Avenue S.E., and some families dissolved. "The pressures of that search were hard on marriages," said Julio DeSantis, the West Pointer and "Rambo of Clearview."

During the search, husbands had barely come home for meals; wives were preoccupied; everyone assessed blame and pointed fingers. "In our little cul-de-sac alone," DeSantis reflected, "there were four divorces, including mine."

Some of Brenda's peers were unable to shake the bad memories and trauma. At twenty, Crista Crownover, an only child, still feared being alone. If her husband went on a business trip of more than a few days, she insisted on accompanying him. Like Mikey Gere, she slept with a kitchen knife under her pillow. Whenever she stepped from her car at night, she sprinted for her front door.

In late 1994, Karen Oberhelman Weir said, "I deal with the case every day." Brenda's closest friend in grammar school now changed TV channels whenever a crime show appeared—*Hard Copy*, *America's Most Wanted*, *Unsolved Mysteries*, *Cops*, anything that might involve human fear and suffering.

She hired only relatives as baby-sitters. It still hurt her that Brenda hadn't been able to carry out a childhood agreement to be her maid of honor.

*   *   *

The Geres' former next-door neighbor Melanie Bonadore struggled to keep her feelings private. In her heart she knew she should have warned Brenda about the man walking down the road.

When Melanie was in her senior year of high school, her mother showed her a magazine article with Brenda's picture. The teenager gasped and started to cry. "Mom," she said, "I'm responsible for two people's deaths."

Gretchen pulled her close and said, "People like Michael Green aren't your responsibility."

That evening Mrs. Bonadore phoned the Geres for advice, and Elaine responded with a letter: "Melanie, we all have this guilt inside of us, all these what-ifs and if-onlys and why didn't I do such and such. That's what killed Mr. Gere. I would be very hurt to know that you're going to continue carrying this guilt around with you."

Melanie wrote a poem, "The Haunting Green Thoughts."

2:30
Don't go home yet, I just saw him
I just saw Green
Looking forward
I turn to the right in hope to catch her
TO CATCH HER
TO CATCH HER
She'll be fine, I said, she'll be fine
The yellow car sped by
I kept shooting baskets
The yellow car sped by again
She'll be fine, I said, she'll be fine
3:30
Pedaling hard
My eyes were open wide
Ready to scream
Ready to witness

Should I go check on her?
She'll be fine, I said, she'll be fine
4:30
An anxiety began to brew

I kept to myself
I visioned him with her
She'll be fine, I said, she'll be fine
5:30
She has never come over to visit
I hope she's not here for that, *please don't be that*
HAVE YOU SEEN BRENDA?
HAVE YOU SEEN BRENDA?
HAVE YOU SEEN BRENDA?
She'll be fine, I said, she'll be fine

The "she" who had "never come over to visit" referred to Elaine Gere, knocking on the Bonadores' door to ask if they'd seen Brenda.

Melanie's mental state improved after she wrote the poem, but she was left with a distrust of men. "I don't take *anybody* for granted," she said later, "and if I start trusting somebody, I think of Brenda."

She planned to work with underprivileged children in Africa after college. Her mother felt it was her way of atoning for a sin she hadn't committed. "We're proud of her," the mother said, "and the way she feels."

As for Gretchen, she discovered that she'd developed an aversion to helicopters. "All the dogs barking, the helicopters flying over our roof looking for a body, hour after hour after hour. To this day I can't stand to hear a helicopter. It makes me want to scream, 'Stop! Oh, Lord, is this happening again?'"

Teachers like Charlene Richardson and Debbie Simmons continued in the habit of jotting down license numbers and memorizing descriptions. At vacation times, they sent their students home with warnings.

Richardson said, "I tell 'em, 'Have a great time, but be careful. I want to see every one of you back here again.'"

She often drove along Thirty-fifth Avenue and noticed that a decade after Brenda's murder, parents still accompanied children to bus stops. Local minors seldom traveled solo on the rural roads, even in daylight. She asked herself, Is this good? Is this *bad*? She wondered what was happening to Clearview, to Snohomish County, to America.

*   *   *

Neither the passage of time nor the solicitude of Elaine Gere or his own loved ones dissolved Gordon Munson's torment. "I looked that Green square on and he smirked at me. I could've driven right over his face and a valuable human would still be in existence. And that piece of shit would be gone. It would've been a public service. But I didn't."

Munson was incensed that Green hadn't suffered the same death as Brenda. "Human beings don't do this kind of thing," he raged. "We're talking about an animal, a beast. We're talking about predators—cougars, hyenas, crocodiles. They look like humans and we treat 'em like humans and that's the fallacy and mistake. We go out and shoot an elephant for rampaging a village, but we give a murderer a life sentence. That's stupid. We should do what's right. People like Green should be put to death."

Wanda Munson tried to convince her husband that he was no more at fault than anyone else involved in the case. She felt sad about her daughter's murdered schoolmate, but she was also aware of the irony involved in her own role in the affair.

"My kids are alive because I forgot a banana," she said, "and because when I got to the hospital, bells and whistles went off in my head. It was like being hit by an anvil—'Call home, call home! *Tell the kids to lock the doors and windows. . . .*'"

Krista Klawa dropped out of her nighttime engineering and computer classes from fear of darkness. For weeks after Michael Green had thrown her over the embankment behind her parking lot, she was afraid to leave her apartment. Friends replenished her refrigerator, and her bosses at the U.S. Navy warehouse granted medical leave.

One sunny morning she shook herself and summoned the courage to walk to the store. In a few days she returned to work, but on the understanding that she wouldn't be assigned to the night shift. She was sure that the rest of her life would be lived in the light.

Dick Cress had searched for the dead and missing for two years before Brenda disappeared, and he continued afterward, but with the added weight of a Colt .38 and a Colt .45. The murder of his son had created a cynicism about his fellow man, and Michael Green's crimes made it worse. "I also felt I might have stirred up some people during searches," he added. "In this violent age, you never know."

He couldn't decide whether to be pleased or intimidated by an anonymous phone call from California. "We owe ya," said the oleaginous voice. "I'm gonna give ya a number. Call if ya need us."

Cress thought about the killer who still walked the streets after taking the life of twelve-year-old Patrick Cress. Maybe the Mafia's muscle could extract a confession. But then he thought, They say they owe me, but if I collect, *will I owe them?*

He didn't write down the number.

2

To the lawmen involved, the Gere case had never been routine. In six years, Joe Ward had seldom gone a week without talking to the family. Joe Gere's suicide and Elaine's courage and persistence kept the case as fresh in his mind as the photograph of Michael Green on his office wall.

In a way, it was an unfair burden. The lead investigator's hair went from thickly dark to thinly light, and some of the resonance left his voice. He started the case skinny and ended it skinnier.

For a long time, Sergeant Tom Pszonka blamed his superiors for allowing Michael Green to "book," but eventually he realized that the problem hadn't been the brass but the budget. The rural county had simply lacked the resources to mount a full surveillance.

Procedures were changed after the Gere case. Dispatchers took missing persons reports immediately, instead of waiting twenty-four hours. Uniformed deputies and detectives rolled at the first suggestion of foul play.

It bothered Pszonka that he still lacked the mental discipline to delete the Gere case from his memory bank and get on with his life in Clearview.

"People think cops lack empathy," he said dolefully. "I wish they were right. I still visualize Brenda struggling and those fingers on her throat and that fist ramming her nose into her brain. I can feel it just as sure as I can feel my own skin right now."

Sometimes he discussed the case with Bryce Siegel, Rick Bart and the others who'd worked the case, and to a man they were still troubled.

3

Life gradually returned to near normalcy in the Pittman house overlooking the Mukilteo lighthouse. With Michael Green no longer around to exacerbate every family tension, Sharon and Donne Pittman became close again, and their sons grew toward healthy manhood without the baneful influence of a bully who slammed them to the floor at the slightest whim.

For Diana Green, money remained the biggest problem. She'd never been able to pay off the amount she'd pledged for her husband's rape defense. The lawyer was patient. She still needed corrective surgery on the nose that Green had broken in Arizona. Bone chips were lodged in her eye socket, and there was a danger they would emerge through the lens. The insurance company refused to pay for what it considered "cosmetic surgery."

Her mother Sharon summed up the family's attitude: "We're just glad she's still alive after what Mike put her through."

Within a few years Diana overcame her compulsive travel urge and returned to work in the mortgage business in suburban Seattle. In mid-1994, she ran into her former father-in-law, Delbert Green, and learned the sad news about Michael's mother. Kathleen Green was in the final stages of Alzheimer's disease.

Diana asked if Mike knew, and Delbert said he doubted it. His son didn't write.

*   *   *

Michael Green was shunted from institution to institution as the Department of Corrections wrestled with the problem of how to handle an overmuscled giant who was disoriented if not insane, and deteriorating daily. At the diagnostic center in the logging town of Shelton, where prisoners were processed after conviction, there were lengthy discussions about returning him to Western State Hospital for still more tests, but the old redbrick hospital's security wards weren't reckoned strong enough to contain the behemoth whose weight now held steady at two-fifty, most of it muscle.

Green was assigned to Walla Walla, the tough penitentiary in the state's southeast barrens, and he'd hardly arrived before he wrote his female pen pal that other inmates had tried to kill him. Administrators realized he would always draw lightning and dispatched him to the relative security of the psychiatric ward, where he remained for a year, wasting reams of paper with diatribes against "The Family," which now included the Lutheran Network, the Aryan Church, Puget Power (the electric company), the State Department of Wildlife, the Supreme Court of the United States, Mikey and Joey Gere, Mother Theresa, the author of this book, and other forces of evil.

His only contact with the outside world was his earth-mother girlfriend from Everett. In one of their nightly phone conversations, he admitted that he'd prowled Thirty-fifth Avenue S.E. to burglarize homes, his usual method of raising cash for the expensive German steroids. But he persisted in his claim that he'd neither entered the log house nor seen a child.

"You want me to keep writing about The Family and maybe one day you'll understand?" he wrote with one of the short, dull pencils issued to psychiatric patients. "What is there to understand? I construct letters of terrible beauty, for it is only to express *their* evil. Maybe you need to visit the holocaust museum in Washington. What is there to understand about Nacht and Nebel?"

He sent lengthy reports to President Clinton, FBI Director Louis Freeh, Attorney General Janet Reno, UN Secretary General Boutros Boutros-Ghali and other prominent figures, patiently explaining in eye-reddening detail how "The Family" had killed Brenda Gere at the behest of her own father. His handwriting was crimped and crabbed, steeply angled, and replete with odd misspellings ("behund," "watter," "alraedy," "swaeting," "sandles").

He remained the center of his own universe, his dissociation so advanced that he began to integrate past and current events—the Manson murders, the killing of Polly Klaas in Petaluma, the collapse of the Soviet Union, the assassinations of John F. Kennedy and Bugsy Siegel, the war in Rwanda, the burnout in Waco, Texas—into his personal conspiracy theories, and relate each happening to his plight. He accused "The Family" of setting off the Los Angeles earthquake with an atomic bomb, and wrote his girlfriend, "I guess the only question which remains is how they did it. Imagine, a network who can produce *Earthquakes* on demand. They arrange crimes which target children."

Early in 1994, he instructed her to compose a narrative poem about his case and send it to officials so he would be treated as a political prisoner and eventually released. When she balked, his letters stopped, and his last close relationship ended.

In 1994 he was transferred to a maximum-security wing in the Clallam Bay facility in the far northwest corner of the state, where he could hear the distant sound of foghorns and ship's bells, the same background noises he'd heard in Mukilteo and Everett. He found Jesus and seemed to be settling down.

Two longtime courtroom antagonists, Michael Magee and Anthony Savage, reached similar conclusions about his fate. Tough prosecutor Magee was no longer certain that Green had been faking insanity. "I suspect he's become mentally ill," Magee said. "I guess paranoid schizophrenia is about as close as you could get to a diagnosis."

Anthony Savage, the philosopher king of the local defense bar, clung to his belief that his client belonged in a mental hospital. But he wasn't disturbed by the outcome.

"I think the corrections people realize he's nuts but he's not gonna hurt anybody," he explained. "Give him a pencil and enough paper and he's happy as a clam at high tide. So in its own way, I guess justice was served. It usually is."

4

In Fontana, the Geres and Mayzsaks kept fresh flowers on the double grave near the Jurupa Hills and held family services on holidays and the birthdays of their lost relatives.

As they reached their forties, Joe's brothers still refused to have anything to do with the firefighters who'd watched from their rig as the enraged Gray brothers broke Joe's head and arm.

"That was the beginning of his trouble," Rick said. He'd idolized his big brother and still suffered over his life and death. "He owned the world till then."

Bob and Rick often visited the youngest sibling, Linda, at her nearby condo in Loma Linda. The ex-schoolteacher was well read in psychology, and she had a different take on the downturning in her oldest brother's life.

"In his heart Joe always thought it was his fault that Mom got burned, and that's why she went three years without hugging him," she theorized. "He punished himself by never sticking to anything long enough to be successful. He was a man against himself, a deliberate failure."

Joe Gere Sr., long retired from the mill locally known as "Kaiser's," avoided discussing the deaths of his son and granddaughter. Whenever the subject came up, he stared out the window overlooking the swimming pool that he'd dug for his children and took no part in the conversation.

The patriarch's main exercise was clubbing spiders with a baseball bat and gesticulating wildly as he talked about World War II or his work in the West Virginia mines or the days when he and Mikey Pompura and his other Kaiser buddies would handle hot and cold steel for eight hours and then carouse in Sierra Avenue bars for eight more.

Years of hard work on his back, knees and feet had mellowed the old man. He phoned his diabetic daughter often, and each conversation ended the same: "I love you, Dad." "I love you, baby."

Linda observed, "That was something new in our family since Joe died. I think Dad realized he never said that to his kids, and maybe if he had, Joe would be alive."

Just before Thanksgiving 1994, Joe Sr. was seated at his dining-room table, gasping from his emphysema as usual. His wife Pat asked how he wanted his spaghetti cooked, and he said, "Thirteen minutes oughta be right, babe."

When she served the food, he said he felt dizzy and stared down the hall as though he saw someone he knew. He moved his lips and slipped to the floor. By the time the aid car arrived, he was dead.

Two days later, a thousand miles north in Coeur d'Alene, Idaho, Evelyn Mayzsak died of a rare blood disease that developed after she moved into a trim little house that Elaine and the boys had built for her behind their own new home. Big Ed's widow had spent the last years of her life playing bingo and mourning the lost granddaughter who'd visited her in Nevada just before stepping off the edge of the earth.

"Mom never got over Brenda," Elaine said later. "She did the crying for all of us. She'd say, 'Oh, Brenda's birthday is coming up,' or 'Wouldn't Brenda love this dress?' I used to tell her, 'Mom, don't be sad. Brenda's still with us. Just think about the good times.' It was like my last years at home in Fontana. I had to be the mother."

5

Elaine agreed with friends and relatives that she was overinvolved with her sons, but she believed it was appropriate to the situation. "We went through the same hell," she explained. "Other people can hear about it, listen to the words, but you can never understand what it's like."

Each of the boys was the other's best friend and unafraid to show it. Love was no longer the four-letter word it had been to earlier generations of Geres.

"You know, Mike," Joey would say to his little brother, "you're my best friend."

"Yeah," Mike answered. "I really love you, Joe." Then they would pummel each other or roll on the floor till one gave up.

Elaine seldom had to raise her voice. "They didn't do anything really bad after the terrible twos and the horrible threes," she recalled. "Raising 'em was easy. I saw what Mom went through with my brother Jimmy, bless his soul—phone calls in the middle of the night, carousing, drinking. I have yet to get a single call from school or anywhere else about my boys. Never! Nothin'!"

She called home from the office three or four times a day, not to spy or check up, but to talk to good friends. She stopped worrying about another incursion by a madman. There were four handguns in the house, plus .30-'06 and .30-'30 rifles for each family member, 16-gauge and 12-gauge shotguns for Elaine and Joe, a .410 for Mike, and several .22s. Every Gere was a marksman; the father had started the tradition, and his survivors would keep it alive.

Elaine also maintained her tradition of tactility, hugged her sons till their ribs ached, then hugged them again. "That little Mikey," she said in mock complaint. "He's got to have three big hugs a day or he won't eat." Mother and sons watched monster movies together, bowled, hiked, sledded, traveled to comic book and movie poster conventions, hunted and fished and shot clay pigeons.

"We enjoy each other," she explained. "What teenage boys still go to the movies with their mom? Sometimes they even sit with me."

When Joe had a tooth pulled, Elaine reminded the dentist that his mouth was sensitive and he required four shots of Novocain instead of the usual two. When he was sent to an endodontist for a root canal, she said, "I'd like to stay and watch. I hope you don't mind."

The dentist looked pleased and the nurse gave her a seat in the corner.

The solicitude seemed to go both ways. "They're my little protectors," she said of the sons who towered over her five feet five inches. When she mentioned the possibility of moving to a warm spot like Laguna Beach after Mike graduated from college in six or eight years, the boys wouldn't hear of it.

"How can I take care of you if you're in California?" Mike yelped. "At least let's be in the same state."

The boys weren't afraid to sit in judgment on her behavior or her attire. One evening she tried on a pair of hot-red pants. "What d'you think?" she asked, pirouetting around the living room.

"Mom," Joe said, "you look like a ho."

Neither son had ever been a whiner, but Joe let something slip on the day he graduated from high school. "You know, Mom," he said, "I didn't have a childhood. I missed it all." He talked as though he were citing an interesting fact rather than registering a complaint.

Elaine understood. Even while she'd been filling their rec room with every imaginable pastime, she knew that possessions could never make up for what they'd lost. In the house were two sets of encyclopedias, hundreds of books by Zane Grey, Edgar Rice Burroughs, and other favorite authors, two color TVs, duplicating VCRs, a water bed for each son, Nintendo, Supernet, Sega Genesis, Game Boy and Game Gear, Amiga computers with the latest upgrade of WordPerfect, a laser printer, CD-ROMs. Mike owned four thousand comic books, and Joe's walls were covered with movie posters and Star Wars memorabilia. Joe drove his own 4x4 short-box Chevy Scottsdale. Elaine bought Mike a blue Camaro IROC-Z two years before he possessed a license. By the time the boys were old enough to drive, they'd spent hundreds of hours crawling in and out of their personal vehicles and knew as much about cars as they knew about guns.

"They're real men," Elaine boasted. "They'd make two of any man."

By college time, she doped out a way to send Joe to the University of Idaho at a profit. First the home-repair woman and former real estate agent made a down payment on a house in the college town of Moscow and furnished it in a style she called "early American Salvation Army."

"It was a mess," she recalled. "We painted the walls, put in carpeting and new cabinets, sanded and painted the kitchen table, replaced some rotting beams and made everything plumb. Joe and I set a new toilet. When the place was shipshape, we rented rooms to three students. We made enough money for tuition and books and sold the house at a ten-thousand-dollar profit."

If Joe carried out his plan to transfer to UCLA to study cinematography, Elaine intended to buy a house in West Los Angeles or Beverly Hills and repeat the maneuver. "He'll have a place to live and he won't have to get mugged every night living in the slums."

Mike remained housebound much of the time, allergic to substances known and unknown. He was a borderline asthmatic, permanently on antibiotics, semipermanently on heavier drugs like Prednisone. He was big and strong, like his father, and a promising football lineman, but every time he went to school he fell afoul of a new bug or allergy and ended up gasping for air. "He just goes to school long enough to get sick," said Elaine. "Then we've got to pull him out. So we had to switch back to home schooling."

She worked days at her government job and spent evenings digesting books, her own and Mike's. She re-enrolled at Lewis Clark State College, and Mike worked on a high school diploma from a correspondence school in Pensacola, Florida. She worried about whether she was shortchanging the son who intended to become a doctor, his father's stated ambition at the same age.

After a year of home schooling, Mike was tested against national averages and scored in the 96th percentile in reading and the 86th in math, the family's bugaboo. Elaine was pleased. She told Joey,

"It certainly proves that home schooling works—if the student's Mikey."

As Elaine approached the end of her first half-century, she still attracted admiring glances. She was sure she'd gone gray, but the boys insisted that she retain her short blond bottle-based shag. Since her high school years in Fontana, she'd added ten or twelve pounds, but they were artfully concealed by the business skirts and pantsuits she wore to work and the sweats and jeans she donned on weekends. Her figure still popped eyes when she walked through the malls of Coeur d'Alene or stepped from her car at the office.

She'd always known what she looked like and dressed conservatively. "I'm not advertising," she explained. "I used to wear big hoop earrings, but they made me look like a Harley mama. So I switched to little studs."

She wasn't compulsive about avoiding men, just uninterested. "After Joe, I never saw anybody that looked halfway decent. The guys my age are falling apart. The younger ones want to take you to rock 'n' roll bars where you can't talk. Shoot, it's all different now. I wouldn't know how to date anymore."

Some of her friends and relatives were convinced she was slavishly obeying a neurotic husband's demand for fidelity after death. "Maybe I am," she admitted. "I never loved Joe more than I love him right now. Maybe I'm just being obedient. Or maybe I don't want to bring a strange man into our house while I'm raising two boys. Didn't they go through enough?"

Most of her acquaintances respected her lifestyle and admired her resilience, but a few wondered if she was being fair to herself. "She's always done for others," her friend Lesley Caveness observed. "When is she gonna start doing for Elaine? It won't happen in this life, will it?"

"The Geres are a Greek tragedy," said Joe's childhood friend Paul Curry, "but Elaine runs too fast to feel it."

The subject of such speculation laughed at the theories and continued on the same path. "I'm sure women are gonna say I've been exploited by men and now I'm being exploited by my sons. 'Let her get a life for herself.' But I've always enjoyed my life, even with Brenda and Joe gone."

She remained so close to her lost loved ones that she often spoke of them in the present tense. "Maybe it looks like I spent all those years under Joe's thumb," she said, "but in his own way he treats me like a queen.

"Of course, I always let him *think* he's in control. It's a trade-off, makes him happy, makes *me* happy. We had nice houses, swimming pools, a yacht, Corvettes and IROCs, closets full of clothes, money in the bank. And even when we lost it all, we had great kids. We had love. We have each other."

Anniversaries and birthdays remained difficult. "When September nineteenth comes around, or Brenda's birthday, or some other important date, I try not to dwell on what happened. But some relative always calls. 'Well, Elaine, how did you do today? Did you know this is the day Joe died?'

"I tell 'em I don't want to hear about it. Joe used to get so depressed on anniversaries. I can't afford that luxury. I have to laugh and giggle and act silly." She paused and looked down. "For the boys."

On Joe Gere's forty-seventh birthday in July 1994, his diabetic sister phoned Elaine to discuss old times. "With all you've been through," Linda said, "I don't see how you keep going."

Elaine didn't know how to respond to this sweet consolation from a severe diabetic who faced blindness and death herself. "Don't you wake up crying at two in the morning?" Linda asked. "How do you cope?"

"I get up and go to work," Elaine said softly. "I tear out a wall. I sew. I bake a cake for the boys."

"It works?"

"It's all I know."

Some thought she was deferring her grief and would fly apart on the final separation from her sons. She disagreed. "I don't sit around and say, 'Oh, my God, they're gonna leave me, I'll be all alone.' We'll always be a family. When Joe and Mike get married, we'll just be a bigger family. I'm already collecting things for my grandchildren. I want to be their buddy. I've got Brenda's Barbies and Kennys all packed for them.

"Those boys may end up in New York or California and me in

Timbuktu, but we'll still be a family. There's phones, letters, visits. There's frequent flyer programs. I'll be as tight with Mike and Joe as I was with my mother. This isn't covered-wagon days, ya know.''

The reference to Timbuktu wasn't inadvertent. In college she'd maintained good grades in math, partly due to the boost she got from home-schooling Mikey and partly from spending more hours on numbers, equations and theorems than she spent on her other subjects combined. On May 19, 1995, two days after her fiftieth birthday, she was graduated with a bachelor of science degree in social sciences and offered a job as counselor to troubled northern Idaho children. She kidded her sons that they could be her first clients.

"Mom," Mike cracked back, "we knew your degree would be in B.S." He'd always been as quick with words as his father.

After going on to a master's degree, Elaine intended to apply for a Foreign Service posting. She hadn't refined the details of her plan, and her knowledge of geography was as hazy as ever. "I need to see the world. Fifty's a good age to start, don't you think? Nigeria, maybe. Singapore. Andorra. Every six months or so I'll send the boys tickets, and we'll meet over in India. I'm sure we can make it work out."

She was equally sure that all the Geres and Mayzsaks would reconvene in another dimension and laugh about old times in Fontana, in West Virginia mines, maybe even back in Eastern Europe. It would be interesting to see great-grandfather Franc out of uniform.

"I believe in heaven and hell," she said. "In my church, suicides are damned, but Joe's not really Catholic. God wouldn't condemn someone in his state of mind. I think he's with Brenda in heaven, where I'll be someday, where we'll all be."

She looked away and then looked back. "Together," she said.